# I Brought You Out

## Studies on the Exodus

# I Brought You Out

## Studies on the Exodus

Edited by Thomas Hamilton

**Florida College Annual Lectures**
**February 2022**

FLORIDA COLLEGE
**PRESS**

ISBN: 978-1-736175-22-4

# Contents

# Foreword

With the exception of the COVID year 2020, each Spring since 1947 simple New Testament Christians from across the country have gathered on the campus of our college to hear a special series of outstanding lessons on matters of vital concern to God's people. The 2022 lectures, "I Brought You Out," are centered on the theme of the exodus as it runs throughout the Scriptures. I commend these lessons to you as a reinforcement of the salvation and deliverance that we have in Christ, a reaffirmation of our full and final redemption that will be realized on the Day of Judgment, and a reminder of our duty before God as we wander through this world that is clearly not our home, living as sojourners in the intervening years between our initial exodus and entrance into the Promised Land.

These lectures point us toward a New Moses who brings New Redemption from the slavery of sin and gives a New Covenant for us to live by. Before our very eyes, these lessons paint a picture of a New High priest entering a new Tabernacle to offer up the New Sacrifice of Himself. As Peter said, "gird up the loins of your mind" (1 Pet 1.13) to join us on a New Exodus and sojourn through a New Wilderness, until we make it to a New Promised Land.

The current year 2021–2022 marks a year of transition and change more than usual. I will be making my own exodus from the presidency of Florida College, completing 13 years of service in that role and another 37 years of service in many different roles before that. It has truly been an honor and a privilege to serve the dedicated faculty and staff who have sacrificed so much, not only to keep this college in existence, but to hold it true to its fundamental mission. It has been gratifying to see the thousands of young people that have passed through our doors, that have been educated, equipped, and nurtured in a godly environment, and that have then gone forth into this world to lead lives of Christ-like service to God and their fellow man. It has been humbling to see the devotion and commitment of our alumni to send sacrificial financial support and something of even greater value, their children, that Florida College might continue to be a Friend to Youth, providing a college education in a spiritual environment where one's faith will be nurtured and encouraged, not neglected or attacked.

From my vantage point, I have all the confidence in the Lord that nothing of significance is really changing at Florida College, and I truly believe with all my heart that I leave in greater certainty of the college's future than when I first came 50 years ago. To paraphrase the apostle Paul in 2 Timothy 2.2, what faithful men had entrusted to my generation has now been entrusted to other faithful men that they may teach others also. May God continue to bless Florida College with such faithful men in every generation to keep the school true to its mission to educate young people to the glory of God!

**H.E. "Buddy" Payne**
*President*
*Florida College*
*Temple Terrace, Florida*

# Preface

The 2022 Florida College Annual Lectureship presents studies based on the Old Testament story of Israel's exodus from Egypt. The lessons presented here are designed to help keep our focus on God especially in the midst of seemingly hopeless situations. Who could have imagined that the enslaved and dispirited Israelites—with no organization, no army, no resources—would prevail over the dominant superpower of their day? Of course, *they* did not conquer Egypt, but their God did! So the exodus became the paradigm for the Lord's deliverance of His people out of circumstances that humans label as "impossible" (Matt 19.26). The exodus event is used by the OT prophets to speak of God restoring His people from Babylonian captivity, not just returning them physically to their homeland, but spiritually renewing the people on the inside. More importantly, this foreshadowed God's deliverance of all humanity from sin and death, just as the NT writers develop this exodus theme more explicitly. Can hope become a reality in these situations that seem hopeless? Will the impossible once again be possible? This series of lessons are particularly relevant and vital for God's people today as we await that Final Exodus, holding fast to our hope in something that the world declares "impossible." This is all the more important as our society continues its descent into madness, calling "evil 'good' and good 'evil'" (Isa 5.20), prompting many to despair, "Can God Himself really restore or deliver anything from something this far gone?"

The evening lectures are designed to draw our attention to God's promises and covenant faithfulness as the foundation of all things (Monday), to our trust as the only possible human response to God's gracious deliverance (Tuesday), and to our patient hope in awaiting the final consummation of God's deliverance from every form of oppression and slavery (Thursday). The day lectures on Tuesday may be described as "Getting Israel out of Egypt," followed by Wednesday's theme of "Getting Egypt out of Israel," and culminating in Thursday's day lectures of "Getting Israel into the Promised Land." Although most of the lessons are drawn from the Book of Exodus and presented in roughly chronological order, this lecture book is not intended to be a commentary on the Book of Exodus itself, especially as it extends into some of the narrative of Numbers as well. Rather, it is a contemplation of the true spiritual significance of the exodus experience of Israel, ultimately fulfilled in Christ and fully realized on the Last Day.

As we have come to expect, the men chosen to present the lessons for this year's lecture program have done an outstanding job in presenting a spiritual feast to nourish our souls. In addition to the work they have put into these lectures, they have given generously of their time and have travelled here at their own expense, and we cannot thank them enough. Please make a conscious effort to show them your appreciation as appropriate.

Of course, there would be no lectureship if it were not also supported by the many brothers and sisters who travel from across the country and around the world, and there would be no college to host the lectureship if we did not have so many ardent supporters who donate their time, money, and enthusiasm for the mission of the school, especially those of you who have entrusted your young people to our care for a short but critical point in their lives. We also cannot thank you adequately, but hope these lectures and this written record of them may serve as a token of our appreciation. For the first time in the history of these lectures, we are making a digital version of the lecture book available free to any who would like to have it. Print copies will still be available on a print-on-demand basis from the Florida College Bookstore.

Finally, I owe a debt of gratitude especially to my colleagues in the Biblical Studies department: Will Dilbeck, Jason Longstreth, David McClister, Ray Madrigal, Doy Moyer, Jared Saltz, Nathan Ward, and John Weaver. They have made my first year as chair of the department a true pleasure, and I am blessed beyond measure by the collegiality and comradery among such exemplary Christians and biblical scholars. I am honored to count them as my fellow workers and friends, and I am indebted to them as always for their part in this annual project. A special thanks goes to Nathan Ward for his work in the preparation of this volume for publication, and to David McClister as the Director of the Florida College Press and Carrie Black as the Manager of the Florida College Bookstore for overseeing the publication of this volume.

My prayer is that this volume of the 2022 Florida College Annual Lectures will be a special blessing to all who read it, and that the lessons it contains will be used to further the cause of Christ to the glory of God.

**Thomas H. Hamilton**
*Chairman, Department of Biblical Studies*
*Florida College*
*Temple Terrace, Florida*

# Part One

The Evening Lectures

# The Covenant Faithfulness of God

## Ben Hall

One of the most prevalent features of human life across time and place is the desire for god. The idea of "god" means and has meant a great many things throughout the history of the world, but the desire and pursuit of god is universal. All people desire something or someone (or some things or some ones) to rely upon in order to navigate the violent turbulence of the human experience. Now, the fundamental reason human beings desire for god is because there actually is a God who made us for him (Eccl 3.11; Acts 17.22–28), but other elements of the human experience such as suffering and pain heighten and intensify the desire. Pagans and saints, the secularist and the spiritual have a common bond in their deep desire and felt need for "god"—someone(s) or something(s) outside of and higher than ourselves that will provide salvation, satisfying the needs of the soul and setting right all the wrongs of the world. Tragically, all the promised glories of the imitation gods that human beings have pursued throughout the centuries in the quest for "god" fail to deliver, and leave an even greater sense of emptiness, frustration, and lostness than what was present before. The glory and saving power of the true God who rules supreme over all others is that he always delivers on what he promises; he is the God of covenant faithfulness.

The story of the people of Israel was that their God, Yahweh, had established a covenant[1] relationship with their forefather Abraham

---

[1] "Covenant" is a rich concept that we are not giving enough treatment here.

3

and his family. The promise of this covenant was that Yahweh would do good through the family of Abraham in order to extend blessing to all the nations. And so Yahweh was watching over Israel to some-day bring his good word of promise to fruition for the salvation of the world. Yet for an Israelite—fighting to survive each day as a disenfranchised, oppressed slave under Pharaoh's wicked rule—nothing could have seemed to be further from the truth. The challenge with embracing the story of Israel's world-shaping heritage would have come with the figure at the center of it all: Yahweh himself. Egypt was filled with a wide variety of images of gods standing in the midst of the seemingly obvious effects of their power and glory, taunting the puny slaves for their impotence and promising that the only hope they had was to bow down in reverence to the gods of this great empire. Meanwhile, no one even knew what Yahweh looked like. The effect of his supposed great power was the enslavement of his people, the murder of their children, and the complete and utter degradation of their worth on the world's stage under the mighty hand of Egypt and her gods. What happened to all the promises that Yahweh was said to have made to Israel's forefather Abraham? The Nile itself would have seemed a more glorious object of reverence and trust than the apparently imaginary God of Israel who allegedly made all those fantastic promises to their people so long ago.

But we know that, for some reason, despite their suffering and oppression, there were people who feared Yahweh more than their masters, trusted in his promises more than their experiences, and found him to be the God that all human beings are searching for. Israel's celebration at the moment of their exodus from slavery powerfully expresses what set their God apart from all others.

---

In short, a covenant is a solemn agreement between parties in which each bind themselves to keep expressed commitments toward the other party(s) and/or receive certain benefits promised by the other party(s). God's interactions with human beings are largely based on the covenants he made with various individuals and groups recorded throughout scripture culminating in the new covenant established through the blood of Christ.

Who is like You among the gods, LORD?
   Who is like You, majestic in holiness,
   Awesome in praises, working wonders?
You reached out with Your right hand,
   The earth swallowed them.
In Your faithfulness You have led the people whom You have
      redeemed;
   In Your strength You have guided *them* to Your holy habitation.
(Exod 15.11–13)[2]

The exodus story (and the book of Exodus as a whole) is the emphatic declaration of the nature of the true God, Yahweh. When Pharaoh asks, "Who is Yahweh?" (Exod 5.2), we as readers should recognize this as the central question of the book which the story and doctrines contained therein will answer (Exod 7.5; 20.1–11; 34.1–9; et al). The text cited above from Exodus 15 outlines the greatness of Yahweh and the belief that Israel had about him. They had come to know that there is no one like him in his peerless rule (15.11). They had experienced the redemptive work of his gracious power (15.2, 13), which was made possible through his judgment upon the forces of wickedness (15.1, 3–10, 12). They knew he had even greater goods in store for their future (15.13, 16b-18).

But the keystone to all of Yahweh's greatness, the quality that sets him apart as the true God over all other gods, is found in the first line of verse thirteen: "In your faithfulness you have led the people." The God of Israel had proven himself to be great in his holiness, power, justice, and redemptive grace which compelled the people to know and trust him as their only God, but there are many "gods" that could (at least in some limited spheres and capacities) embody these qualities to benefit those who believe in them. The significant difference between Yahweh as opposed to all the other gods is that he exercises all his beautiful, saving characteristics through his covenant faithfulness.

---

[2] Unless noted otherwise, all quotations of scripture are from the 1995 update to the NASB.

In order to properly explore the truly awesome covenant faithfulness of God, we should take a moment to define the concept biblically. When we say that God is faithful, we are saying that he consistently does what he says he will do so that his loving purposes are accomplished for his people. Yahweh is not simply a loyal sort of God in his general disposition (though he is that). Rather, his faithfulness is a measurable, testable commitment he has made to always follow through with what he has promised to do and to be. He is always true to the solemn words of his covenant.

One of the predominant words used throughout the scriptures to describe this vitally fundamental aspect of God's character is the Hebrew word *ḥesed*. The rich, multi-faceted nature of this word is conveyed by the various ways it is translated into English: "loving-kindness" (ASV, NASB), "faithful love" (CSB), "steadfast love" (RSV, ESV), "goodness" (KJV, NKJV), "unfailing love" (NLT), "loyal love" (NET). Throughout the scriptures, particularly in the exodus story, *ḥesed* is a key word used to describe the heart behind Yahweh's deep and lasting commitment to faithfully keep the covenantal promises that he has made for the good of the world.

The *ḥesed*-driven covenant faithfulness of Yahweh is the essence of what makes him uniquely glorious over all other gods. Near the end of the book of Exodus, soon after Israel's deliverance, they faltered in their commitment to Yahweh and turned their hearts away from him to worship a god they made for themselves (Exod 32). Yahweh took this opportunity to awaken the people to his greatness and goodness, to show them what sets him apart from all the other gods that they (like all humanity) had been and would be tempted to turn to instead of him. We might imagine several aspects of himself that Yahweh could have highlighted as he acquiesced to Moses' request, "Show me your glory!" (Exod 33.18). Of all the reasons that God could have given for what makes him glorious, he pointed to the fact that he is faithful, full of *ḥesed*: "Then the LORD passed by in front of [Moses] and proclaimed, 'The LORD, the LORD God, compassionate and merciful, slow to anger, and abounding in [*ḥesed*] and truth; who keeps [*ḥesed*] for thousands …'" (Exod 34.6–7). Yahweh's goodness in character, his greatness over all other gods, and the glory that he uniquely possesses to satisfy the needs of the human soul and save us from the evils of the sinful world are rooted in his covenant faithfulness. Yahweh is the God that each person of every nation should embrace as their God because he is truly glorious, full of *ḥesed*, faithful.

The covenant faithfulness of God (rooted in his *ḥesed*) is profoundly featured throughout the story of the exodus in order to impress upon us the incomparable weightiness of his glory. The book opens with a reminder of his faithfulness by listing the names of the family of Israel which Yahweh had watched over, cared for, and grown just as he had promised to do centuries earlier (Exod 1.1–7; cf. Gen 15.1–5). Though it seemed that he had abandoned Israel to the evil Pharaoh who sought to eradicate them through harsh slavery and infanticide, the truth was, "God was good to the midwives, and the people multiplied, and became very mighty" (Exod 1.20). At the height of their suffering, the text tells us that Israel's prayers were answered by their God who was indeed remaining true to his ancient promises to them even in their darkest hour: "And the sons of Israel groaned … and their cry for help because of *their* bondage ascended to God. … and God remembered His covenant with Abraham, Isaac, and Jacob. And God saw the sons of Israel, and God took notice *of them*" (Exod 2.23–25). As Yahweh called Moses into the ministry of deliverance, he did so by introducing himself as the God who was still loyal to the long-dead Abraham, Isaac, and Jacob and to the covenant of promise he had made with them (Exod 3.1–9, 3.16–17, 4.4–5). Even the identity that God used to reintroduce himself to Moses and Israel ("I AM") spoke to his continual reliability—what he was is what he is and is what he will be (Exod 3.13–15).

But there was a critical moment when it looked like Israel would not believe in the covenant faithfulness of Yahweh nor would they trust in him as their God at all. In Exodus 5 we find Moses going to

Pharaoh to demand Israel's release. Naturally (or divinely), Pharaoh refused and then made the labor of Israel even more burdensome than it previously had been. The Israelites—Moses included—did not take this turn of events too well (Exod 5.22–23). Yahweh had given his word that he would save his people, but now that they had trusted in him things had gone from incredibly bad to far, far worse. Could Israel trust in Yahweh and the promises of his covenant? Would he actually be the one to satisfy the needs of their souls and save them from the evils of their sin-sick world?

Yahweh had some work to do to convince Israel to fully rely upon him as their God. What would be his argument? He could have performed great works of power. He might have offered profound insights from his treasury of wisdom. He had the authority to execute swift justice upon any and every evil that he saw among the Egyptians or Israelites. But instead of leveraging any of these character traits to cause the people to see his glory, Yahweh reasserted his covenant faithfulness. This was the reason he said that they should trust him, and would learn to do so:

> I am [Yahweh]; and I appeared to Abraham, Isaac, and Jacob as God Almighty, but *by* My name, [Yahweh], I did not make Myself known to them. I also established My covenant with them, to give them the land of Canaan, the land in which they lived as strangers. Furthermore, I have heard the groaning of the sons of Israel, because the Egyptians are holding them in bondage, and I have remembered My covenant. Say, therefore, to the sons of Israel, 'I am [Yahweh], and I will bring you out from under the labors of the Egyptians, and I will rescue you from their bondage. I will also redeem you with an outstretched arm, and with great judgments. Then I will take you as My people, and I will be your God; and you shall know that I am [Yahweh] your God, who brought you out from under the labors of the Egyptians. I will bring you to the land which I swore to give to Abraham, Isaac, and Jacob, and I will give it to you *as* a possession; I am [Yahweh]. (Exod 6.2–8, edited).

The LORD had previously shown himself to be powerful and wise, just and kind, but he had not yet fully revealed himself, his true identity as Yahweh, the God of covenant faithfulness. The thing about God that he believed Israel needed to know, and what all people of every place and time need to know, about him is that he does not mess around when he makes promises. He means every word, and he will employ all his power, wisdom, justice, and grace to prove himself faithful to his covenantal promises. That covenant faithfulness is what makes him truly glorious, setting him apart from all the other gods—the somethings and someones that people turn to for satisfaction and salvation in this world. Other gods may tempt human beings to trust in them rather than in Yahweh, but none of them are full of *ḥesed*. None of those other gods can be counted on to make and keep covenant for the good of their people. Just like many people today, Israel at that time did not see God's glory or believe in his name (Exod 6.9), but they would soon change their tune.

The plagues, Passover, and Israel's rescue through the Red Sea proved the glorious covenant faithfulness of God as he brought about his judgments upon Egypt for the redemption and restoration of his covenant people. Once they were saved, Israel sang and danced in praise to Yahweh because he had done what he said he would. He kept the covenant he had made with Abraham. He had been true to the word of salvation that he had promised to and through Moses. He had proven himself faithful, full of *ḥesed*. Israel had come to know their God as one who was full of power, justice, wisdom, and saving grace, but the true weight of his glory that they now beheld in the joys of salvation was his covenant faithfulness (Exod 15.13).

From the time of the exodus moving forward, the covenant faithfulness of Yahweh is what Israel held up as the reason that their God had been proven as the only God who satisfies the yearnings of the human soul and who can save the sinner and sufferer from the brokenness of this world. When the ark of the covenant was brought into Jerusalem, the remembrance of God's covenant faithfulness caused David to evoke the exodus celebration, calling on all the nations to, "Proclaim the good news of his salvation from day to day" (1 Chron 16.23). It was Yahweh's *ḥesed* that gave David confidence that his house and its place in God's purposes was secured for all generations (1 Chron 17.13; Psa 18.50). At the dedication of the temple, God's covenant faithfulness was the centerpiece of the worshippers' praise, king Solomon's prayer of dedication, and Yahweh's hope-inspiring response (2 Chron 5.13–14; 6.14, 42; 7.3, 6; 7.11–22). Years later, when Israel found themselves in battle against insurmountable odds, they marched to victory singing the song of Yahweh's *ḥesed* (2 Chron. 20.20–21). Even after the nation fell into idolatry and the discipline of captivity, the servants of God who led the people into restoration did so by constantly reminding themselves and their comrades that their strength and song and salvation were to be found in the covenant faithfulness of their God (Ezra 3.11; 7.27–28; 9.9; Neh 1.1–11; 9.17, 32). The history of Israel is a story of a people who were repeatedly seeking, finding, realizing, forgetting, remembering, and ultimately learning to trust more and more in the covenant faithfulness of Yahweh their God.

The Psalms—Israel's collection of divinely inspired songs, prayers, and meditations on their God and their relationship with him—contain a number of vivid descriptions of the glory of Yahweh proven through his covenant faithfulness (Psa 23.6; 36.5–10; 63.1–5; 98.1–3; 107.1–3, 43; et al). One could argue that the central theme of the Psalms is the covenant faithfulness of Yahweh, God of Israel. At the exodus, the covenant faithfulness of God was the epicenter of God's work to save his people, and so the psalmists had a keen interest in remembering and reminding Israel that this is what made their God uniquely glorious, singularly trustworthy among all the gods of the world. If Israel ever lost sight of Yahweh's covenant faithfulness, then they would lose their entire understanding of him, which would result in losing the salvation he so richly provided them.

There is another concept that is key to understanding the significance of God's covenant faithfulness for the salvation of his people. In Psalm 85, the psalmist cries out for God to once again bring the salvation and joy that he is uniquely able to provide (vv. 4, 7). The psalmist then turns to exhort the worshippers to remember and recognize what makes Yahweh able to save. We are not surprised that the first thing that he identifies about Yahweh is that he is the God of *ḥesed* and truth, that he is faithful to his covenantal promises (Psa 85.10). But then there is a curious turn in the language. The rest of the Psalm underscores a seemingly different dimension of God's glory: his righteousness.

> Graciousness and truth have met together;
>> Righteousness and peace have kissed each other.
> Truth sprouts from the earth,
>> And righteousness looks down from heaven.
> Indeed, the LORD will give what is good,
>> And our land will yield its produce.
> Righteousness will go before Him
>> And will make His footsteps into a way. (Psa 85.10–13)

Three times the text emphasizes to us that what satisfies and saves the people of God is the righteousness of God. This scripture along with a number of passages throughout the Psalms and prophets teaches that salvation is made possible only through the righteousness of God (Psa 65.5; 98.1, 9; 118.19, 25; 132.9, 16; Isa 41.10; 51.5; 61.10; Jer 23.6; 33.16; et al). To put it another way, the scriptures teach that God is the only reliable source of salvation—he alone can set right what is wrong in our lives—because he himself is righteous. Apart from the righteousness of God, there is no hope of salvation. This might seem like a new concept in contrast or at least in addition to the notion that it is Yahweh's covenant faithfulness and *ḥesed* that save, but actually God's faithfulness and righteousness are interdependent partners of his nature and work of salvation (Psa 36.5–10;

40.7–11; 48.9–10; 85.7–11; 89.1–2, 14; 98.3, 9; Jer 33.11, 16; Hos 2.19; 10.12). What we are finding here is a clarifying definition of what makes the covenant faithfulness of God so important and why it is the essence of his glory. The scriptures are teaching us that the covenant faithfulness of God is the proof of his righteousness, securing his position as the one and only glorious God who is capable and willing to save all those who entrust their lives to him alone.

But like the days when Israel was enslaved in Egypt, there were many times when the glory of Yahweh and the promise of his saving righteousness was shrouded from human eyes. Psalm 89 captures the despair of the apparent chain of broken promises left behind by Yahweh, the so-called glorious God of covenant faithfulness whose supposed righteousness was to be the salvation of his people. Israel had been completely broken down, overrun by enemy forces, and vulnerable. No one was sitting on the throne of the great King David. None of the glory that had been promised to Abraham's family was anywhere to be found. The once-noble, liberated people whom God had said would bless all the nations now found themselves once again in shambles and shackles just like they were in Egypt so long ago. The psalmist writes as one who had spent his entire life listening to all the old people sing the songs and tell the tales of Yahweh's salvation, yet from his vantage point there was not a bit of God's glory in sight. The psalmist had heard of Yahweh's saving righteousness in his covenant faithfulness (Psa 89.1, 3, 5, 8), and he knew about the promises made to David's house which were supposed to finally establish what God had initiated with Abraham's family in the exodus (Psa 89.19–37). But when the psalmist looked at his world, all he could see was a landscape as dark and hopeless as the shores of the Nile where his ancestors had cried to their God with the same groanings that he now felt centuries later (Psa 89.46–51). It sure seemed like Israel's faith in the glory of the saving righteousness of their God, who they had thought would always maintain *hesed* for their good, was just a fantasy after all. The psalmist's disillusionment over the apparent abandonment by his God is an all too familiar echo of the same sort of discouragement and despair that fills the world we find ourselves in today among those still on the quest for God.

And yet Psalm 89 ends not with despair but a ray of hope (v. 52). Despite the doubts and fears that perhaps the glory of God had simply been a figment of Israel's imagination, there was still a hopeful belief in the saving righteousness of Yahweh who was full of *hesed,* faithful to his covenant. God had proven his glory through the saving righteousness of his covenant faithfulness to Israel at the exodus, and he would prove it again. When troubles arise and make it difficult to see the glory of God, it can become especially and extremely tempting to turn to the gods of this world that seem more immediately useful and helpful to save and satisfy. But even today when God's people are beckoned by the false promises of other gods, we must learn like the writer of Psalm 89 to wait for God to prove himself faithful to his promises yet again. Abraham, the exodus, and David were the stories that the prophets constantly turned to as they reminded Israel (and people of all the nations who would listen) of the hope that one day Yahweh would come to be ultimately faithful to his covenant, proving himself righteous once and for all, bringing eternal salvation for the peoples of any and every nation who would recognize and rely upon his glory alone over all the other gods of the world. The word of the prophets to Israel is one that God's people in every place and time must hold firmly: He will save those who patiently wait for the hope of his glory.

Eventually that hope was fulfilled through the most unexpected and shocking turn of events imaginable. A Bethlehem-born carpenter from Nazareth (who had been raised during his early years in Egypt, of all places) came proclaiming that he was working out the fulfillment of all righteousness (Matt 3.15) and that Yahweh was being faithful to the words of his covenant through him (Matt 5.17). Those who witnessed the deeds that this man did and heard the words that he spoke found in him the fulfillment of all the promises of God. They saw God's covenant faithfulness coming to the climactic height that the prophets had pointed them toward for centuries (Matt 1.23; 2.4–5; 2.15; 2.16–18; 4.12–17; 8.10–12; 8.14–17; 12.15–21; et al). In the righteousness of God brought about by Jesus the Christ, lost and sinful people beheld the glory of God and found the joy of salvation greater than what the redeemed slaves on the shores of the Red Sea could have ever imagined (Matt 1.21). The God of Israel had not forgotten or forsaken his people; he had been faithful to his covenant all along. His righteousness was fulfilled in the life, death, resurrection, and ascension of Jesus the Christ. True and lasting salvation had come to mankind, and the glory of God was filling the earth.

One of the greatest biblical texts that helps us to understand the covenant faithfulness of God through Christ is the book of Romans, the apostle Paul's grand treatise on "the gospel of God" (Rom 1.1). In Romans, Paul demonstrates that the "good news" for the world is that God has faithfully fulfilled all his covenantal promises through Christ thereby proving his righteousness and making his glory known to all nations in order to save all who are willing to believe and pledge their loyalty to Christ (Rom 1.1–7; 1.16–17; 3.21–26; 5.1–11; 16.25–27). He sums up this message—directly connecting salvation to God's faithfulness-based righteousness—by saying, "For I am not ashamed of the gospel, for it is the power of God for salvation to everyone who believes, to the Jew first and also to the Greek. For in it *the* righteousness of God is revealed from faith to faith; as it is written: 'But the righteous *one* will live by faith'" (Rom 1.16–17). The "good news of God" (Rom 1.1) is that the perfectly obedient life, atoning sacrifice, and justifying resurrection of Christ have proven God to be faithful to the words of his covenant. His expectations for mankind have been fulfilled in Christ, the penalty for man's sins were paid by Christ, and his vision of eternal life has been accomplished by Christ. Christ's work has proven God to be faithful, thus revealing God's righteousness that in turn produces faithfulness to

God among all those who believe in the gospel, so that they can now be made righteous in God's sight.

Just as Israel was redeemed from slavery in Egypt, now all people can be saved from sin and death through Jesus Christ, who is the ultimate embodied expression of the covenant faithfulness of God and the power of his saving righteousness. Besides presenting us with this majestic doctrinal argument for the glory of the righteousness of God proven through his covenant faithfulness in the person of Christ, Paul also spends a great deal of energy in Romans making us understand what kind of life those who have pledged themselves to Yahweh, the God of covenant faithfulness, must lead in response to him.

The first subject that Paul addresses in Romans is the devastation of idolatry among those that do not recognize and submit to the glory of God (Rom 1.18–32). All the horrifying evils that have defined the human story find their roots in rejecting, ignoring, and exchanging the glory of the true God for something or someone lesser. Saints living in contemporary Western culture may think that warnings against idolatry like this are only meaningful for ancient people or more "primitive" cultures than their own. Nothing could be further from the truth. Idolatry is alive and well throughout the world as it always has been, and the fact that the people of God often do not realize its presence around us is the reason that we too often fall prey to the empty promises of imitation gods.

God, help us see your glory more clearly each day and crush the idols of the world that only ever disappoint and destroy! Material wealth offers security and prominence but will eventually rot or be stolen, and in the meantime will never be enough. Pleasures of the flesh initially produce sweet blossoms of happiness only to fall dead off the vine after providing only temporary comfort and strength. Human lovers seem powerful, transformative, and everlasting, worthy of forsaking all others including the God who is and made love itself, yet they will only betray their vows or eventually pass away.

Political forces and social movements that promise justice and righteousness (at whichever end of the political spectrum one might bow down) inevitably show their true colors as either intentionally manipulative and deceptive or as empty dreams. There are no gods besides our God who makes and keeps covenant. His glory surpasses all others. Those who have submitted themselves to the saving righteousness of God found in the gracious reign of Christ must reject all the other gods of this world and be loyal to him to the same degree that he has been loyal to us.

Loyalty expressed through obedience to God is the purpose of the preaching of the gospel and is the essence of genuine, saving, righteousness-producing faith in Christ (Rom 1.5; 2.4–11; 6.12–23; 10.16; 16.26). Without faithful obedience, a saint cannot truly say that they are a believer in the gospel of God. Paul's argumentation in Romans demonstrates that the faithfulness of God (doing what he said he would do) is what has proven him to be righteous, and therefore our faithfulness in response to God (by obediently doing what he has told us to do and what we promised to do from the day we were baptized into Christ, confessing him as Lord) is what makes us righteous in his sight. Granted, God never fails at all in his faithfulness and is therefore righteous, while in our sin we often fail to live up to the standard of faithfulness that righteousness would require. We depend upon his mercy and grace each moment in pursuit of his righteousness. But we must never make the mistake of thinking that our faith can be anything less than a life of constant obedience to the one who has faithfully loved us and given himself for us.

All those who practice the obedience of faith in response to God's faithfulness can only do so by embracing the self-sacrificial love of God (Rom 12.1–2). God's faithfulness has always been fueled by his steadfast love (*hesed*) which he ultimately expressed through the sacrifice of his Son (Rom 5.6–11; 8.31–39). By revealing his glory through the love of the cross of Christ, God has transformed and renewed our perspective so that we are no longer conformed to the world that is ruled by self-interest. Rather, we are being transformed more and more each day into the image of Christ himself (Rom 5.1–5; 8.28–30; 12.1–2; 12.9–10; 13.8–14). God's sacrificial love has been poured into our hearts to cause us to be faithful in obedience to him even as he has been faithful in his covenant with us.

God's faithfulness not only compels followers of Christ to loyally love and obey him in return, but it also demands that we be devoted to one another in brotherly love. Perhaps the most pressing issue that Paul was writing to address among the saints in Rome as the proper and necessary response to the faithfulness of God is that those who have been saved in Christ must learn to be faithful to one another as the family of God (Rom 14–15). The saints in Rome were a culturally diverse group with individuals coming together from varied and even opposing backgrounds. Their differing social standings, probable political leanings, and certainly religious and spiritual perspectives serve as an instructive mirror-image of the culture that saints living in a pluralistic society find ourselves in today.

What are we to do with the wide variety of persons that God brings together in his family? Are we to subdivide and segregate the kingdom of Christ according to generations, political convictions, socio-economic standing, or ethnic heritage? I imagine that nearly all of God's people living in the contemporary Western social climate would say no. But whatever words may come from our lips, what do our actions say? Do we prioritize the fellowship of our social, cultural, and political identities in the world more than the bond we share by God's Spirit with one another? How do we regard, speak about, and relate to brothers and sisters in Christ that would have been opposed to us in the things of the world (and perhaps still differ with us on several significant matters)? Do we claim to have love and harmony with all those who are in the family of God even as we despise or judge the socio-political opinions, cultural circumstances, or ethnic burdens of our brethren with whom we differ in the flesh? Have we done what Jesus commanded when he told us to "deny self" at the foot of the cross so that the only affiliation that matters to us is what we have found in Christ?

At the climax of this great discourse on the saving righteousness made possible by God's covenant faithfulness in Christ, Paul's bold exhortation to the saints is that they (we) learn to operate together as family, refusing to allow personal preferences or differing opinions (even over some significant matters) to drive them (us) apart or allow them (us) to look down upon one another. Saints must—I repeat, must—remain true and faithful to one another as members of the covenant family because God has been true and faithful to the words of his covenant for us and our good. "Therefore, accept one another, just as Christ also accepted us, for the glory of God. For I say that Christ has become a servant ... in behalf of the truth of God, to confirm the promises given to the fathers" (Rom 15.7–8). The gospel is for all so all who share in the joys of the salvation that the gospel provides must share their lives together as a witness to the life-altering, world-changing power of God's covenant faithfulness. So now, even in such a terribly self-absorbed, fractured, unloving place as the United States of America, we who are in Christ must obey the Lord's command to accept one another in the faith and love found in the covenant faithfulness of God and in so doing we will serve the purpose of God to bring hope to the nations (Rom 15.13).

Audacious hope is the guiding light for those that have entrusted themselves to the saving power of God's covenant faithfulness. If we truly have been saved by the power of the righteousness of God, if we believe in his glory, if we have come to know his faithfulness through the gospel of Christ, then how can we ever be anything less than supremely confident both in our present salvation in Christ and the new life we will one day share with him in the resurrection? Fear, despondence, and anxiety that come from the world have no place in the hearts and minds of those who know the gospel of God's covenant faithfulness: "Therefore, having been justified by faith, we have peace with God through our Lord Jesus Christ, through whom we also have obtained our introduction by faith into this grace in which we stand; and we celebrate in hope of the glory of God" (Rom 5.1–2). Paul repeatedly exhorts saints to be a people of steadfast hope for our future in Christ, rooted in the confidence that we have through the salvation we have found in Christ (Rom 8.9–11, 24–25, 28–39; 15.8–13). God has been faithful to the word of his covenant to take what was wrong in us and make it right, and so we live each moment with confidence in his grace. We also live in hope that one day he will fulfill his covenant of promise, returning to set all things right in heaven and on earth and bring us to himself for eternity. We are people of hope who proclaim that hope to all who will hear so that they too can be saved.

And make no mistake about it, proclaiming the hope of the good news of the glory of God is why we are here. Paul plainly tells us both at the beginning and ending of Romans that the mission of preaching the gospel was the impetus for writing the letter in the first place (Rom 1.8–17; 15.14–33). Paul's intention was to come to Rome in order to make it his new mission base for further expansion in the preaching of the kingdom of Christ, so he wrote to the saints there about the saving righteousness of God proven through his covenant faithfulness in Christ in order to clarify their understanding of the true doctrine of the gospel and to exhort them to live in such a way that would align with the gospel. All this was so that they would be prepared upon his arrival to share in fruitful partnership with him in the mission of preaching the gospel to the nations.

Why was Paul so obsessed with continually reaching new frontiers with the gospel and to constantly draw other saints into that work alongside him? Paul truly believed that, through his covenant faithfulness from the waters of the Red Sea to the shores of Galilee, the God and Father of Jesus Christ had proven himself to be the God who surpasses all others and that his name must be made known until the earth is filled with the knowledge of the glory of his name. This is why Paul said at the outset of this letter,

For God, whom I serve in my spirit in the *preaching of the* gospel
of His Son, is my witness ... [how I am] always in my prayers requesting if perhaps now, at last by the will of God, I will succeed in
coming to you. ... I am under obligation both to Greeks and to the
uncultured, both to the wise and to the foolish. So, for my part, I
am eager to preach the gospel to you also who are in Rome. For I am
not ashamed of the gospel ..." (Rom 1.9–17)

Paul devoted every moment of his existence to the mission of bringing
the gospel of Christ to more and more people who had not yet heard it
because deep down in the bones of his soul he believed in the glorious
truth about the God of heaven who has always kept his covenantal
promises, proving himself to be righteous and able to save and satisfy
lost human beings faced with the consequence of their sins and the
burden of their suffering in the world (Rom 1.16–17; 3.21–5.11).

Imagine what God would accomplish through his people if we
all believed in his faithfulness as strongly as the Israelites did when
they passed through the sea and as strongly as Paul did when he
found salvation in Jesus Christ. What if all God's people everywhere
made it our highest priority—not just in word, but in practical action, using every resource at our disposal every moment of every day,
individually and communally—to preach the gospel to all nations?
What if rather than seeking ways to bring in greater strength to help
ourselves, our goal and proactive work was to train up, build up, and
send out workers to all the corners of the globe where there are still
souls who have yet to see the glory of God in the face of Christ? If
the preaching of the gospel of God became such an obsession, we
would certainly have to make significant sacrifices of our finances
and comforts, reorient our personal schedules and social agendas,
be mocked and ridiculed in society, and suffer any number of loss-
es in this world for Christ. But for those who believe, all these are
a perfectly reasonable expectation in the service of proclaiming the
good news about our God who has proven his glorious righteousness
through his covenant faithfulness in Christ.

Now to Him who is able to establish you according to my gospel and the preaching of Jesus Christ, according to the revelation of the mystery which has been kept secret for long ages past, but now has been disclosed, and through the scriptures of the prophets, in accordance with the commandment of the eternal God, has been made known to all the nations, *leading* to obedience of faith; to the only wise God, through Jesus Christ, be the glory forever. Amen. (Rom 16.25–27)

There is a world out there full of people—some across the street, some across the seas—who are looking for someone or something to save them from the dangers of this world and the disappointments they face daily. They are searching for the God who has what it takes to save them. Most will believe in false gospels of imitation gods who promise redemption and joy but will deliver sorrow in this realm and everlasting death in the next. You know the tragedy of their story; it used to be our story. Now we know the glory of the true God whose faithfulness and righteousness has provided salvation to all of us who have pledged ourselves in loyal obedience to him. But how will they hear the good news unless we who have received the joy of his salvation go and tell them so that they also might believe (Rom 10.5–17)? Through his faithfulness from Egypt to Calvary, God has made known the glories of his saving righteousness, his covenant faithfulness. Only one question remains for the fate of the lost world: Will the people of God be as faithful to their work in his saving purpose as he has been faithful to them?

# "By Faith"

## Jason Longstreth

Without question, the exodus served as the centerpiece of Israel's history and provided a unifying experience through which the nation of Israel would share a common narrative and heritage. However, more importantly, it also provided the theological background for nearly everything the Israelites understood about their relationship with God. It was through this event that Israel had become known as the chosen people of God whom He had brought up out of the land of Egypt, and it was a result of this event that these people would experience God's favor and enter into the land of promise. Therefore, Israel's identity was intimately connected to the exodus.[1]

However, the exodus was not only connected to the identity of Israel, it also formed the foundation for many of Israel's activities and rituals. That certainly was the case when it came to the commemoration of the Passover itself and the command to "Remember this day" (Exod 13.3) throughout future generations. It was also one of the most significant collective memories for the nation of Israel. The term "exodus" came to represent a number of different aspects of what God had done or would do for Israel. On the one hand, it represented God's deliverance as He brought them out of Egypt and destroyed Pharaoh's army. In another respect, it represented the elec-

---

[1] Ruth A. Reese, "Joseph Remembered the Exodus: Memory, Narrative, and Remembering the Future," *Journal of Theological Interpretation* 9:2 (2015) 277.

tion of Israel as God's chosen people, unique among all the nations of earth. The exodus served as a reminder of the covenant God had made with Israel and the obligations that were a part of the covenant. In addition, the exodus represented the promise that God had made to Israel, especially in light of His relationship with the patriarchs.

Therefore, it is not surprising that the exodus would find its way into the narrative of Hebrews 11. It would be astonishing if it did not appear in that history of those men of old who gained approval by faith. Certainly, we cannot have a list of individuals from Israel's history who demonstrated faith and not include Moses. After all, the Hebrews writer had already indicated that Moses was faithful in all His house, twice in a span of only four verses (Heb 3.2, 5). Furthermore, it is nearly impossible to discuss the life of Moses without discussing the exodus. Thus, the Hebrews writer introduces his narrative concerning Moses almost exactly in the middle of Hebrews 11 and, after giving details regarding his birth, his upbringing, his choice to be identified with his people, and his leaving Egypt (as well as the motivation that led Moses to make these choices), he tells us, "By faith he kept the Passover and the sprinkling of the blood, so that he who destroyed the firstborn would not touch them. By faith they passed through the Red Sea as though they were passing through dry land; and the Egyptians, when they attempted it, were drowned." (Heb 11.28–29) [2] This passage emphasizes the fact that the exodus was accomplished "by faith." Such an assertion carries with it a number of implications. It is also connected to the context of Hebrews 11.

## What Is Faith?

Although Hebrews 11 is itself connected to the greater context of the entire epistle, we will not do a broad examination of Hebrews at this time. However, I do believe it is important to understand the context of this particular chapter in order to understand what the author of Hebrews was implying when he talked about the exodus

---

[2] Unless noted otherwise, all quotations of scripture are from the 1995 update to the NASB.

occurring "by faith." Of course, it is well established that this chapter contains a detailed examination of faith. It begins, "Now faith is the assurance of things hoped for, the conviction of things not seen." (Heb 11.1) It then proceeds to give further descriptions of what faith does, how faith was manifested in the lives of various individuals, and the necessity of faith in those who seek to please God. However, faith is not the only theme or thread that runs throughout this chapter, as McClister identifies at least two additional threads,[3] both of which are also related to the exodus.

The first of these auxiliary themes is the idea of holding to a sure conviction concerning the things God has said. The people of faith not only believe in God, but they also believe in the promises of God. Therefore, if God has said that something will happen, the people of faith accept it as a certainty. This concept is clearly demonstrated in the lives of Noah, the patriarchs, Moses, Joshua, and Rahab. Their complete acceptance of God's promises led them to act—often putting themselves at risk. This dedication toward acting on God's word also caused them to have a forward-looking faith. The exodus experience embodies this conviction.

The second of the additional threads that runs through Hebrews is the idea of escape from death. The Israelites believe God will deliver them from the living death of slavery, death in the wilderness, and the death from starvation and invasion that results from not having a land of one's own. This is what caused Israel to set out from Egypt, not only escaping death during the exodus itself, but also throughout the aftermath of the exodus.

These connections to the exodus are also seen in what is commonly called the definition of faith in Hebrews 11.1: "the assurance of things hoped for and the conviction of things not seen." While it is widely recognized that this is not meant to be a comprehensive or exhaustive definition of faith, it highlights certain characteristics of

---

[3] David McClister, *A Commentary on Hebrews* (Temple Terrace: Florida College Press, 2015) 277.

faith that are important to the theme that is developed throughout the chapter. God's people of faith possessed an assurance concerning those things for which they hoped. They also felt a conviction regarding those things they had not yet seen. This served as their motivation to take action and press on toward those better things. In the same way, the Israelites believed in God's promise regarding the Promised Land and they were willing to risk their lives based on the assurance that God would be with them and would deliver them from their enemies. This concept is an integral part of the exodus narrative and fits into the overarching theme of Hebrews 11.

However, faith implied much more than just the assurance of things hoped for and the conviction of things not seen. It also meant much more than just belief. We have already noted that the people of faith in Hebrews 11 believed not only in God, but also in what God said or what He promised. This is consistent with how the word is used throughout the New Testament. In this way, belief was placed in scripture, the Law, the prophets, Moses, or anything God was saying at any moment.[4] In addition, the word "faith" came to be the most commonly used term in early Christianity to describe the relation of man to God.[5] This relationship was based on the idea of man turning to God as a result of some revelation that was given by Him. The response to the revelation represented a deeper connection.

This same kind of response and relationship is also what James describes as "faith" in James 2.20–26. This faith involves the whole person. It engages the intellect, the emotions, and the will. It has sometimes been described in this way: the mind comprehends or understands the truth and accepts it as such, the heart desires and rejoices in the truth, and the will acts upon the truth. Therefore, true faith leads to action, not just intellectual contemplation or emotionalism. James provided two great examples to demonstrate this kind of faith—Abraham and Rahab. The pairing of these two examples is

---

[4] TDNT, πιστεύω et al., 6:205.
[5] Ibid.

a bit shocking, because Abraham and Rahab represent a stark contrast in just about every aspect. However, they shared faith in God. Furthermore, Abraham demonstrated his faith through the works that he performed. In the same way, Rahab demonstrated her faith through the works that she performed.

In some ways, this serves as a good introduction to our deeper discussion regarding Hebrews 11, because it is generally accepted that the Hebrews writer is making the same kind of argument when presenting those individuals who accomplished great feats by faith. Yet Hebrews 11 does not provide examples of people who were perfect. In fact, on some level the narrative that is provided in this chapter is not really about this great cloud of witnesses at all. Instead, it is about faith and what faith does. So, what is the connection between the exodus and faith?

## Remembering the Exodus

As has already been mentioned, the primary reference to the exodus in Hebrews (or at least the reference that most people consider when examining the exodus in Hebrews) is found in the midst of the Moses account (vv. 23–29). However, this is not the only time the exodus is mentioned in Hebrews 11. In fact, it is not even the first reference to the exodus in Hebrews 11. Instead, that honor is found in a verse that is describing the faith of Joseph: "By faith Joseph, when he was dying, made mention of the exodus of the sons of Israel, and gave orders concerning his bones" (v.22).

This passage is interesting because the exodus had not yet occurred when Joseph died. What makes this even more interesting is the fact that the Greek word translated "made mention" in the NASB (and many other translations; Gr. *mnēmoneuō*) is not usually translated that way. Instead, the word ordinarily conveys some sense of recall or memory and is normally translated as "remember" (e.g., Exod 13.3; Heb 13.7).[6] However, since there is no way that Joseph could have

---

[6] The basic idea is calling something to mind. See BDAG, μνημονεύω. Notice its usage earlier in Hebrews 11.15.

remembered an event that was not yet a historical fact, the translators changed the verb. Furthermore, to explain why this particular verb was used in this passage, some have argued that Joseph could not have remembered the exodus itself, but he could have remembered the promise of the exodus or he may have reflected on what God had said. In fact, there is no doubt that this sort of reflection was involved. Consider what was said in Genesis 50.25, "Then Joseph made the sons of Israel swear, saying, 'God will surely take care of you, and you shall carry my bones up from here.'" Why was Joseph so certain that the sons of Israel would carry his bones up from Egypt? This is directly connected to the promise that God had made to bring the children of Israel out of Egypt. Joseph's instructions are also referenced when Moses finally does lead Israel out of Egypt. "Moses took the bones of Joseph with him, for he had made the sons of Israel solemnly swear, saying, 'God will surely take care of you, and you shall carry my bones from here with you'" (Exod 13.19). However, neither Genesis nor Exodus say Joseph *remembered* the exodus.

Is it possible that Hebrews uses the word that is usually translated "remembered" for another reason? Reese argued that this term is used in Hebrews 11 because the Hebrews writer wanted to make a strong connection to the collective memory of Israel.[7] In other words, whenever an Israelite thought about the exodus or even heard the word "exodus," they immediately connected it to the concept of remembering, analogous to our reaction to "the Alamo" or "Pearl Harbor." However, the exodus served as far more than just a motivational symbol or a battle cry. Instead, it is the central event in all of Israel's history. By remembering the exodus, they remembered everything that it represented.

Therefore, the significance of this "remembrance" is not found in the mental recollection of historical events, even though that type of memory played a part when the Israelites remembered the exodus. Instead, this remembering was much more of an exercise in reflecting

---

[7] For a longer discussion on the use of "remembered" in Hebrews 11.22, see Reese, 267–286.

on the significance of these events and a commemoration of the relationship that existed between God and his people. We may compare this to what we experience when we partake of the Lord's Supper "in remembrance" of Jesus. Certainly, the Christian is expected to mentally recall the Lord's death when we partake, but we also do more than this. In our proclamation of the Lord's death until He comes, we are reminded of the significance of His death, we recognize the relationship we have with God because of what Christ did, and we conform our actions to that recognition accordingly. We renew our promise to Jesus, pledging to live out that commitment more thoroughly and consistently than we have in the past.

Another demonstration of this multi-faceted meaning for the concept of remembrance can be seen by considering what was meant when we are told that God "remembered" Israel while they were in Egypt. This clearly does not mean that God had forgotten them in the sense of having no recollection of them. He had not misplaced Israel and then remembered where they were. Instead, He was moved to act based on His relationship with them, consistent with His promises. In the same way, when we are told that Israel forgot God, they were not suffering a mental failure, but a moral failure. Had they remembered the exodus, they would have remembered their relationship with God and acted accordingly.

One final note that can be made concerning the mention of the exodus in relation to Joseph is the fact that the exodus serves as the event that connects the first half of Hebrews 11 to the second half of Hebrews 11. It was also the event that joined all the Israelites together.

## By Faith *They* Passed Through

As it has already been noted, the main text concerning the exodus in Hebrews 11 is generally considered to be the portion that discusses the life of Moses(vv. 23–29). Here the Hebrews writer examines various aspects of the Moses story and presents a narrative of faith. This account also includes the theme of escape from death (beginning with Moses escaping from death as a child and culminating with the Passover and exodus). It is in the conclusion of this account that we read, "By faith they passed through the Red Sea as though they were passing through dry land; and the Egyptians, when they attempted it, were drowned" (Heb 11.29).

One of the details that stands out in this account is the fact that the subject switches from a singular person to a collective entity. Throughout most of the chapter up to this point, the subjects were singular: Abel, Enoch, Noah, Abraham, Sarah, Isaac, Jacob, Joseph, and Moses. The only exceptions were a collective "men of old" in verse two, the "worlds" in verse three, and several references to "these" and "them" (taking a collective view of the individuals that had been mentioned in the chapter) in vv. 13–16. However, in v. 29 we are told "*they* passed through the Red Sea." In this way, the entire nation participated in this act of faith.

Another significant element of this text is the fact that the Israelites were willing to take action even though the outcome of passing through the sea was far from certain. In this way, it was an act of faith. Furthermore, the narrative points out the fact that when the Egyptians attempted to do the same thing, the outcome for the Egyptians was death. This additional detail emphasizes the real danger that was involved in passing through the sea. However, their faith motivated them to do so. As McClister noted, "…the more immediate point of this verse is to further illustrate that faith overcomes any fear we may have because of our earthly circumstances. Moses' faith (and his parents') consists of one example after another of how faith conquered fear, and here the Israelites as a nation joined in that same faith." [8]

## Faith in Action

In considering the actions of the Israelites at the time of the exodus, the necessity of faith manifesting itself through action is clearly seen. This concept of faith doing something or acting in some way is often

---

[8] McClister, 420.

considered the central theme to Hebrews 11. In addition, James tells us, "Even so faith, if it has no works, is dead, being by itself" (2.17), and "…are you willing to recognize, you foolish fellow, that faith without works is useless" (2.20)? However, we must also recognize that the type of works in which we engage ourselves also matters. God does not just want us to do *something*—He wants us to do what He has commanded us to do. This requires certain qualities on our part. We must be humble enough to seek out God's guidance and instruction. We must also be committed to obeying God and trusting in Him.

God has always demanded obedience of His people, whether in the Old Testament or in the New Testament. In fact, this characteristic of obedience is implied anytime we are examining a people of faith, because believing is equated with obeying. This is particularly true when examining the concept of faith in Hebrews 11.[9] It was only by obedience that the Israelites would reach the Promised Land (and their lack of obedience resulted in them falling in the wilderness). In the same way, it is only by obedience that the people of God today will reach their goal.

As to the idea of trust, this concept is also implied when talking about faith, whether in the Old Testament or in the New Testament. However, this is especially true when dealing with matters such as the exodus. The Theological Dictionary of the New Testament makes the point that in Judaism the sense of trust was combined with faith and while references to trusting in God were comparatively rare in scripture, the ideas of trust and obedience are part of the faith that was demonstrated by the Old Testament characters in Hebrews 11.[10] They trusted that God would fulfill His promises and they trusted in His miraculous power. This is what led them to pass through the sea.

Jesus shared His thoughts on the idea of a false faith (one that lacks both trust and obedience) in Luke 6.46 when He asked, "Why do you call Me, 'Lord, Lord,' and do not do what I say?" It is worth

---

[9] TDNT, 6:205.
[10] Ibid., 6:206.

noting that this passage is located right between a statement concerning the idea of bearing fruit (Luke 6.43–45) and Jesus' exhortation to act on His words and thus establish a firm foundation (Luke 6.47–49). Those who do not act upon the words of Jesus will not have the kind of faith that will serve them well. Instead, they will experience the ruin of their house.

An example of insufficient faith is found in Numbers 20.12. The most interesting part of this text is probably the fact that Moses serves as the example of a worthless faith. After Moses struck the rock twice, the Lord responded, "Because you have not believed Me, to treat Me as holy in the sight of the sons of Israel, therefore you shall not bring this assembly into the land which I have given them" (20.12). True faith obeys God and treats him as holy. Given everything that we know about Israel and her history, it may be difficult to associate this kind of true faith with the Israelites. Certainly, they had a history of disobedience. However, they remembered the exodus, because in that event they did obey the Lord.

Another aspect of faith that is very closely related to trust is hope. It is also clear that when Hebrews 11 uses the term "faith," it includes the idea of hope, because faith in God's promise is the essence of hope.[11] Those Old Testament characters in Hebrews 11 understood that they were just strangers and pilgrims. They were headed to a heavenly dwelling. This forward-looking faith is exactly what Israel demonstrated in the exodus and it serves as an example to all of us. In a sense, it is faith that causes us to press on toward our mission. Faith also leads the believer to focus on the eternal instead of the temporal.

In addition, it is by faith that we participate in the activity of God. This may be one of the most significant items when it comes to Israel and the exodus. Ordinarily, we would think about the exodus in terms of what God had done for Israel. This is certainly appropriate. However, there is also the aspect of what the children of Israel

---

[11] Ibid., 6:207–208.

did themselves. By faith they were active participants and played a part in what was accomplished. This characteristic of faith is often connected to the idea of faithfulness.[12] Once again, we may struggle with thinking about Israel as being faithful to God. She often fell short in that regard. However, this is what made the crossing at the Red Sea such a special event. Israel was faithful on this occasion. As a result, they are given credit for their faith. This idea of being credited because of what they did by faith often leads individuals into discussions of merit and grace.[13] However, what we must understand is that God has allowed us to participate with Him in His works. Furthermore, He not only allows us to participate, but He has also called us for this purpose. When we respond by faith, we engage in those activities God has prepared for us to do.

## They Came Out of Egypt

By faith Israel came out of Egypt. At the time of the exodus, they were willing to place their trust in God and they believed in His promises. As a result, they were willing to obey Him and they looked forward to the reward that was set before them. In many respects, this event may be seen as the high-water mark of Israel's relationship with God. That was why it was the event that Israel remembered. However, they did not remember it enough. This event should have motivated Israel to a greater faithfulness to God and a deeper relationship with Him. If only they had continued to walk by faith. May we learn from these examples set before us.

We must also remember that the true purpose of everything in Hebrews 11 was not a "looking back" but a "looking forward." By faith Moses was looking to the reward. By faith Joseph looked forward to the exodus. By faith Isaac regarded things to come. The patriarchs died in faith, without receiving the promises, but having

---

[12] Ibid., 6:208.

[13] For a discussion on the relationship between merit and participation as it relates to salvation, see Charles D. Raith, "Aquinas and Calvin on Merit, Part II: Condignity and Participation," *Pro-Ecclesia* 21.2 (2012) 195–210.

seen them and having welcomed them from a distance. They desired a better country, a heavenly one. In each of these instances, faith caused them to look forward to what God would do through Jesus Christ. Jesus is the true focus of Hebrews 11.1–12.3, although it is obscured by the artificial man-made chapter division. The Hebrews writer climactically encourages his readers to focus on Jesus as the true "author and perfector of faith" (12.2). In other words, Jesus is the very definition of faith from beginning to end.

We should also note that these examples of faith in Hebrews 11 were foreshadowing Christ. After all, more than Adam, Jesus is the one who offered the better sacrifice and still speaks to us after his death. More than Enoch, Jesus was taken up by God, being found pleasing to Him. More than Noah, Jesus provided the means of salvation inheriting righteousness by faith, while simultaneously condemning the world by its rejection of that salvation. More than Abraham, Jesus left His home, lived as a stranger among us, and brought forth many children of promise, though being as good as dead. More than Isaac, Jesus was the Son of Promise offered up by God and raised from the dead. More than Isaac, Jesus was the one who has blessed both Jacob (Jew) and Esau (Gentile). More than Jacob, Jesus bestowed this blessing upon all of Abraham's offspring while dying on a piece of wood. More than Joseph, Jesus talked with Moses and Elijah about His exodus before He died. More than Moses, Jesus was the Special Child that was beautiful in God's sight, that chose to endure ill treatment with God's people, that endured rather than fearing the wrath of any earthly king, that kept the True Passover and saved the firstborn of God's people, and that delivered God's people in the True Exodus, while bringing divine judgment upon their enemies. More than Joshua, Jesus has prepared a Promised Land where Israel, including pagan idolatrous Canaanite prostitutes like Rahab, may dwell. This is why we must fix our eyes on Jesus and run the race that is set before us, so that we do make it to that Promised Land.

# The New Exodus and the Final Exodus

## Tom Hamilton

One of the most unusual scriptural arguments for the resurrection of the physical body is found in Jesus' use of Exodus 3.6:

> But that the dead are raised, even Moses showed, in the passage about the bush, where he calls the Lord "the God of Abraham and the God of Isaac and the God of Jacob." Now he is not God of the dead, but of the living, for all live to him (Luke 20.37–38).[1]

A common explanation for the logic of the passage is sought in the grammar, where Matthew's account records the words "I am the God of Abraham," etc. (22.32), reflecting his underlying Greek text, *egō eimi* ("I am"), taken over verbatim from the LXX. The point, it is argued, is that God *is* (present tense) the God of the patriarchs and, therefore, they must still be alive somewhere. In addition, it is often cited along with Galatians 3.16 as an example of how careful we need to be in our Bible study, even down to observing the number of a noun (e.g., singular or plural) or the tense of a verb.

However, there are several problems with this argument. First, it is not clear how a mere affirmation that the patriarchs are still alive in any way argues for the necessity of the resurrection; at best it affirms that their spirits have not been annihilated. Second, the grammar simply cannot carry the weight some are trying to place

---

[1] Unless otherwise noted, all quotations of scripture are from the ESV.

upon it. For example, if an atheist father identified himself at his son's funeral with, "I am so-and-so's father," would the Christian be logically justified in concluding that the atheist does in fact, after all, believe in the resurrection? Or if a Christian father of the deceased identified himself with, "I was so-and-so's father," would the Christian be logically justified in rebuking the father for disbelief of the resurrection? Or is it more likely that we should simply not assume that these words are intended to convey such nonsense? Third, if the argument hinges on the tense of the verb, it is incredible that Mark leaves the verb entirely out of his Greek text (12.26). Of course, the verbal idea could still be understood from the context, as reflected in the fact that all of our English versions still say "I am" without the *eimi* in the original text, but its omission when it is the focus of the argument would be almost inexplicable. This is even more telling when one recognizes that the original text of the LXX includes the verb and Mark must intentionally omit it (Exod 3.6 LXX). But most decisive of all is the fact that Luke's account is recorded in such a way that the verb "to be" (*eimi*) cannot be understood or supplied into the sentence at all (Luke 20.37). But if Jesus is not making a grammatical argument, then what is his point?

### The Critical Importance of the Promise to Abraham

When Yahweh first gave His promise to Abraham in Genesis 12, He was articulating the divine redemptive plan that was established before the creation of the cosmos, that is, His eternal purpose to save humanity (Eph 1.3–14; 3.1–13). Paul refers to this Abrahamic promise as nothing less than the "gospel" (or "good news") proclaiming that eternal purpose to save all people: "And the Scripture, foreseeing that God would justify the Gentiles by faith, preached the gospel beforehand to Abraham, saying, 'In you shall all the nations be blessed'" (Gal 3.8).[2] Here Paul is conflating the three instances

---

[2] While it is obvious that the Greek word *ethnē* from Genesis 18.18 and 22.18 can be translated as either "nations" or "Gentiles," it is not equally obvious how Paul in Galatians 3.8 justifiably reads salvation into the Greek word *eneulogēthēsontai*

where Yahweh specifically indicated to Abraham His intention to bless all human beings through Abraham and his family (Gen 12.3; 18.18; 22.18), which intention was repeated to Isaac (Gen 26.4) and Jacob (Gen 28.14). From this point on throughout the remainder of the Old Testament, the three-fold reference to "Abraham, Isaac, and Jacob" is always a shorthand way of indicating this foundational covenant or promise and all that it entailed.[3]

This is one key to understanding the logic of Jesus' resurrection argument noted above (Matt 22.29–32; Mark 12.24–27; Luke 20.34–38). If all the covenant promises of Yahweh to Abraham, Isaac, and Jacob—none other than the singular divine purpose God has for mankind—end with those patriarchs (and everybody else) as worm food, what good are they? If death is the ultimate power and authority in the universe, if death has the final say, and if death is the decisive determiner of everybody's fate, God's covenant faithfulness is meaningless, merely secondary and conditional, and subject to being vetoed and overturned by death.[4] To read of God's covenant with Abraham, Isaac, and Jacob and think that death will be allowed to be victorious in the end is truly to "err, not knowing the scriptures nor the power of God" (Mat 22.29 KJV).

---

("will be blessed"). The answer is found in context. While a large screen television might be considered a blessing in one context, to a man drowning in the middle of the Atlantic Ocean it would be a liability and not a blessing. Similarly, if humanity's singular problem is sin, the only thing that could qualify as a "blessing" in that context would be the forgiveness of sins.

[3] See Gen 50.24–25; Exod 2.23–25; 3.1–4.17; 6.1–8; 33.1–3; Lev 26.40–45; Num 32.6–15; Deut 1.8; 6.4–12; 9.1–29; 29.10–14; 30.15–20; 34.4; 2 Kng 13.22–23; Jer 33.23–26.

[4] Paul makes a similar argument in the synagogue at Antioch of Psidia from Isaiah 55.3: "And as for the fact that he raised him from the dead, no more to return to corruption, he has spoken in this way, 'I will give you the holy and sure blessings of David'" (Acts 13.34). While the passage does not mention resurrection directly and the context of Isaiah 55 cannot be construed to supply it, Paul's argument remains valid: how can the blessings of David be "sure" or "certain," if death can trump them? Note also that the "you" in both Isaiah 55.3 and Paul's quotation in Acts 13.34 is plural, indicating the promise extends to more than just Jesus personally, but to all who can lay claim to the Davidic promise (including Christians today).

## The Critical Importance of the Exodus under Moses

However, there is a second critical key to understanding Jesus' point to the Sadducees about the resurrection. Of the nineteen different passages in the Old Testament that Jesus could have used to speak of Yahweh's covenant with "Abraham, Isaac, and Jacob," Jesus selected the occasion of the burning bush to make his point ("in the passage about the bush;" Mark 12.26; Luke 20.37). As has been demonstrated throughout this lectureship, the exodus from Egypt is Yahweh's greatest act of salvation in the Old Testament, the paradigm for all other redemptive acts in the history of Israel, and that story begins in earnest at the burning bush. Here we are told that "God remembered His covenant with Abraham, Isaac, and Jacob" (Exod 2.24), which does not refer to God's mental recall after a lapse of memory, but being "mindful" of something in such a way as to act in a manner to make the idea a reality. In other words, the exodus from Egypt would become God's first major effort to fulfill His promise to Abraham in any substantial way and thereby to reveal Himself as living up to His covenant name, Yahweh:[5]

> Then Moses said to God, "If I come to the people of Israel and say to them, 'The God of your fathers has sent me to you,' and they ask me, 'What is his name?' what shall I say to them?" God said to Moses, "I AM WHO I AM." And he said, "Say this to the people of Israel, 'I AM has sent me to you.'" God also said to Moses, "Say this to the people of Israel, '[Yahweh], the God of your fathers, the God of Abraham, the God of Isaac, and the God of Jacob, has sent me to you.' This is my name forever, and thus I am to be remembered throughout all generations (Exod 3.13–15, edited)

From Abraham down to Moses, the patriarchs were—to use the words of the writer of Hebrews—merely "heirs of the promise" (Heb 11.9), who "died in faith without receiving the promises" (Heb

---

[5] See V. J. Benson, "The I AM Remembers His Covenant with Abraham," in Thomas Hamilton, ed., *Florida College Annual Lectures 2022* (Temple Terrace: Florida College Press, 2022) xx-xx

12.13) and "did not receive what was promised" (Heb 12.39). However, with what Yahweh purposed to accomplish through Moses, the exodus was to become God's definitive exhibition of redemption and salvation for all the world to see. Yahweh's covenant faithfulness in fulfilling His promise to Abraham was openly displayed for almost 1500 years, as the later prophets hearkened back time and again to the exodus as the ultimate paradigm of divine deliverance for Israel.[6]

Yet as great as this salvation was, the exodus could only foreshadow the as-yet-unrealized true deliverance from death, both physical and spiritual, and inherently points us toward the need for an even greater exodus. One must understand Jesus' reference from Exodus 3.6 to serve two purposes: (a) it demonstrates God's past faithfulness in working out His divine promises to Abraham, Isaac, and Jacob down to Jesus' day; and (b) it simultaneously assures us of God's future faithfulness in bringing those promises to total and complete fulfillment, including the defeat of death by means of the resurrection of the dead. Little did the Sadducees understand that the dawning of that new and greater exodus was already bursting upon them in the very person of Christ. After all, to use the words of the writer of Hebrews again, Moses himself along with all other faithful Israelites were also merely "heirs of the promise" (Heb 11.9), who "died in faith without receiving the promises" (Heb 12.13) and "did not receive what was promised" (Heb 12.39) either. Only with the arrival of this New Moses, Jesus, to inaugurate a New Exodus would the promise to Abraham be more truly fulfilled and God's eternal purpose realized.

## The Shadow and the Body

It seems that most Christians have at best an ambiguous relationship with the Old Testament scriptures. On the one hand, they have been told that the "law" has been "abolished" or "nailed to the cross" (Eph 2.14–15; Col 2.13–17), so that the Old Testament scriptures

---

[6] See Ben Hall, "The Covenant Faithfulness of God," in Thomas Hamilton, ed., *Florida College Annual Lectures 2022* (Temple Terrace: Florida College Press, 2022) xx-xx.

are no longer authoritative, but only to be used for (a) historical background information to the NT; (b) familiarity with OT quotations in the NT; or (c) basic moral teaching akin to Aesop's fables. On the other hand, they have been told that the "law" is still scripture, revealing the character and mind of God, and it is also still obviously authoritative for some things such as child training (just try preaching a sermon on that topic without using Proverbs). The confusion seems to lie in a wide-spread misunderstanding of the word "law" as it is used by NT writers and a corresponding failure to differentiate two particular uses of "law."

This difference is easily seen in Romans 3.21: "But now apart from the Law the righteousness of God has been manifested, being witnessed by the Law and the Prophets" (NASB). Here Paul affirms that God's righteousness has nothing to do with the "law," but it is also at the same time revealed in the "law." To clue to the distinction is found in the phrase "Law and Prophets," the standard way by which Jews referred to their scriptures (they obviously did not call them the "Old" Testament), while the other "law" must be the Mosaic covenant, the relationship God formed with Israel beginning at Mt. Sinai. The latter, the old covenant, has been abolished and one cannot have this covenant relationship with God if one wanted to. In distinct contrast, the Old Testament scriptures, the books of the Bible from Genesis through Malachi, retain their authority as the very words of God that reveal His eternal purpose to us:

> But as for you, continue in what you have learned and have firmly believed, knowing from whom you learned it and how from childhood you have been acquainted with the sacred writings, which are able to make you wise for salvation through faith in Christ Jesus. All Scripture is breathed out by God and profitable for teaching, for reproof, for correction, and for training in righteousness, that the man of God may be complete, equipped for every good work (2 Tim 3.14–17).

The sacred writings known to Timothy from his infancy could only have been the Old Testament scriptures, which Paul here affirms to be inspired and therefore authoritative. In fact, people can only be thoroughly equipped as God's people when these scriptures are used as they should be to (a) teach people what they do not know; (b) rebuke people about what they are doing wrong; (c) correct people about how to fix what they are doing wrong; and (d) give people practice in living right. This agrees with Jesus' own words about the Old Testament scriptures:

> Do not think that I have come to abolish the Law or the Prophets; I have not come to abolish them but to fulfill them. For truly, I say to you, until heaven and earth pass away, not an iota, not a dot, will pass from the Law until all is accomplished. Therefore whoever relaxes one of the least of these commandments and teaches others to do the same will be called least in the kingdom of heaven, but whoever does them and teaches them will be called great in the kingdom of heaven. For I tell you, unless your righteousness exceeds that of the scribes and Pharisees, you will never enter the kingdom of heaven (Matt 5.7–20).

It is obvious that not "all things" foretold in the Old Testament scriptures have been "accomplished" yet (Gr. *genētai* "happened"),[7] so the assurance of Jesus stands that nothing has been abolished or passed from this "Law" (the Old Testament scriptures), unlike the other that has now been abolished (the old covenant relationship).

Not only does the NT explicitly demand our recognition of the authority and purpose of the Old Testament scriptures, but this is also made clear by the example of the apostles and early disciples. Beginning on Pentecost, the early Christians preached the gospel of Jesus Christ with no other scriptures than the Old Testament, and they used these scriptures authoritatively. For example, in Acts 13.46–47

---

[7] At the very least, Paul argues that neither Isaiah 25.8 or Hosea 13.14 will be fulfilled completely until the final resurrection has "happened" (1 Cor 15.54–55; Gr. *genēsetai* "will happen").

Paul cites Isaiah 49.6 as a binding command from the Lord that requires him to evangelize the Gentiles. With Paul's argument in Galatians 3.10–29 about the inferiority and passing of the "law" (old covenant)—which employs several Old Testament scriptures to abrogate the "law," the validity of the argument directly depends upon those Old Testament passages retaining their authority as scripture.

In addition to direct statements of scripture and approved apostolic examples, one should consider the implications of God's eternal purpose and its relation to the Old Testament scriptures. If all scripture is intended to reveal the character and mind of God, especially His single unchanging plan developed before the foundation of the world, one might expect that both the Old and New Testaments would be disclosing aspects of this same message, as opposed to contradictory messages. In fact, this is affirmed repeatedly in the NT. For example, the saving work of Jesus Christ that has been accomplished for all people is said to have already been "preached beforehand to Abraham" (Gal 3.8), and since the entirety of the Old Testament is the outworking of God's promise to Abraham, the OT must really be about Christ. This agrees with what Jesus Himself declared in Luke 24:

> And beginning with Moses and all the Prophets, he interpreted to them in all the Scriptures the things concerning himself (v. 27). … Then he said to them, "These are my words that I spoke to you while I was still with you, that everything written about me in the Law of Moses and the Prophets and the Psalms must be fulfilled" (v. 44)

Do not be deceived: if one abolishes, nullifies, or discards the Old Testament scriptures, one thereby has abolished Christ, nullified God's promise to Abraham, and discarded one's own salvation.

Yet it must be recognized that there is a distinct difference in the way God has revealed Himself in the Old Testament and the way He has revealed Himself in the New Testament. Understanding this difference is necessary to avoid the error of using OT scripture to require animal sacrifice, bind circumcision, or legislate several other old covenant features (e.g., instrumental music, clean and unclean food regulations, a separate intercessory priesthood of fallible humans). The key is found in two concepts the NT uses to describe the OT scriptures: (a) "shadow" (Gr. *skia*; Col 2.17; Heb 8.5; 10.1); and (b) "type" (Gr. *typos*, Acts 7.44; Rom 5.14; 6.17; 1 Cor 10.6, 11; Phil 3.17; 1 Thess 1.7; 2 Thess 3.9; 1 Tim 4.12; Tit 2.7; Heb 8.5; 1 Pet 5.3) or "copy, example" (Gr. *hypodeigma*, Heb 4.11; 8.5; 9.23; Jam 5.10; 2 Pet 2.6; Gr. *hypotypōsis*, 1 Tim 1.16; 2 Tim 1.13; Gr. *antitypos*, Heb 9.24; 1 Pet 3.21).

The idea of a "shadow" is that one can discern some basic features of the object casting the shadow, which can be helpful if one cannot see the object itself directly (e.g., around the corner of a building). One can estimate the object's size, distinguish a person from an animal, etc., but many details, such as the color of the object, are not discernible or are "hidden." In Colossians 2, Paul affirms that the old covenant features (e.g., sabbath keeping, food regulations) were merely shadows of Christ, who is the actual object (Gr. *sōma* "body") casting the shadow: "Therefore do not let anyone judge you with respect to food or drink, or in the matter of a feast, new moon, or Sabbath days—these are only the shadow of the things to come, but the reality [Gr. *sōma* "body"] is Christ" (Col 2.16 NET). The writer of Hebrews also uses this imagery to speak of the entire Levitical priesthood and sacrificial system (Heb 8.5; 10.1), which point us to the true high priest and sacrifice, Jesus Himself (Heb 7.26–8.2; 9.23–10.18). Note that this does not mean that the "shadow" is without value or, worse yet, is somehow false, because it does reveal true details about the object of which it is a shadow. Nor is the shadow superfluous now that one can see the object itself directly, because sometimes one might notice a detail from the shadow that causes one to look back to the object with greater scrutiny. Yes, a shadow by definition is incomplete, but it also captures our attention and directs it toward the One casting the shadow.

The idea of a "type" can be conveyed by the more colloquial term "model." Like the model airplanes I built and painted as a child, they were patterns, examples, or copies of the real objects they were modeling. Since I was not allowed to have an actual Boeing 747 or a Saturn V rocket in my bedroom, I had to be content with an inoperative plastic replica that was the wrong size. Yet in every other facet, it was "just like" the "real" thing, and this is how the Bible speaks of the Old Testament items being "models" of their "true" counterparts. For example, when the writer of Hebrews speaks of the "true tabernacle" (Heb 8.1–5; cf. 9.24), it is not in contrast to a "false" tabernacle, but the one Moses built, which itself was a "pattern" or "model" of heaven. In the same way, the true, spiritual worship which is now possible in Christ (John 4.23–24) is not contrasted with false worship, but the incomplete and inadequate worship under the old covenant system, no matter how sincerely or correctly it had been performed (cf. Josh 24.14). The model is "just like" its true counterpart, except for having the wrong size, being made of the wrong material, and/or lacking functionality.

This is the key to reading the Old Testament: (a) seeing how all of the Old Testament ultimately points us to Christ and is fulfilled in Him; and (b) discerning the limitations of the Old Testament models in regard to size, material, and functionality limitations (e.g., animal sacrifice, instrumental music). What is important to remember, however, is that the ways in which the model is "just like" the real thing, it is communicating the truth of God's eternal purpose and that truth does not cease to be true simply because one can now see the actual object more directly. In fact, a continued scrutiny of the model may reveal aspects of the actual object that one failed to recognize or appreciate when only looking at the object itself.

Therefore, as we study the exodus we must appreciate that it is the most important, most fundamental, and most fully developed model of divine redemption that is only surpassed by the true redemption that we have in Christ. The exodus in all its various dimensions constantly points us to the salvation that we now have in Jesus and that we will realize more fully on the Day of Judgment.

## The Exodus: Old and New

As has been demonstrated throughout this lectureship, the exodus from Egypt is Yahweh's paradigm for all His other redemptive acts in the history of His dealings with humanity, culminating in the greatest act of salvation of all, our deliverance from the bondage of sin into the true Promised Land of heaven. This lectureship gives us the opportunity to pause, to reflect upon, and to marvel at how the most prominent aspects of the exodus story foreshadow and point toward their fuller realities in the New Exodus accomplished in Christ.

First, Jesus Christ is the New Moses. This model or paradigm was established in Deuteronomy 18.15–19 and ever since that time God's people had been anticipating a second Moses:[8]

> The LORD your God will raise up for you a prophet like me from among you, from your brothers—it is to him you shall listen—just as you desired of the LORD your God at Horeb on the day of the assembly, when you said, "Let me not hear again the voice of the LORD my God or see this great fire any more, lest I die." And the LORD said to me, "They are right in what they have spoken. I will raise up for them a prophet like you from among their brothers. And I will put my words in his mouth, and he shall speak to them all that I command him. And whoever will not listen to my words that he shall speak in my name, I myself will require it of him."

The parallels between Moses and Jesus cannot be merely coincidental: (a) a special child rescued from an evil king bent on his destruction; (b) one who leaves a place of glory to cast his lot with the lowly; (c) one who works signs and wonders; (d) a savior and

---

[8] Note the NT references anticipating "the Prophet" (John 1.21, 25; 6.14; 7.40; cf. Matt 21.11; Luke 7.16) or referring to the Deuteronomy passage (Matt 17.5; Mark 9.7; Luke 9.35; John 1.45; 5.46; Acts 3.22–23; 7.37). Also note Jewish extra-biblical sources (4Q175 4–8; *Midr. Rab.* Exod 2.4; Jos. *Ant.* 20.97–99).

redeemer who delivers God's people from bondage; (e) one who provides bread and water to the people; (f) one who sees the form of God and hears God's voice on behalf of the people; (g) one who reveals the will of God to the people; (h) a mediator of a new covenant and gives the law to the people; (i) one who builds a tabernacle for God to dwell among the people; (j) one who institutes the priesthood and sacrificial system to provide for forgiveness of sins; (k) one who leads the people to the Promised Land; and (l) one who is disobeyed, despised, and rejected by the people.[9] It is this last point that Stephen uses to such great effect in his defense in Acts 7.2–53, as he subverts the traditional first-century view of Moses. They were looking for another prophet like Moses—or even greater, and in their imagination that could only mean one that was even more respected, revered, and exuding glory. However, Stephen argues effectively that the Jews should have been looking for one rejected and mistreated like the real Moses, and such a search could only lead them to Jesus Christ. This New Moses, the Prophet par excellence, continues to speak to us and guide us toward that final rest in the Promised Land until we see Him as He is and are like Him (1 John 3.1–3). It is Jesus as the Word of God (John 1.1–3, 14; Heb 1.1–4), the very self-disclosure of God's nature and character to us that has most fully revealed to us what this God is like, that God is love (1 John 4.8, 16), "full of grace and faithfulness" (John 1.14–18), and one who fully lives up to the Name He chose for Himself using every Hebrew descriptor for forgiveness (Exod 34.5–7).[10] Truly one can only know the Father because of Jesus' ability to reveal Him to us (John 1.18; 14.6–7), something neither Moses nor any other prophet could truly do (John 1.17; 3.13; 6.44–46; Heb 1.1–4).

---

[9] See D. C. Allison, *The New Moses: A Matthean Typology* (Minneapolis: Fortress, 1993).

[10] See Marc Hinds, "God Declares a New Name for Himself," in Thomas Hamilton, ed., *Florida College Annual Lectures 2022* (Temple Terrace: Florida College Press, 2022) xx-xx.

Second, we have experienced the True Redemption by means of the True Sacrifice.[11] The truth spoken by this New Moses sets us free from our slavery to our sin (John 8.31–34; cf. Rom 6.6–23), because by means of His own blood Christ Jesus has redeemed us (Rom 3.24;Gal 3.13; Eph 1.7; Col 1.14; Heb 9.12). In fact, it may truly be said that Jesus Christ is Himself our redemption (1 Cor 1.30), the very Lamb of God who takes away our sins (John 1.29, 36; 1 Pet 1.18–19; Rev 5.5–6). However, we also await the final completion of this redemption with the resurrection of the body (Rom 8.23) and the reception of the fullness of all that God has promised us (Eph 1.13–14; 4.30).

Third, we have received a New Covenant and a New Law.[12] Just as was foretold in the Old Testament (Jer 31.31–34; Isa 42.1–9; 49.5–13; 59.20–21; 61.1–9; Ezek 16.60–63; 37.24–28), Jesus as the New Moses has become not only the "mediator of a better covenant" (Heb 8.6–13) or "new covenant" (Heb 9.15; 12.24), but also the "guarantor of a better covenant" (Heb 7.22). It is probably not coincidental that the giving of the new covenant coincided with the timing of Pentecost, fifty days after the Passover, just as Jewish tradition affirmed that the giving of the Torah was seven weeks after Pascha (Passover) on the first Shavuot (Pentecost).[13]

Fourth, we have a New Tabernacle where we experience the presence of God dwelling with us, both in Jesus Christ (John 1.14; 2.19–22) and in His church (1 Cor 3.16–17; 6.19–20; 2 Cor 6.16; Eph 2.19–22; Rev 3.12). Even so, we still await the full realization

---

[11] See Russ Roberts, "Redemption from Slavery," in Thomas Hamilton, ed., *Florida College Annual Lectures 2022* (Temple Terrace: Florida College Press, 2022) xx-xx; and Andrew Dow, "The Sacrifice of the Lamb," in Thomas Hamilton, ed., *Florida College Annual Lectures 2022* (Temple Terrace: Florida College Press, 2022) xx-xx.

[12] See John Weaver, "God Gives the Law," in Thomas Hamilton, ed., *Florida College Annual Lectures 2022* (Temple Terrace: Florida College Press, 2022) xx-xx.

[13] Jubilees 1.1; cf. Exod 19.1. Note also the interesting contrast between the 3000 who died at Sinai in connection with the giving of the old covenant (Exod 32.38) and the 3000 who were saved in connection with the giving of the new covenant (Acts 2.47).

of God's presence more directly and more intimately in that True Tabernacle of heaven itself (Heb 8.1–5; 9.11–12, 23–28), which is not really a place separate from God, but is in fact God Himself (Rev 7.15; 21.1–4, 22). In eternity, we shall know the fullness of the glory of being with God, a reality to which the tabernacle of Moses could only provide a fraction of foreshadowing.[14]

Fifth, we have Jesus Christ as our True High Priest with a sacrificial system that can actually take away our sins (Heb 2.17–18; 3.1–6; 4.14–16; 5.1–10.25), and He stands ready to make intercession for us (Rom 8.34; Heb 7.25). Jesus Christ, being both fully human and fully divine, is the one able to serve as the one and only mediator to bring God and people into a direct relationship with one another, meaning that there is no one standing in between them, which would indicate that both God and humanity are still actually separated from one another (1 Tim 2.3–7).

Sixth, we have embarked on a New Journey through the wilderness of this life, being both tested by God and led by His divine providence. Through Christ's victory over the spiritual forces that enslaved us (Col 2.15; Eph 1.19–23; Phil 2.9–11; 1 Pet 3.22),[15] we have been freed and separated from our former way of life by being immersed into Christ and partaking of His spiritual food and drink (1 Cor 10.1–4).[16] However, we must heed the warning of the exodus generation, not to repeat their mistake of disbelief and disobedience

---

[14] See Gianni Berdini, "God with His People: The Tabernacle," in Thomas Hamilton, ed., *Florida College Annual Lectures 2022* (Temple Terrace: Florida College Press, 2022) xx-xx.

[15] See Mark Russell, "Conquest over the Kingdom of the World," in Thomas Hamilton, ed., *Florida College Annual Lectures 2022* (Temple Terrace: Florida College Press, 2022) xx-xx.

[16] See Roger Polanco, "'Through the Water': The Parting of the Red Sea," in Thomas Hamilton, ed., *Florida College Annual Lectures 2022* (Temple Terrace: Florida College Press, 2022) xx-xx; Chris Huntley, "God Tests His People," in Thomas Hamilton, ed., *Florida College Annual Lectures 2022* (Temple Terrace: Florida College Press, 2022) xx-xx; and John Gibson, "God Leads and Provides for His People," in Thomas Hamilton, ed., *Florida College Annual Lectures 2022* (Temple Terrace: Florida College Press, 2022) xx-xx.

(1 Cor 10.5–13; Heb 3.7–4.13; Jude 5).[17] Indeed, this world is not our home because, although we live here as "resident aliens" (Gr. *paroikos*; Eph 2.19; 1 Pet 2.11), "sojourners" (Gr. *parepidēmos*; Heb 11.13; 1 Pet 1.1; 2.11), and "strangers" (Gr. *xenos*; Eph 2.19; Heb 11.13), our true citizenship is in heaven (Eph 2.19; Phil 1.27; 3.20). Until we make our way to our true home, we must be faithful and pass the tests along the journey (Rom 5.3–5; Jam 1.2–4, 12; 1 Pet 1.6–7), having our loins girded like the exodus generation long ago (1 Pet 1.13; cf. Exod 12.11).

Finally, at the end of this journey we have a New Promised Land, a place of True Rest that awaits us, far greater than a plot of dirt in Canaan (Heb 11.13–16, 39–40; 12.18–29; 13.14).[18] It is a "New Heavens and a New Earth" (Isa 65.17; 66.22; 2 Pet 3.13; Rev 21.1), a New Jerusalem (Rev 21.1–27), and a New "Garden of Eden" of Paradise regained (Rev 22.1–5). There we will dwell in peace and security with our every need provided for by God.

## The New Israel

The biblical typology that unites all of these aspects of the exodus together is the foundational theme that God's people in Christ are a New Israel and are, therefore, called to live out the original purpose for Israel in deeper, more consistently faithful ways. In addition to the specific typologies detailed above, this point is established more broadly in a variety of ways in the New Testament: (a) several passages use "Israel" in such a way to demonstrate that it is redefined in Christ (Matt 2.6; 15.24; 19.28; 27.42; Mark 15.32; Luke 1.54, 68; 2.25, 52; 22.30; John 1.49; 12.13; Acts 1.6; 5.31; Rom 9.6, 27; 11.26; Gal 6.16; Eph 2.12; Heb 8.8, 10; Rev 7.4; 21.12); (b) followers of Jesus are "Jews inwardly," circumcised in the heart (Rom

---

[17] See Reagan McClenny, "'They will not Enter My Rest,'" in Thomas Hamilton, ed., *Florida College Annual Lectures 2022* (Temple Terrace: Florida College Press, 2022) xx-xx.

[18] See Caleb Churchill, "'There Remains a Sabbath Rest for the People of God,'" in Thomas Hamilton, ed., *Florida College Annual Lectures 2022* (Temple Terrace: Florida College Press, 2022) xx-xx.

2.28–29; Phil 3.2–3; Col 2.9–14), redefining what it means for Jesus to be lauded as "King of the Jews" (Matt 2.2; 27.11, 29, 37; Mark 15.2, 9, 12, 18, 26; Luke 23.3, 37–38; John 18.33, 39; 19.3, 14, 19); (c) the metonymy "New Jerusalem" (Rev 3.12; 21.2), especially as the bride of Christ (John 3.29; Eph 5.21–33; Rev 19.7; 21.2, 9), suggests this same connection; and (d) the depictions of Jesus' disciples as the true offspring of Abraham (Matt 3.9; 8.11–12; Luke 3.8; Rom 4.1–25; 9.7; Gal 3.6–29; 4.21–31; Heb 2.16; cf. 1 Pet 3.6: "Sarah"; Rev 7. .4; 21.12: "Israel"), as well as other common descriptors of Israel ("[God's] people": Rom 9.19–33; 15.7–12; 2 Cor 6.16; Heb 4.9; 8.10; 10.30; 1 Pet 2.10; Rev 18.4; 21.3; "[God's] possession": Eph 1.14; Tit 2.14; 1 Pet 2.9), place the depiction of the church as the New Israel beyond question. Indeed, those who belong to Christ are "heirs according to the promise" (Gal 3.29) that was made to Abraham, Isaac, and Jacob, which brings us back full circle to where we began with Jesus' use of Exodus 3.6 (Luke 20.37–38; cf. Matt 22.32; Mark 12.26).

## The Same, Ancient, Original Calling

Therefore, while Christians comprise a New Israel, their purpose and calling is rooted in the original promise to Abraham almost four thousand years ago: to be a blessing to all the families or nations of the earth (Gen 12.2), the same good news (or "gospel") preached beforehand to Abraham so long ago (Gal 3.8). It is important to note that the fourth (or central) clause of the seven clauses of Yahweh's address to Abram in Genesis 12 is in fact an imperative: "be a blessing!" This places the central focus of the Abrahamic promise on the reality that "the blessings of God are not all to be turned in on Abram. A great nation, blessed, a great name—yes. But Abram must be more than a recipient. He is both a receptacle for the divine blessing and a transmitter of that blessing."[19] Because this promise was not just to Abraham personally

---

[19] Victor P. Hamilton, *The Book of Genesis: Chapters 1–17*, NICOT (Grand Rapids: Eerdmans, 1990), 373. The complexities of Hebrew grammar are beyond most

but also to his heirs, both the blessings and the responsibility of being a blessing were passed down as well.

This integral connection between blessings and being a blessing, rights and responsibilities, grace and works, is what accounts for the embellishment of the Abrahamic promise in Isaiah 40–55. Here Isaiah develops the emphasis that being the "Seed of Abraham" entails being the "Servant of Yahweh (or the LORD)," yet national Israel had failed in her calling; she neglected God's command to be a blessing to the nations of the earth. In fact, Israel was a servant that was so blind and deaf herself (Isa 42.18–25) and so disobedient and ineffective (Isa 43.22–28) that Yahweh would need to raise up another servant to repair what was broken with Israel (Isa 49.5–6; 50.10).[20] But even this great work would not be enough for God, because the original task of blessing the nations (i.e., the Gentiles) still had to be done: "It is too light a thing that you should be my servant to raise up the tribes of Jacob and to bring back the preserved of Israel; I will make you as a light for the nations, that my salvation may reach to the end of the earth" (Isa. 49.6; cf. 42.6).

All of the gospels portray that Jesus Christ is the truest and most complete fulfillment of the Promise to Abraham and the Promise to David, but Matthew is perhaps the most obvious, starting with the first verse: "The book of the genealogy of Jesus Christ, the son of

---

readers of this essay, but Hamilton provides an easily accessible and defensible explanation of the imperative in Genesis 12.2.

[20] The Ethiopian's question in Acts 8.34 ("Of whom does the prophet speak? Himself, or some other?") demonstrates that he had been reading this section of Isaiah with great thoughtfulness and perception, as this is the fundamental question to get at the point of Isaiah 40–55: is this Servant of Yahweh (a) a group of people (41.14; 42.18; 43.10) or a single individual (42.1–4; 49.6); (b) the nation of Israel as often explicitly identified (41.8; 44.1; 49.3) or someone other than Israel (49.5–6; 50.10); or (c) a disobedient servant (42.18–25; 43.22–28) or a faithful one (42.1; 52.13–53.12)? To understand how it can be both, it may be helpful to picture the "Seed of Abraham" and the "Servant of Yahweh" as roles (like those in a theatrical performance) which different actors may attempt to fill with varying degrees of success. In this case, however, Jesus is not merely filling a role or playing a part, but He is the reality after which the role was modeled.

David, the son of Abraham" (Matt. 1.1). He is the true "Seed of Abraham" and true "Servant of Yahweh" that has come to fix what is broken with Israel and bring the Gentiles in to be part of this New Israel. Jesus' fulfillment of Hosea 11.1 ("Out of Egypt I called My Son.") is not rooted in the obscure fact that both of these "sons of God," Israel and Jesus, geographically relocate from a plot of dirt called "Egypt," but rather is more deeply rooted in God raising up Jesus to complete the work that He had raised up Israel to do, but which they had failed (Matt 2.15). It is not by coincidence that this is shortly followed by the Temptation story (4.1–11), in which Jesus is taken into the wilderness to be tested as God's son, just as Israel was (Deut 8.1–5), but Jesus passes the test while Israel failed. The gospel of Matthew culminates with Jesus having accomplished the work of the perfect "Servant of Yahweh" envisioned in Isaiah, that by His crucifixion and resurrection the brokenness of Israel could be fixed and the nations (or Gentiles) brought in and made part of this New Israel.

However, if we are part of this New Israel restored by Christ and also heirs of the Promise to Abraham, is not the obligation of that original promise also ours just as much as the blessings? Is not the imperative to "be a blessing" to the nations just as binding upon us today? Is it any wonder that the gospel of Matthew therefore ends with these words:

> All authority in heaven and on earth has been given to me. Going, therefore, ***disciple all the nations***, by immersing them in the name of the Father and of the Son and of the Holy Spirit, by teaching them to observe all that I have commanded you. And behold, I am with you always, to the end of the age (Matt 28.18–20, edited)?

The only real question is, will we be any more faithful than national Israel? Will we fail, like they did, to be an influence upon this world for good, destroying our ability to be a blessing to our world because we allowed it to have a greater influence upon us, converting us to its philosophy, its values, its lies? Or will we by God's strength be the conduit of His blessing, bringing salvation to those looking for it?

To fully appreciate how we might try to answer these questions, consider why 1 Peter 2.4–10 is the singularly most compelling text that deals with evangelism directly. Peter calls us to be living stones just like Jesus is a living stone, and just as Jesus was rejected by the world but chosen by God, so we too might be rejected by the world as we seek to be like Him and share His message. But all that matters on that last day is what God thinks, that is, that we are chosen and precious to Him. Peter' choice of words, of course, echoes Isaiah 28.16, but also connects with the description given of Israel in Exodus 19.6 (via Isaiah 43.20–21): "But you are a chosen race, a royal priesthood, a holy nation, a people for his own possession, that you may proclaim the excellencies of him who called you out of darkness into his marvelous light" (1 Pet 2.9).[21] Ultimately, the proclamation of the gospel is not a five-step improvement plan, but the proclamation of a person, the message of the very nature and character of God Himself. It is the joyful cry of thanksgiving and praise for all the world to hear because Yahweh has blessed me as the Seed of Abraham and called me to be the Servant of the Lord to glorify Him by sharing that blessing with all who will hear, being that blessing for all those separated from God, discipling the nations by immersing them in the name of Jesus and teaching them what He has commanded.

---

[21] Note that Israel's description as a "nation of priests" (Exod 19.6) is not a reference to the fact that Israel had a separate Levitical priesthood, nor is it that all Israelites are priests in the same sense as the Levitical priests. Rather, the point is that just as a priest stands between the sinner and God to mediate on the sinner's behalf, so the nation of Israel was supposed to function in a similar way on behalf of the world, mediating the knowledge of the true God to the polytheistic pagan Gentiles that did not know Yahweh. Peter is not teaching a "priesthood of all believers" wherein Christians are subordinate priests within the atoning priesthood of Jesus as High Priest. Hebrews makes it clear that there is only one priest who atones for sin once-for-all and only one member of that priesthood, who alone is sufficient to accomplish its work. Instead, Peter by analogy is pointing out we bear the same priestly duty as Israel of old, mediating the knowledge of the true God to those yet in the darkness.

The world desperately needs to know the I AM, Yahweh, the God of Abraham, Isaac, and Jacob. But before I can proclaim the excellencies or outstanding qualities of this God, I must first truly know Him myself. When I do, I cannot but be that blessing to others.

# Part Two

The Day Lectures

# The I AM Remembers His Covenant with Abraham

## V. J. Benson

The book of Exodus records the birth of Israel as a nation. It is an account of God's faithfulness in fulfilling His promise to Abraham made in Genesis 12. It also shows the inception of God's provisional scheme of redemption for the nation of Israel. In the first chapter of Exodus, we see God's blessings upon the children of Israel as they were fruitful, increased abundantly and the land of Egypt was filled with them. This chapter describes the oppression of the Israelites by the Egyptians and how Israel prospered despite the fact. This caused the Egyptians to be jealous and at the same time fearful that the Israelites might join Egypt's enemies in case of war. This presumptuous fear caused them to further oppress and enslave the Israelites. They appointed task masters who treated them ruthlessly. The king ordered that any male child should be cast into the river to curb the population growth of Israel. These are the circumstances under which Moses was born. We can see how God spared his life and he was raised as the son of Pharaoh's daughter in the second chapter. After Moses became an adult, he identified himself with his people, but circumstances led him to flee Egypt as he had killed an Egyptian who had wronged an Israelite. Moses fled to Midian and encountered the daughters of a Midianite priest named Jethro. He married one of Jethro's daughters and settled in Midian, tending his father-in-law's sheep for forty years (Acts 7.30).

## Significance of Names in the Bible

The Hebrew title for the book of Exodus is simply the first words of the text "*we'elleh shemoth*," meaning "Now these are the names," as it begins by listing the names of the children of Israel. Names have great significance in the Bible. A person's name often signifies his character or ability or mission. "And Adam called his wife's name Eve, because she was the mother of all living" (Gen 3.20).[1] Names sometimes can be tied to people's origins or traditions, such as naming one in honor of an ancestor (e.g., Luke 1.60–62). Names can also sometimes allude to the circumstances at birth. When Rebekah gave birth to the twins in her womb, "the first came out red. He was like a hairy garment all over; so they called his name Esau. Afterward his brother came out, and his hand took hold of Esau's heel; so his name was called Jacob. Isaac was sixty years old when she bore them" (Gen 25.25–26). Esau acknowledged how Jacob had lived up to his name, by deceiving their father and stealing his blessing: "Is he not rightly named Jacob? For he has supplanted me these two times. He took away my birthright, and now look, he has taken away my blessing!" (Gen 27.36)

Because of the importance of names, the names of some people in the Bible were changed to highlight something significant. God changed Abram's name to Abraham to reflect God's purpose to make him a father of many nations (Gen 17.5). Sarai's name was changed to Sarah ("princess"), as God similarly made her the mother of nations. (Gen 17.15). Jacob was renamed as Israel following his conversion experience at the Jabbok River, marking the dramatic change in his character from one of grasping to one of trusting (Gen 32.28). In the New Testament, when the Son of God was incarnated, he was given the name Jesus because he would save His people from their sins (Matt 1.21). He would also be known as Immanuel in keeping with Old Testament prophecy (cf. Isa 7.14): "'Behold, the virgin shall be with child, and bear a Son, and they shall call His name Immanuel,' which is translated, 'God with us'" (Matt 1.23). In John

---

[1] Unless noted otherwise, all quotations of scripture are from the NKJV.

1.42, Jesus changed Simon's name to Cephas (in Aramaic) or Peter (in Greek), meaning "rock," a name that might have been intended by Jesus foreshadow how Peter would live up (or down) to this name in both positive and negative ways. Names are also sometimes associated with power and authority, because of who wears the name. Paul describes the significance of the name given to Jesus in Philippians 2.9–11: "He humbled Himself and became obedient to the point of death, even the death of the cross. Therefore, God also has highly exalted Him and given Him the name which is above every name, that at the name of Jesus every knee should bow, of those in heaven, and of those on earth, and of those under the earth, and that every tongue should confess that Jesus Christ is Lord, to the glory of God the Father." Here the point is not that the name "Jesus" (or "Joshua," the English form of the name that is closest to the Hebrew) is itself inherently important, as it was the fourth most common name for a Jewish male born in the first century. Rather it is because this particular Jesus also bears the name "Yahweh (the Lord)," the name that is above every name, and this is what all must confess: "Jesus Christ is Lord" (or Yahweh).

## The Meaning of God's Name in Exodus 3

This name of God, Yahweh, is prominently introduced to us at the beginning of the exodus story at the burning bush in Exodus 3. God gave Moses a new revelation of his name: "I AM WHO I AM" (v. 14), "I AM has sent me to you" (v. 14), and "the Lord (YHWH or Yahweh) God of your fathers, the God of Abraham, the God of Isaac, and the God of Jacob, has sent me to you" (v. 15). The most crucial name for God in the Old Testament is what God revealed here to Moses and is most often translated in English as "the Lord." In Hebrew, the tetragrammaton consists of a sequence the four consonants *Yod, Heh, Waw*, and *Heh* (*YHWH*), and with its accompanying vowel sounds is thought to be pronounced "Yahweh." At some point in Jewish history, the Jews began to avoid pronouncing

*YHWH* because it was the closest thing to a proper name for God, so when they encountered this name in their reading of scripture, they substituted the Hebrew word for "lord," *'adonai.* This has led to the literary convention in English Bibles of translating the name Yahweh as "the LORD," using a large capital letter "L" and small caps for the remaining letters (in contrast to those times when the word "Lord" is actually a translation of *'adonai* instead of *YHWH*). The name "LORD" (or *YHWH*) is only used of the true God, appearing 6828 times in the Hebrew Bible as the most common designation of God. In 891 of those occurrences the name appears in the familiar Old Testament phrase "LORD God (*YHWH 'elohim*)," and this is the form in which the name YHWH first occurs in scripture (Gen 2.4). In fact, God declared this is His name forever (Exod 3.15), and the fact that Abraham was aware of the name *YHWH* and used it frequently (Gen 14.22; 15.2, 8; 22.14; 24.3, 7) shows that God is not revealing a previously unknown name to Moses in Exodus 3, but God is revealing Himself more fully in such a way that others will recognize a new significance to the ancient designation. Through Yahweh's deliverance of Israel by His mighty power displayed in all the plagues and the exodus from Egypt, both Israel and the other nations would have a fuller recognition of, and fear of, His name spread throughout the region.

It is profitable to spend some time to understand the meaning of these words by which God chose to reveal Himself. Different explanations have been given and scholars do not agree on every point, but the facts as generally accepted are that the phrase "I AM" is from the word "to be" (Heb. *hyh*). The idea is that God is the one who is always in existence, the Self-existing One, the ever present One, the Eternal One who does not have a beginning or an end. He is a true God that transcends time and place. He is and continues to be. He is a living God. He is the source of all life and gives to all life, breath, and all things (Acts 17.25), while He Himself does not depend upon another for His existence.

The phrase "I AM THAT I AM" (KJV) translates from the Hebrew into one of the Indian languages, Telugu, in a way that seems to bring out the meaning more clearly for me: "I AM the one who exists," emphasizing the fact that God exists without any time or place or limitations, always existing. The phrase "I AM THAT I AM" is also translated as, "I AM the one who speaks", expressing the power of the word of the One who spoke all things into existence. The LORD is not only the One who spoke at the beginning in creation, but is also the One who spoke to Abraham and verbally communicated a covenant with him, to which Abraham responded in faith. Now this same God speaks from a burning bush to Moses about those same covenant promises and how all will witness how the LORD will live up to His covenantal name, Yahweh (the LORD).

The notes of Matthew Poole concerning the meaning of the names of God in Exodus 3.14–15 are worth considering:

> Verse 14: *I am that I am*; a most comprehensive and significant name, and most proper for the present occasion; it notes:
>
> 1. The reality of his being; whereas idols are nothings, (1Cor 8.4), all their divinity is only in the fancies and opinions of men.
>
> 2. The unnecessariness, eternity, and unchangeableness of his being; whereas all other beings once were not, and, if he please, they shall be no more; and all their being was derived from him, and wholly depends upon him; and he only is by and from himself.
>
> 3. The constancy and certainty of his nature, and will, and word. The sense is, I am the same that I ever was, the same who made the promises to Abraham, &c., and am now come to perform them; who, as I can do what I please, so I will do what I have said. Heb. *I shall be what I shall be*. He useth the future tense also...."
>
> Verse 15: *The Lord*, Heb. *Jehovah*; a word of the same root and signification with *I am*. See Exod 6.3. This he adds, because God was best known to the Israelites by that name; and to show, that though he identifies himself a new name, yet he was the same God. This is my memorial, by which I will be remembered, owned, and served by

my people, and distinguished from all others. See Psa 102.12 ("But
You, O Lᴏʀᴅ, shall endure forever, and the remembrance of Your
name to all generations); Psa 135.13 (Your name, O Lᴏʀᴅ, endures
forever, Your fame, O Lᴏʀᴅ, throughout all generations.")[2]

The following attributes are implied by this name of God:

1. *God exists:* God's existence is evident from the creation. Paul
stated in Romans that what may be known of God is manifest in
the creation "for God has shown it to them. For since the creation
of the world His invisible attributes are clearly seen, being understood by the things that are made, even His eternal power and
Godhead" (Rom 1.19–20 ɴᴋᴊᴠ). God's existence is not based on
anything else, but everything else exists because of His existence
and His will.

2. *God created everything:* God created all things by His will,
they exist and were created, and nothing exists without him. Because
of this, He is worthy to receive glory and honor and power (Rev
4.11). All the creation trembles in His presence. He is the source for
all creatures for life and sustenance. It is He "who gives food to all
flesh, for His mercy endures forever (Psa 136.25).

3. *God is unchanged:* "For I am the Lᴏʀᴅ, I do not change;
Therefore, you are not consumed, O sons of Jacob (Mal 3.6). Because of God's unchangeable nature He kept the covenant made to
Abraham in regard to multiplying his seed and will now keep His
covenant to bring them into the promised land. For the purpose of
instilling trust in Him and His power He exalted His name for Moses to tell the people of Israel and for them to recognize His character.

4. *God is faithful:* When God made this revelation, the people
of Israel should have recognized that the promise to Abraham was
already fulfilled by God granting Isaac to Abraham when he was 100

---

[2] Matthew Poole, *Annotations upon the Holy Bible, vol. 1, wherein the sacred text
is inserted, and various readings annex'd, together with parallel scriptures, the more difficult terms in each verse are explained, seeming contradictions reconciled, questions and
doubts resolved, and the whole text opened* (London: John Richardson, 1683), sub
versa Exod 3.15.

years old, multiplying his descendants, and providentially caring for them over these centuries. They know how the LORD through Joseph preserved the entire family of Jacob from the famine, and there had to be some great divine purpose for that. Now God's name is to build Israel's confidence in His faithfulness and power to deliver them from bondage and lead them to the Promised Land.

## What does God's Name have to do with the Exodus?

Gods revelations to Moses in Exodus 3 are the beginning of God's plan for the nation of Israel to separate them out of the land of Egypt and consecrate them for His purpose. By giving Moses His name, God is reintroducing Himself to the people of Israel, showing them the significance of His name and His abilities, that He is the God of their fathers, and that He is the one who made the covenant with Abraham. God shows the people of Israel that He is the "I AM", the one who always existed and will exist forever going into the future. God through His miracles shows that He is the one who speaks, the one who is all powerful who can speak things into existence. God is showing His direct involvement in bringing them out of Egypt.

We see that the incident of the burning bush had enormous impact on the life of Moses. It is the initiation of God bringing the people of Israel out of Egypt. It begins with a new revelation of God and His name to Moses from the burning bush and develops with the commissioning of Moses to go back to Egypt and to Pharaoh in order to deliver God's people from their harsh oppression and slavery. However, it is colored with Moses' excuses for not taking up the great task given by God, because of his fundamental failure to understand the One with whom he was dealing, the Self-existing One, YHWH.

The most significant event in the exodus of the people of God began with the burning bush in Exodus 3. This chapter talks about the great turn that has taken place in the life of Moses (from shepherd of sheep to shepherd of God's people). In the first six verses, we can see

that our God sees, He listens, and He responds. God not only saw
Moses coming closer to the burning bush and warned him, but God
saw the oppression of His people by the Egyptians. As Moses was
walking to see the wonder of why the bush was not consumed by the
fire, God told him to take his sandals off his feet for the place where
he stood was a holy ground. It is the presence of God which makes
the place holy, and the putting off the shoes is to acknowledge that
fact.[3] Removing the sandals is a sign of reverence to the holy God,
and such a removal of sandals at places of worship is still practiced
among many eastern countries including India.

God identified Himself, "I am the God of your father, the God of
Abraham, the God of Isaac, and the God of Jacob" (Exod 3.6), and
Moses hid his face for he was afraid to look upon God. By identifying
Himself with the patriarchs, God is indicating that He is faithful in
fulfilling the covenant made to them (vv. 7, 8), but He is also laying
the groundwork to strengthen Moses to accept the commission that
He was going to give him. God said He has seen the oppression of
His people, He has heard their cry because of their taskmasters, and
He has known their sorrows. Therefore, He has come down to deliv-
er them out of the land of the Egyptians, and to bring them up from
that land to a good land, to a land flowing with milk and honey.
God repeats that He has heard the cry of the children of Israel, and
He has seen the oppression with which the Egyptians oppress them,
but then delivers what must have been a most terrifying message for
Moses: "I will send you to Pharaoh that you may bring My people,
the children of Israel, out of Egypt" (v. 10). Moses had fled for his life
from Egypt and now God not only wants him to return to this realm
of danger, but to confront Pharaoh and demand he release the Israelites from bondage. The most natural response is exactly what Moses
said to God, "Who am I that I should go to Pharaoh, that I should
bring the children of Israel out of Egypt?" (v. 11) There was proba-

[3] See also Joshua's experience with the Captain of the Yahweh's army (Josh 5.15),
as well as the fact that no footwear was prescribed for the Levitical priests in the Law
of Moses.

bly no Israelite who could better appreciate the power of Egypt, the depth of Egyptian cruelty, and the obvious hopelessness of the situation in the face of impossible odds. If there was any man up to such a task, it certainly was not him, Moses thought. The meaning of his question "Who am I?" focused on *his* ability and *his* credentials that *he* should go to talk to Pharaoh and *he* should deliver the people of Israel. God's answer to Moses' question awakened his understanding that he is merely an instrument in God's powerful hand and Moses needs to obey the word of Yahweh.

## How God Empowered Moses for the Great Work

God's presence is promised to Moses. God knew that this great task of bringing out the people of Israel was not possible for Moses without the LORD's divine presence and guidance. Moses needed to recognize this fact, so God gave him sign to assure him that he will be successful that they "shall serve God on this mountain" (v.12). Now Moses must trust God and act in faith. It is at this point that he asked God's name. "Then Moses said to God, 'Indeed, when I come to the children of Israel and say to them, "The God of your fathers has sent me to you," and they say to me, "What is His name?" what shall I say to them?'" (v. 13). Why would Israelites ask for God's name? Perhaps to distinguish Him among other gods because they were living in the pagan land where there were many pagan gods such as Hapi, Oriris, Iris, etc. They needed to trust and obey Yahweh to be delivered from the Egyptian slavery. God reveals Himself to Moses, demonstrating His character and His authority, under which Moses is to return to Egypt to deliver the Israelites. God's answer to Moses' question was incredible and a great assurance to them, that they shall be brought out of Egypt. "And God said to Moses, 'I AM WHO I AM.' And He said, 'Thus you shall say to the children of Israel, "I AM has sent me to you."' Moreover God said to Moses, 'Thus you shall say to the children of Israel: "The LORD God of your fathers, the God of Abraham, the God of Isaac, and the

God of Jacob, has sent me to you. This is My name forever, and this is My memorial to all generations"'" (vv. 14–15).[4]

### Moses' Objections and Excuses

God's commission to bring Israel out of Egypt was a great blessing to Moses, but he was still reluctant. God promised His presence shall be with him and said the people of Israel will heed his voice (v. 18), but Moses was not ready to take up this responsibility. It was necessary to convince the children of Israel that Moses was indeed sent of God, but he used this as an excuse instead of asking God's help and guidance: "But suppose they will not believe me or listen to my voice; suppose they say, 'The Lord has not appeared to you'" (Exod 4.1). God answered his objection and strengthened his faith by empowering him to perform miracles. Two of them were performed on the spot, to build confidence in him for the great mission he was to take up. God assured him that if the Israelites do not believe him nor heed his message after the first miracle (turning his rod into to serpent and back again), then they would believe after the second (making his hand leprous and back again). Even if they still did not believe him, God equipped him to perform a third miracle: pouring some water from the river on the dry land and witnessing it turn to blood.

Moses used the anticipated unbelief of the Hebrews and his overstated ineloquence as excuses to avoid God's commission to bring Israel out of Egypt. God answered Moses' objections by promising His power and His presence (Exod 4.11–12). Yet, Moses was still fearful to take up the great task, although it should be evident that one cannot escape God's commands by excuses. God's anger was kindled against Moses, and He reproves him for his unbelief. God provides Aaron his brother, to be his spokesman in this

[4]Note the translation of Exodus 3.15 in the Complete Jewish Bible: "God said further to Moshe, 'Say this to the people of Isra'el: "*Yud-Heh-Vav-Heh* [*ADONAI*], the God of your fathers, the God of Avraham, the God of Yitz'chak and the God of Ya'akov, has sent me to you."' This is my name forever; this is how I am to be remembered generation after generation."

commission and instructs him to take his rod to be the instrument for working miracles (Exod 4.13–17).

The lessons to be learned from Exodus 3 and 4 are many: Do we truly know what it means for God to be Yahweh? On the one hand, the LORD is truly sovereign and powerful in ability, and on the other hand, the LORD is truly loving and compassionate in covenant faithfulness. He is truly an unstoppable force for good for His people. When we are prompted to ask, "Who am I?" in the midst of suffering, difficulty, or even the "impossible," we would do well to remember what Moses had to learn: it is not about us, but whoever Yahweh says we are.

# The Sacrifice of the Lamb

## Andrew Dow

The exodus from Egypt is the most significant event in Israel's history. The book which tells this story finds itself commonly listed among the top five most quoted Old Testament books in the New Testament. But lists of Old Testament quotations in the New Testament cannot do justice to the array of allusions back to this event in both halves of the Bible. Few Biblical events can capture the character of God, the human predicament, and the nature of salvation as clearly as Israel's departure from Egypt.

Among the most striking features of this event is the prominence which death plays in Israel's deliverance. Though it seems counterintuitive, God uses death to propel the events forward which lead to life. Moses came to the house of Pharaoh's daughter due to Pharaoh's order to kill the Israelites' children (Exod 1.15–16, 22; 2.1–10). Moses travelled to Midian due to the death of an Egyptian and a threat on his own life (Exod 2.11–15). Similarly, Israel's journey into the wilderness began with the deaths of cattle, firstborn, and the Passover lamb.

With this lecture, we intend to examine the sacrifice of the Passover lamb as found in Exodus 12–13. This is not a discussion of modern Passover practices or how various traditions have unfolded over time. Rather, our goals are simple: (1) examine the context and structure of the Passover texts, (2) identify and describe a few key elements among the Passover stipulations and (3) recognize how this ritual serves as a shadow for the Christ.

## Context and Structure

Before we embark on an analysis of the stipulations concerning the Passover lamb, we should say a few things about the context and structure of the text at hand. Beginning in the nineteenth century, critical scholars began to question the unity of the Pentateuch and, thus, the book of Exodus.[1] Though these challenges to the text's unity have changed over time, scholarship has continued to dissect these books with an aim to deduce their origins. Whether God used multiple authors or sources to preserve these texts should not be overly concerning to Christians with a high view of inspiration. Regardless how the document came to be, it was handed down as a complete unit.[2] Therefore, readers should interpret Exodus 12–13 as an integral part of the continuation of the story of deliverance from bondage.

The Passover event is part of the Ten Plagues narrative. Exodus 7–13 records the increasingly powerful acts of God against the Egyptians while highlighting His increasingly obvious protection of the Israelites.[3] From a narrative standpoint, these plagues appear to happen in quick succession—one right after another. This pace continues until chapter 12 in which the Ten Plagues narrative is paused while Israel receives the LORD's command. Therefore, the text containing the Passover requirements creates a sense of anxious anticipation as the reader awaits the climax of the tenth plague to arrive. Perhaps

---

[1] Curious readers can find a summary of the documentary hypothesis debate, for instance, in Tremper Longman III and Raymond B. Dillard, *An Introduction to the Old Testament,* 2nd ed. (Grand Rapids: Zondervan, 2006) 40–51.

[2] Brevard Childs advocated strongly for this canonical approach to interpretation. He wrote, "It is the final text, the composite narrative, in its present shape which the church, following the lead of the synagogue, accepted as canonical and thus the vehicle of revelation and instruction." *The Book of Exodus*, OTL (Louisville: Westminster, 1976) xv.

[3] For a discussion concerning these plagues, see Mark Russell, "Conquest over the Kingdom of the World," in Thomas Hamilton, ed., *Florida College Annual Lectures 2022* (Temple Terrace: Florida College Press, 2022) xx-xx.

this helps us sympathize with the Israelites who anxiously awaited their own deliverance as they prepared and ate the Passover meal.

The unity and flow of Exodus 12–13 has challenged commentators because the text transitions between instruction speeches (12.1–20, 21–27, 42–49; 13.1–16) and narrative sections (12.29–41; 13.17–22). However, the stylistic differences allow us to form a functional—even if oversimplified—outline of the text:

A   Passover Instructions (12.1–28)

   B   Ten Plagues Narrative continued (12.29–41)

A'  Passover Instructions continued (12.42–13.16)

   B'  Ten Plagues Narrative continued (13.17–22)

The repetition of these Passover instructions may seem redundant. However, it may be that both sets of instructions serve a different purpose. The instructions in 12.1–28 serve as an explanation of how God first communicated the Passover ordinances to Israel through Moses and Aaron. After Israel's departure from Egypt, however, the author reiterates and expands upon the instructions as they must now maintain this ritual going forward into the Promised Land.[4]

### An Overview of the Passover Stipulations

As we examine the Passover instructions, we would do well to notice the significance placed on this event throughout the text. God begins with a bold declaration: "This month shall be the beginning of months for you; it is to be the first month of the year to you" (Exod 12.2).[5] Israel's freedom from bondage is so significant that the event marks the beginning of their calendar year.[6] This feast and all that sur-

---

[4] Douglas K. Stuart observed, "What links all the material of 13.1–16 together especially is this sense of preparation for inhabiting the land—and not forgetting once there to keep covenant with Yahweh, who had made it possible for his people to have all that they would enjoy in their new land." *Exodus*, NAC 2 (Nashville: Broadman and Holman, 2006) 312.

[5] Unless noted otherwise, all quotations of scripture are from the 1995 update to the NASB.

[6] John J. Davis writes that this was a new year in a "spiritual sense" while suggesting that Israel kept both a "civil calendar" and a "religious calendar." *Moses and*

rounded it was a reminder of "the beginning of Israel's life as a nation."[7] The narrator adds that "this night is ... to be observed by all the sons of Israel throughout their generations" (Exod 12.42). This memorial is crucial for Israel's identity as a nation and their understanding of God's role in their deliverance. Consequently, the elements which make up the observance of the Passover must be equally significant and infused with meaning. We will summarize these instructions in three broad brushstrokes: the lamb, the meal, and the participants.

## The Character of the Passover Lamb

The centerpiece of the Passover meal was the sacrificial lamb. Each household was to sacrifice their own lamb (except for a household too small to eat a whole lamb, Exod 12.3–4). The emphasis of this sacrifice is not so much on the kind of animal (it could be "from the sheep or from the goats," Exod 12.5), but on the quality of the animal. "Your lamb shall be an unblemished male a year old" (Exod 12.5). Everything about this animal was to represent purity from defilement. God would later demand that all future sacrifice under the Law must likewise be visually perfect (e.g., Lev 1.3, 10; 23.12).

It was not enough, however, to select the perfect specimen. That spotless animal must die for Israel to have life. "The whole assembly of the congregation of Israel is to kill it at twilight" (Exod 12.6). A few features of this death are noteworthy. First, the death of this animal is "a Passover sacrifice" (Exod 12.27). This is not merely a meal cooked and eaten by the Israelites before their journey. To the contrary, this was a ritual slaughter with the intent to make a covenant or establish peace with a deity. Second, each household among the Israelites killed its own Passover lamb. Of course, the norm under

*the Gods of Egypt: Studies in Exodus*, 2nd ed. (Winona Lake, IN: Brethren Missionary Herald Books, 2011) 144. Nahum Sarna corroborates this claim that Israel had several ways of dividing the year but emphasizes that the text "unmistakably points to an innovation, to a break with the past." *Exploring Exodus: The Origins of Biblical Israel* (New York: Schocken Books, 1996) 81.

[7] R. Alan Cole, *Exodus: An Introduction and Commentary*, TOTC 2 (Downers Grove: Inter-Varsity, 2008) 111.

the Law of Moses would be that only the Levitical priesthood could offer sacrifices.[8] But the Passover sacrifice was unique and far more personal. Finally, in killing this animal the instructions are clear: the animal's bones are to remain unbroken (Exod 12.46).

After slaughtering the lamb, each household took "some of the blood and put it on the two doorposts and on the lintels..." (Exod 12.7). This application of the sacrificial blood marked the house as containing God's people (Exod 12.13). It was proof that a sacrificial lamb had died in the place of the firstborn in that household. When Moses passes this instruction along to the Israelites, he adds this detail: "You shall take a bunch of hyssop and dip it in the blood which is in the basin, and apply some of the blood..." (Exod 12.22). The use of hyssop is a strange but meaningful detail. Beyond hyssop's inclusion in the Passover ritual, it also finds itself used to cleanse leprosy (Lev 14), create purifying water (Num 19.1–10), and purify someone who has touched a corpse (Num 19.11–19). David would later use hyssop poetically to describe the cleansing he desired from his sin (Psa 51.7). The application of the lamb's blood by hyssop is symbolic of ritual purity that this sacrifice brings to the people.

## The Character of the Passover Meal

More than a sacrifice, the Passover was a feast. Stuart uses a helpful analogy for our modern minds by pointing out that we have similar celebratory feasts today—e.g., Christmas ham or Thanksgiving turkey.[9] Feasting in the ancient world was about more than good food and good company. Feasts served a function. For example, Jacob and Laban made a covenant in part by eating a meal together (Gen 31.46, 54). This solidified their peace agreement. So too did the sacrificial Passover meal establish a covenant of peace and protec-

---

[8] Though this is the norm, it cannot be stated as an absolute rule. For example, David appears to offer a burnt offering in 2 Samuel 24.25. That said, the Law of Moses only directs Levitical priests to offer sacrifices (e.g., Lev 1–7) and the Israelites seem to acknowledge this (cf. Jdg 17.7–13).

[9] Stuart, *Exodus* 273.

tion between God and His people. Through the sharing of this meal, God would save Israel from death.

The recipe for this meal, however, may not be the most appetizing dish ever devised. The instructions for preparation seem to include a blend of both symbolic and functional ingredients. God gave precise instructions to the participants: "Do not eat any of it raw or boiled at all with water, but rather roasted with fire" (Exod 12.9). Davis suggests that "the command not to eat the meat raw was significant because many of the surrounding pagan peoples often ate raw flesh at their sacrificial meals."[10] Additionally, roasting the animal may have purified the creature of its blood and fat,[11] or been commanded as "the fastest, quickest way to cook meat."[12]

The text goes on to explain that the meat was to be prepared with "bitter herbs" (Exod 12.8). Paul R. House finds theological significance in this detail: "[The Israelites] are to eat foods that remind them of the plainness and bitterness of their bondage."[13] In addition to the bitter herbs, the meat was to be eaten "with unleavened bread" (Exod 12.8). Household bakers could easily and quickly bake bread of this kind because it did not require time for the leaven to rise. But this element of the meal takes on further significance when the LORD established another feast in conjunction with the Passover celebration—the Feast of Unleavened Bread (Exod 12.14–20). The Israelites would rid their homes of all leaven and eat unleavened bread for seven days. To explain why God rejects leaven in this (and other) Old Testament sacrifices, Sarna points to a late Jewish tradition that "the process of fermentation was associated with decomposition and putrefaction, and so became emblematic of corruption."[14]

---

[10] Davis, *Moses* 148.

[11] Cole, *Exodus* 114.

[12] Stuart, *Exodus* 277.

[13] Paul R. House, *Old Testament Theology* (Downers Grove: InterVarsity, 1998) 102–103.

[14] Sarna, *Exploring Exodus* 90–91.

Finally, God expected Israel to leave no remnant of the Passover feast behind them. "You shall not leave any of it over until morning," God commanded, "but whatever is left of it until morning you shall burn with fire" (Exod 12.10). Israel's departure would be sudden. They need not burden themselves with gathering leftovers or cleaning up.

## The Character of the Passover Participants

God intended that only a particular kind of people shared the Passover sacrifice and feast. While in Egypt, the people who partook of this meal were to be eager and ready to leave their old life of slavery behind them. The LORD said to eat "with your loins girded, your sandals on your feet, and your staff in your hand; and you shall eat it in haste" (Exod 12.11). This posture of readiness was only heightened by the speedy preparation of the meal. By eating in this way, the people showed a level of trust in God to deliver them that very night.[15]

God also specified who could participate in the Passover memorial in future generations. "No foreigner is to eat of it … A sojourner or a hired servant shall not eat of it" (Exod 12.43–45). To the contrary, all future observances would be for "the congregation of Israel to celebrate" (Exod 12.47). Consequently, the only way for one of these rejected groups to participate in the Passover feast is for them to become a part of the Israelite community through circumcision (Exod 12.44, 48). The Passover was a special memorial for a holy people.

## A Shadow of Sacrifices to Come

The Passover sacrifice—with all its detailed rituals—was the first sacrifice God demanded of His new covenant people. The fundamental idea behind the Passover lamb's sacrifice is one of substitution. If each household faithfully slaughtered their Passover lamb,

---

[15] Note the expression "faithful readiness for a speedy departure" in Stuart, *Exodus* 278. Peter's use of "gird," combined with his other exodus imagery, is also probably an allusion to the original exodus (cf. 1 Pet 1.13), emphasizing the need for the Christian's own readiness of mind.

God would spare that household from death. The lamb, therefore, stands in for each household's firstborn to die in his place. Many of the sacrifices within the Law of Moses follow this same pattern: the offerer can be ritually purified from his wrongdoing by offering an animal to suffer the consequences of sin in his place. This is not, however, where the similarities end.

The most complete description of Mosaic Law sacrifices resides in Leviticus 1–7. The sacrifice of the Passover lamb prefigures many of these sacrificial rituals. Consider the following examples. The Passover lamb was unblemished; this became a requirement of all future sacrifices (Lev 1.3, 10; 3.1, 6, etc.). The offerer ate the Passover lamb just as with the peace offering (Lev 7.15–18). The Passover lamb must avoid contact with leaven. An Israelite's grain offering was also to avoid leaven (Lev 2.11). The Passover lamb was entirely consumed just as the burnt offering would be reduced to ashes (Lev 6.8–13). The offerer spread the blood of the Passover lamb on his doorposts, while the blood of other sacrifices would be sprinkled on the altar and the doorway of the tent (Lev 4.7). The Passover lamb pointed forward to the sacrifices the Israelites would regularly perform. But, of course, the Passover sacrifice points to a greater sacrifice revealed in the New Testament.

## The Passover as a Shadow of the Christ

Old Testament quotations and allusions fill the pages of the New Testament. Jesus' life and ministry—in fact, the whole Gospel—brings to completion the work God set out to do through Israel. As a result, Jesus could assert, "all things which are written about Me in the Law of Moses and the Prophets and the Psalms must be fulfilled" (Luke 24.44). Characters, places, events, and rituals in the Old Testament were mere shadows of what Jesus offers in the Gospel (Heb 10.1). Therefore, the Passover rituals discussed previously cast a shadow which resembles and highlights Jesus' own "once for all" sacrifice on the cross (Heb 7.27).

## The Lamb of God

The central feature of the Passover rituals was the sacrificial lamb chosen by each household. It is noteworthy that John introduces Jesus to the public with this announcement: "Behold, the Lamb of God who takes away the sin of the world!" (John 1.29; cf. 1.35–36). This designation is broad enough to encompass many Old Testament concepts.[16] Among the many sacrificial lambs which find fulfillment in Jesus, readers should call to mind the prominent Passover lamb.

Peter also described the Christ in the language of a sacrificial lamb, but his descriptions create stronger connections between Jesus and the Passover lamb:

> If you address as Father the One who impartially judges according to each one's work, conduct yourselves in fear during the time of your stay on earth; knowing that you were not redeemed with perishable things like silver or gold from your futile way of life inherited from your forefathers, but with precious blood, as of a lamb unblemished and spotless, the blood of Christ (1 Pet 1.17–19).

Peter describes Jesus as an "unblemished" lamb. This is, of course, the same idea found in the Passover lamb. Jesus fulfills this in a perfect way by being "tempted in all things just as we are, yet without sin" (Heb 4.15). While the Passover lamb represented moral excellence, Jesus embodied moral perfection. Peter also draws special attention to the "precious blood … of Christ." This is another prominent feature of the Passover ritual—the blood used to redeem the Israelites' firstborn from certain death.[17]

John revisits the lamb imagery in the book of Revelation. When the heavenly host waited expectantly for someone to open the sealed scroll, one of the twenty-four elders told John to stop and look at "the Lion that is from the tribe of Judah, the Root of David" (Rev

---

[16] For a list of possible allusions, see D. A. Carson, *The Gospel According to John*, PNTC (Grand Rapids: Eerdmans, 1991) 149–150.

[17] Although this lecture has not taken the time to explore it, redemption language features prominently in Exodus 13.13, 15 in connection to the Passover event.

5.5). This powerful, Messianic figure was coming to open the scroll. When John turned around, however, he saw "a Lamb standing, as if slain" (Rev 5.6). Throughout the book of Revelation, John sees this meek, slaughtered animal as a vibrant and powerful victor. Like the Passover lamb which guaranteed Israel victory over the dominant world power, Jesus—the living lamb—guarantees His people victory over the powers of the world.

## The Memorial Meal

The Passover involved a sacrifice, but it was also a feast. After the first Passover feast, Israel was to mark the occasion by taking part in an annual memorial meal. Jesus' death on the cross functions as a new sort of Passover event—a sacrificial death which delivers humanity from bondage to sin. It is noteworthy that Jesus died during the time that the Israelites were celebrating the Passover and the Feast of Unleavened Bread (e.g., Mark 14.1). Surely there can be no doubt that Jesus' crucifixion is the intended fulfillment of the Passover sacrifice.

Before Jesus offers Himself as a slaughtered lamb, he eats the slaughtered Passover lamb with His disciples. This is the meal popularly known as "the Last Supper." It was during this Passover celebration that Jesus instituted a new kind of memorial meal. Matthew records the event this way:

> While they were eating, Jesus took some bread, and after a blessing, He broke it and gave it to the disciples, and said, "Take, eat; this is My body." And when He had taken a cup and given thanks, He gave it to them, saying, "Drink from it, all of you; for this is My blood of the covenant, which is poured out for many for forgiveness of sins" (26.26–28).

Jesus uses the Passover feast—the memorial of Israel's exodus from Egypt, freedom from bondage, and beginning of nationhood—to create a new memorial meal. This new memorial does not commemorate the Passover lamb as that which brings safety, but it commemorates the sacrifice of Jesus.

Shortly after Jesus shared this meal with His disciples, Judas betrayed Him and the Jews led Him away to be sacrificed as our perfect Passover Lamb. As He was dying, onlookers offered Jesus sour wine "upon a branch of hyssop" (John 19.29), the same kind of branch used by the Israelites to smear the lamb's blood on their doorposts. After He died, Jesus' blood poured out on the ground, but—just as with the Passover lamb— "they did not break his legs" (John 19.33–34). As a result, we can share the memorial meal Jesus instituted by symbolically consuming His body as our own sacrificial Lamb.

Paul used this same Passover language when discussing the problem of sin in the Corinthian church. He wrote, "For Christ our Passover also has been sacrificed. Therefore let us celebrate the feast, not with old leaven, nor with the leaven of malice and wickedness, but with the unleavened bread of sincerity and truth" (1 Cor 5.7–8). In this passage, Paul is addressing the problem of immorality existing unchecked in the local church. This cannot be allowed, Paul argues, because we are celebrating Christ's Passover and we need to have purged the leaven from our lives and from our churches. So long as "leaven" exists among us, we are unworthy of celebrating Jesus' freedom from sin and death.

## Conclusion

For Israel to have life, God required death. Mercifully, God allowed the Passover lamb to die in the place of Israel's firstborn. God designed the Passover lamb with its feast to keep the exodus event in Israel's collective mind throughout the years. But above all else, the Passover pointed Israel forward to the need for a greater deliverance, a greater sacrifice, and a greater exodus.

For you and me to have life, God required a death. Mercifully, God sent His Son—the Lamb of God—to die in our place. Now we who are in Christ celebrate a new kind of Passover. We celebrate freedom from bondage to sin and the hope of victorious life with the Lamb. May we never forget the cost of our freedom. May we forever remember our Passover Lamb.

# Redemption from Slavery

## Russ Roberts

Two dreams and a colorful robe help set the cogwheel of Jehovah's promise in full churning motion. He had established a unilateral covenant through the patriarchal lineage of Abraham, Isaac and Jacob to "give them the land of Canaan" (Exod 6.3–4),[1] but it would be almost four and a half centuries before the promise is realized. Jacob demonstrates his love for his son Joseph over his siblings by giving him a coat of many colors. This coat, along with Joseph's two divine dreams of his family bowing down to him, triggers his envious brothers to sell him to a band of Ishmaelites passing by, thus initiating the providential events which lead Abraham's descendants from Canaan, "the land of their pilgrimage," to Egypt.

God uses personal events in the lives of His people to teach heavenly truths. Without an understanding of these divine concepts, such as mercy, grace, atonement for sin, faith, hope, obedience, and redemption, His creation will never fully appreciate the blessings received through His promises. During the Divided Kingdom period of Israel's history, the northern nation of Israel betrayed God through their constant disobedience. God embedded Israel's repetitive defiance into the life of the prophet Hosea by instructing him to take a "wife of harlotry" (Hos 1.2). His passionate preaching to this arrogant and ignorant nation demonstrated his appreciation

---

[1] Unless noted otherwise, all quotations of scripture are from the NKJV.

of God's feeling to Israel's act of betrayal. Hosea learned the truth about God's love, mercy, and obedience through his marriage to Gomer, an unfaithful wife. In Egypt, the Israelites learn the necessity of being redeemed.

## From Royalty to Servitude

Genesis closes with a near Utopian setting, portraying Israel as a small population of shepherds-turned-farmers in Goshen, located in the Nile River delta's fertile riches. Because of Joseph's nearly limitless authority, these seventy descendants of Abraham were well protected by Egypt, one of the most powerful empires on earth. Joseph could not live forever, and the Pharaohs who brought him to his position could not continually remain in power. Joseph died, and the dynasty which surged Joseph to prominence over Egypt was overthrown.

The opening verses of Exodus rehearse the favorable status of Israel and explain that God had blessed the descendants of Joseph as they had become "fruitful and increased abundantly, multiplied and grew exceedingly mighty; and the land was filled with them" (Exod 1.7). Israel was no longer small; it had grown to a number easily exceeding two million in population.[2] The scriptures, however, are silent about the affairs of Israel between the writings of Genesis and Exodus. In just eight verses within the opening chapter of Exodus, the social status of Israel plummets from being "exceedingly mighty" in the land of Egypt, to one of servitude under "hard bondage" (Exod 1.7–14). Though it appears the transition was swift, decades must have passed to reach the full rank of slavery. Moses did not record the extraordinary occurrences between his writings of Genesis and Exodus which completely reshaped the lives of the Israelites. Events so dramatic are left to our own imagination and wonder. Edersheim reflects, "This silence of three and a half centuries is almost awful in its grandeur, like the loneliness of Sinai, the mount of God."[3]

---

[2] Israel's population can be reasonably estimated at two million using the total of men at 603,050 (Num 2.32).

[3] Alfred Edersheim, *Bible History: Old Testament* (New York: Revell, 1876; rep.

Though historians speculate concerning the events of the nation's uprisings and Egyptian dynasties that allowed Joseph's rise of authority, they do not all agree. This secular history is only important to this study in the fact that God raised up Joseph, fulfilling His promise to the patriarchs. Just as abrupt as Joseph's rise to power, his descendants were reduced to the status of slaves to their Egyptian governing power. A new Pharaoh, "who did not know Joseph," feared that the ever-growing population and power of the Israelites would someday challenge the rule of the Egyptians, so he instigated cruel and harsh bondage upon the Israelites. Great cities and storage vats were constructed through rigor and inhuman treatment geared to discourage and decrease the Hebrew populace. Additional decrees were established to kill the male children at birth, furthering the effort to stunt population growth. The more the Egyptians afflicted God's people, the more they grew in number. By the end of the first chapter of Exodus, the descendants of Abraham who flourished during the days of Joseph were significant in number, but now diminished to the status of full-fledged slavery. The Utopian days were over.

## Slavery in the Ancient World

When mentioned in the Pentateuch, slavery is acknowledged as a condition "in which a person is deprived of freedom, a least for a period of time, by being in subjection to a master in order that the master may benefit from the labor of the slave."[4] Slavery can be either voluntary or involuntary. Voluntary servitude is normally under the dire situation of an unpayable debt or an attempt to survive poverty. Involuntary servitude is what usually comes to mind when we hear the term slavery. Involuntary enslavement may be broken down even further into the "chattel slave" and the "forced labor slave," when considering ancient slavery. The chattel slave is one who is complete-

---

ed., Peabody: Hendrickson, 1994) 149.

[4] Gene Haas. "Slave, Slavery" in T. Desmond Alexander and David W. Baker, *Dictionary of the Old Testament: Pentateuch* (Downers Grove: InterVarsity Press, 2003) 778–781.

ly owned by a master and, by law, is considered movable property to that master. This slave has no rights or possessions, only duties, though they can attain freedom through the grace of the owner. The forced labor slave is one used by his owners primarily for manual work, mainly to farm the land or construct facilities and large structures. The servitude described in Exodus of the Israelites to the Egyptians is one of forced labor (Exod 1.11–14).

Slavery was prevalent in the ancient world.[5] It was a part of everyday life, in almost every ancient culture. Slavery, whether voluntary or involuntary, whether chattel or forced labor, insinuates by the very term that the one in servitude has lost his or her freedom and a significant portion of their human dignity. Even the Law of Moses, bilaterally established and ratified between Jehovah and the children of Israel, distinguished between the free and the slave. Injuring or killing a free person resulted in a "life for life, eye for eye, hand for hand, etc." punishment. However, restitution for a killed or injured slave was determined more closely aligned with the repayment of property or an animal, not of human life (Exod 21.20–27). Although some slavery in the ancient world was voluntary, being a slave has always limited freedom and human dignity.

## The Concept of Redemption

Redemption is a simple and familiar concept. The broad spectrum in which we use this word today ranges from compensating for a past fault or performance, to rescuing an animal fallen into a storm drain, to claiming a prize with a winning ticket. Another common occurrence of this term in our lives today is seen as we proceed to the final checkout when purchasing an item online. Prior to the completion of the transaction, we are often prompted with the option to redeem a gift card to reduce the cost of the items being bought. We check our wife's cloak and our hat at the theater's concierge before enjoying a Broadway play, receiving a ticket stub

---

[5] Michael McHugh, "Slavery" in E. Ferguson, *Encyclopedia of Early Christianity* (New York: Garland Publishing, 1990) 854–855.

so that we can "redeem" our possessions as we leave the theater. The verb redeem today means to "to vindicate, to buy, to rescue, to deliver or to retrieve and give back to its rightful owner." We use this same term "redeem" in all these circumstances. Redemption is a common term today, and it is a simple concept.

In our Bibles, the idea of redemption is used the same way. The three primary Hebrew words often translated in some form of our English word redeemed are (1) *ga'al* which means "to redeem, deliver, avenge, and act as a kinsman," (2) *padah* meaning "to redeem, ransom," and (3) *kapar* used to describe the act "to ransom, atone, expiate, and propitiate."[6] The term *ga'al* best fits the focus of our thoughts in this essay. It is the Hebrew word used by the LORD when He declared, "I will redeem you with an outstretched arm," foretelling His rescue of Israel from the bondage of Egyptian slavery (Exod 6.6).

The Old Testament offers many examples of the Hebrew word *ga'al*. It conveys the concept of deliverance from harm (Gen 48.16), of an avenger of a murdered relative associated with the laws surrounding the cities of refuge (Num 35.19), and of a kinsman redeeming property and another relative from their disastrous circumstance (Ruth 2.20). The usage of *ga'al* in the story of Ruth is important to our topic in that it demonstrates three aspects of the kinsman-redeemer; it shows that the redeemer must have the authority to redeem (i.e., the right of redemption), the willingness to redeem, and the ability to redeem (Ruth 4.1–12). Ruth and her mother-in-law, Naomi were childless widows who, under Jewish law, had no legal right to the property previously owned by their husbands. The Law of Moses did stipulate that the nearest kinsman had the responsibility to redeem one of these women to perpetuate the name of the dead through the inheritance (Deut 25.5–10; Ruth 3.12–13). A wealthy Jewish landowner named Boaz was related to Naomi, but he was not the closest kinsman; he had neither the authority, nor the responsi-

---

[6] William Vine et al., "Redeem," *Vine's Complete Expository Dictionary of Old and New Testament Words* (Nashville: Thomas Nelson, 1996) 1:194–96.

bility to redeem these women. At the climax of Ruth's story, Naomi's closest relative, who had the authority to redeem, was unwilling to redeem because he felt he did not have the ability due to his current inheritance (Ruth 4.6). Boaz had the capacity to redeem Ruth and was more than willing; when the nearest of kin refused to redeem Naomi, Boaz then had the authority and ability to redeem Ruth and the inheritance of Naomi's land. Boaz willingly redeemed Ruth. It is important that we understand this concept; God has the authority or sovereignty, and ability or omnipotence, to redeem Israel. In Exodus 6.6, He also expresses His willingness.

One more idea of redemption should be acknowledged before the situation of the Israelites in Egypt is discussed. The more personally involved we are in the "redemption" process, the more thought provoking it becomes for us, and the more astute we are to the terms of its process. A good illustration of this can be seen in the familiar story of Jessica McClure. In 1987, at the age of eighteen months, the baby referred to as Baby Jessica, fell twenty-two feet down an 8-inch water well casing in her aunt's backyard. The whole nation watched for the next fifty-six hours as rescuers pulled this innocent baby safely from her apparent doom in a backyard in Midland, Texas. During the entire process, the parents of Baby Jessica pleaded for prayers and help as they listened to their toddler's songs echoing up through the shaft of the well. When Jessica was rescued, everyone rejoiced, especially those in Midland. As nerve-racking as those two and a half days were to those who kept up with the story, our compassion for her and her family was limited since we were not personally involved. I am not saying that our hearts did not melt with every news update. All of us who watched placed ourselves in the shoes of Jessica's parents, but the experience was not the same because we were not personally involved with the disaster. If, however, the toddler who fell down the well was one of ours, or, if we were the victim of a similar horrifying circumstance, our yearning for redemption would be that much greater. It would be real. We must feel the need to be rescued before we will appreciate this redemption process. The more personally one is involved, the more the helpless situation is sensed and the more the act of the redeemer is understood and appreciated.

## Redemption Becomes Personal to Israel

Before the Israelites were chosen as God's peculiar people, they had to first be redeemed, or rescued from Egyptian captivity. Before they were redeemed, they had to cry for a redeemer. Before they cried for a redeemer, they had to appreciate an urgency to be redeemed. Redemption needed to become personal to them. We may understand better why, centuries before our current story, God providentially and methodically guided His people to a most unlikely setting where the teaching process of redemption could be cultivated. They lived among the powerful and intimidating people of Egypt; first associated with the ruling class of Egyptians, and then as slaves to this ungodly and pagan nation. Among the privileged class, the Israelites would grow in number and confidence. Under slavery, this enormous populace learned redemption. They understood firsthand the idea of slavery and developed a yearning to be redeemed. God demonstrated a divine concept to His people by again placing them right into the process. He forced them to live in the definition, so to speak; Israel was forced to realize the need for redemption firsthand. God was still in control when Abraham's descendants were mysteriously reduced to servitude. This transition was necessary. God would teach these people they needed a redeemer which He would mercifully provide.

To the successor of the Egyptian throne in the first chapter of Exodus, the name Joseph or the Hebrew culture was more of a national threat than the amusement of past folklore. The Pharaoh had to stop the continual growth of these mighty foreign infiltrators, so he ended all privileges of the Hebrews. The Hebrews did not possess weapons or have military experience. Pharaoh's fear was sheerly born out of the growing population of the Hebrew nation. Their lands and liberties were exchanged for forced labor and their situation became undeniably hopeless with no end in sight.[7] The constraints of slavery, no matter what culture or circumstance, is a degradation of self-worth. The slavery was intended to break the spirit of these men, "reducing to a mind-set that would have made their escape impossible."[8] Their labor was severe. It was rigorous work; they had the back-breaking task to construct the store cities of Pithom and Raamses (Exod 1.11). From archeological findings, some scholars consider the Israelites' survival during this period of history as somewhat miraculous, given the conditions of slavery frequently in temperatures exceeding 130° Fahrenheit.[9]

Of course, the Egyptians had more slaves than just the Israelites, but these Hebrew slaves were different. They were a people of promise and "destined for deliverance, not by some unexpected benevolence of the Pharaoh, but by an act of Yahweh, their God."[10] This is why at the end of Genesis, Joseph on his deathbed tells his family, "I am dying; but God will surely visit you, and bring you out of this land to the land of which He swore to Abraham, to Isaac, and to Jacob" (Gen 50.24). He knew the Israelites would one day return to the Promised Land and he insisted that they take his body with them. However, this divine destiny was a two-edged sword. On the one hand, God multiplied the Israelites despite Pharaoh's best efforts, thwarting his plans, but at the same time, Pharaoh multiplied the servitude of the Israelites, causing them to cry out even more to God. Now, with no relief in sight and heavy bondage seemingly guaranteed for all future generations, God will hear the cry of Israel and raise up a redeemer in answer to their prayers and His promises.

---

[7] James Burton Coffman, *Exodus* (Abilene: ACU Press, 1985) 5.

[8] *Ibid.* 5.

[9] *Ibid,* 6.

[10] Henry Flanders et al., *People of the Covenant: An Introduction to the Old Testament* (New York: Ronald Press Company, 1973) 127.

## Crying Out for a Redeemer

As the book of Genesis closes, it is difficult to imagine that the descendants of Joseph, the one God used to develop Egypt's prosperity during a devastating famine, would find themselves as forced slave laborers in their host nation. But slavery is exactly what initiated their cry for help, their cry for a redeemer.

"Now it happened in the process of time that the king of Egypt died. Then the children of Israel groaned because of the bondage, and they cried out; and their cry came up to God because of the bondage" (Exod 2.23). From the wording in the first part of this verse, it appears that the Israelites anticipated some relief of oppression upon the death of the present Egyptian king, for it was only after this occasion that the urgent yearning for freedom was provoked. Their hope was possibly founded upon the changed attitude of the new ruler; surely, he would ease the pain of bondage, or even restore the good fortune that was once enjoyed decades ago, but it was not to be. Whomever this new Pharaoh was, the oppression remained. The Hebrew nation, buried deep in the Egyptian culture and continuing in brutal slavery, had lost all sense of hope. In their awakened desire for freedom, the Israelites poured out their remorseful and repentant hearts toward heaven, to God, toward whom they had become calloused and complacent.

God heard their cries (Exod 2.24–25), and with His divine covenant to the patriarchs firmly in mind, God turned His attention to the slaves in Egypt as if to say, "This is the genuine cry I was waiting for and the reason I brought you to this foreign land." These cries were an integral part of God's redemptive plan. Slavery affected all aspects of their lives, and Israel could not save themselves. Now the entire Hebrew people understood the need for redemption and cried out loud for a redeemer.

## Redeemed as Conquerors

As stated earlier, the usage of the Hebrew word *ga'al* (redeem) in the story of Ruth demonstrates three aspects of the kinsman-redeemer; it shows that the redeemer must have the authority, the willingness, and the ability to redeem. Not everyone who has authority to act also possesses the ability to act on that authority. Authority and skills do not always coincide. A newly appointed manager of a small business firm may have been given instant authority but has yet to learn the managerial skills needed to perform all functions under this authority. And even if one possesses the authority and the ability to perform the required tasks, he or she may not have the willingness or desire to act upon these responsibilities. Ruth was redeemed by Boaz because he possessed all three aspects of the kinsmen-redeemer: he gained the authority, and he already had the means and the willingness to redeem Ruth.

Back to our story in Egypt, Moses—the Hebrew raised as a royal prince—had assumed a role of a rescuer, but with no authority or plan, he could not redeem his Hebrew people. He left for Midian and returned to Egypt forty years later. This time he arrived with the authority of God to redeem the Hebrew people from their cruel and brutal bondage. God not only possessed the authority (or sovereignty) to govern all the things of this earth (Isa 45.18); He had the ability (or power) to alter and sustain all things of this earth (Job 42.2); and His love and mercy toward His creation demonstrated His willingness to act upon His authority and power (Exod 6.5–6). The rescue of the Israelites from Egyptian bondage validated all three aspects of God's redemptive power.

The rescue from slavery, however, was not simply a release into the desert plains of Egypt or a return to the local Goshen community. It would not have fully profited the Israelites if they were rescued from bondage with no place of their own to dwell securely. The Israelites' release from bondage is unlike the prisoners in the Philippian jail whose chains and doors were unleashed by a divine earthquake. The jailer in charge of those prisoners was concerned because he knew that they could have escaped and scattered haphazardly into the city of Philippi and throughout the adjacent countryside of Macedonia

(Acts 16.25–28). The Israelites in Egypt left with a pre-determined, prophetic, and divine direction. They were heading for the land "flowing with milk and honey" (Exod 3.8), the land which they had heard about all their lives in captivity.

Israel was not forcibly displaced from Goshen in shackles and fetters; nor did they leave destitute or in a state of poverty. The Hebrew people (approximately two million) departed Egypt victoriously. Seizing the gold, silver, and livestock from their neighbors, they aligned with Moses in singleness of purpose and marched toward Canaan, the great portion of land promised to their forefathers over four hundred years before. The redemption was all by the power, foresight, and orchestration of Jehovah, their God. He, through the voice of Moses, explained to Israel that they would "exit only to enter" a new relationship with God: "I will take you as My people, and I will be your God. Then you shall know that I am the LORD your God who brings you out from under the burdens of the Egyptians" (Exod 6.7). Every generation existing after the exodus will understand the details of Israel's escape from Egypt. Even the inhabitants of Canaan would be warned of the events which led to the Hebrew nation's rescue (Josh 2.9–11). They were now redeemed as God's victorious people. They did not leave Egypt as fugitives; they left as conquerors.

## Sin Makes Redemption Personal Today

The apostle Paul reminds us that the writings of the early inspired authors can be applicable to increase our faith today. The scriptures were written for us to meditate upon the text so we can envision our hope more clearly and patiently (Rom 15.4). So many lessons can be learned from the events recorded in the book Exodus, but the clearest and most direct correlation between the Israelites and us is one of redemption.

God has given mankind a promise of eternal life to those who believe on Him and His Son, Jesus Christ (John 3.16). Before one can enter into a relationship with God as He has prescribed, one must recognize his or her lost condition, separated from God. The most challenging part of teaching the gospel to the lost is convincing them that they are sinners. Many who I speak with are good and honest people. They cannot recall any activity in their lives that would cause a loving and merciful God to turn His face from them. However, before one can be redeemed, one must feel the need to be redeemed.

The transition from the Israelite social status of royalty to full-fledged slavery must have been gradual. Even if the transitional phases were marked with milestones of excessive afflictions (Exod 1.11), their anxious cry for help was not fully realized until Israel reached the abyss, the nadir of misery and depression. It is the same today with sin. Many people turn to God as a last resort. I am not referring to the selfish who only cry for help when their physical health or security is in jeopardy, I am talking about the true believer who finally recognizes the dire condition of their sinful state and is searching for the true avenue of salvation. The wider the chasm between sin and holiness sensed, the louder the cry is for help. Until we acknowledge our separation from God, and understand the results of an eternity without Him, we too will not yearn for redemption.

Jesus told an audience of Jewish believers that they needed to be set free if they wanted to be His disciples. As descendants of Abraham, they were confused because they had never recalled being under bondage to anyone. Jesus explained, "Most assuredly, I say to you, whoever commits sin is a slave of sin" (John 8.34). Sin is the restraint that keeps us bound to this world. We will not feel a need to be set free or redeemed until we recognize our state of separation. Once sin is personally recognized and personally acknowledged, one can then search for the true redeemer; the redeemer who has the authority to redeem, the ability to redeem and the willingness to save.

## Jesus Christ is Our Kinsman-Redeemer

It is no coincidence that the Hebrew word *ga'al* (redeem) is used in the Old Testament to foretell the coming of our Messiah. The common meaning of *ga'al* among the Israelites was that of a kinsman and redeemer, and Isaiah uses this word to describe the "Redeemer" coming as an intercessor and rescuer for the righteous (Isa 59.16–20). No man, the prophet writes, is suitable for the task of redeemer, so God uses His own arm and own righteous garments for the judgement and vindication in Zion.

All men "have sinned and fall short of the glory of God" (Rom 3.23). Our only hope of reconciliation to God is through a near kinsman, with the ability and the willingness to fulfill his duties as the redeemer. The prophetic words of Isaiah foretold that God would come to earth, because no other man is suitable to redeem us. He came in the form of His Son, both as deity and as a man (John 1.1, 14). In this role, God served as our nearest kinsman in the flesh, and with the ability to save as God.

The women who witnessed the redemption process for Ruth rejoiced by telling Naomi, "Blessed be the LORD, who has not left you this day without a close relative" (Ruth 4.14). Boaz, the close kinsman, was willing to pay the full price for Ruth's redemption. Jesus, as our kinsman had to be willing to pay the full price for our sins. The price for our redemption has not been paid with "corruptible things like silver or gold," but with His own blood, as the only unblemished sacrifice (1 Pet 1.18–19; Rom 3.23–25). It is through this redemption that we have the forgiveness of our sins (Eph 1.7).

Jesus had the authority as our kinsman, the power to save us through His deity (Col 1.15–17) and was willing to humble Himself on the cross to pay the full debt (John 15.13; Phil 2.8). Jesus Christ is our kinsman-redeemer and has asked us to remember His sacrifice for us each Lord's Day (1 Cor 11.23–26).

## The Joy of Redemption

Sing, O heavens, for the LORD has done it!
  Shout, you lower parts of the earth;
Break forth into singing, you mountains,
  O forest, and every tree in it!
For the LORD has redeemed Jacob,
  and glorified Himself in Israel (Isa 44.23).

We do not meditate enough upon our redemption. Man's sins have separated him far from God, and through His perfect justice, man's punishment is everlasting separation. Man cannot save himself. Hidden for thousands of years, God revealed His scheme to reconcile man through the only price that could pay the debt. The price was paid in the death of God's only heavenly son, Jesus Christ.

As the Hebrews gathered their belongings and precious possessions of their Egyptian neighbors, it must have been a solemn scene. There was the constant noise of over two million Israelites ordering themselves intertwined with the sounds of transport and thousands of livestock being prodded along. Distant instructions were heard to ensure that Joseph's bones were among their assets, and God Himself would soon be plainly visible before them, either by cloud or fire. He was directing them on a special route to fulfill a promise recounted to every traveler since they were young. It was a day unimaginable months before, but now a reality. God has recued them. It was indescribable joy.

The Old Testament prophet Isaiah appropriately expressed the joy at the knowledge of God's people being redeemed and returning home from Babylonian captivity: "Sing, O heavens, for the Lord has done it!" (Isa 44.23). Seven decades had separated them from the temple and the familiar sounds and smells of their past worship. What a joyous occasion when God's people were redeemed to return from seventy years of Babylonian captivity. They were heading home to rebuild their temple, their capital city of Jerusalem, and their homeland. It was indescribable joy.

Can you imagine the unveiling of God's redemptive plan for mankind? Man is enslaved to sin just as the Israelites were in bondage to the Egyptians and the southern nation of Judah was captive to Babylon. The departure days of Egypt and Babylon cannot compare with our final rescue. Isaiah's description in the verse above, though the context is plainly referencing the release from Babylon, foretells the revelation of God's redemptive plan for man. All heavenly and earthly realms harmonize in joyous song: "Sing, O heavens, for the Lord has done it!" The unimaginable plan is a reality. It is the "things which angels desire to look into" (1 Pet 1.12). It is indescribable joy, unparalleled!

# "Through the Water"

## *The Parting of the Red Sea*

### Roger Polanco

The parting of the Red Sea is perhaps the most significant event of the entire Old Testament. This one event became the foundation of Israel's faith in Yahweh for thousands of years to come, and for some, it is still that today. Through the Law, the Prophets and the Psalms, God continually reminded Israel of what he did when he parted the sea and delivered his people from insurmountable odds. In fact, the event is so momentous that it is only surpassed by the death, burial and resurrection of Jesus in the New Testament, which may arguably be identified as the true fulfillment of the exodus. The exodus, especially the parting of the Red Sea, is the gospel or "good news" of the Old Testament. What can we learn today from this momentous event? We will divide the story into three parts: the exit (Exod 13.17–22), the chase (Exod 14.1–12), and the parting (Exod 14.13–31).

### The Exit (Exodus 13.17–22)

When the Hebrews marched out of Egypt, they had already experienced manifestations of God's power. After the tenth and climactic devastating plague, Pharaoh decided to let the people go (Exod 13.17), just as God had intended from the beginning (Exod 4.22–23). It was truly a remarkable display of God's power that compelled Pharaoh to free them. If you have ever read the exodus story, you have wondered what would be necessary for this evil man to relinquish power over the Israelites? He was determined to keep his slaves no matter the cost, even if it meant the destruction of his own kingdom for all practical purposes. Finally, after the death of his first-born, and not only his, but the firstborn of every Egyptian, even the cattle (Exod 12.29), it became obvious that God had prevailed. The defeated ruler dejectedly relinquished the people he had lost everything to keep. God had finally shown him that he was powerless. He could not even protect his own child. God humbled him to the point that after his concession, he begged for a blessing from the God who had taken it all away (Exod 12.32).

God did not only show his power by his defeat of Pharaoh, but also by the fact that he enabled the Israelites to plunder Egypt. Exodus12.36 says, "Thus they plundered Egypt."[1] The word "plunder" in this text is military language, referring to what armies traditionally did to nations that they conquered. In this case, we have a group of newly freed slaves, particularly the women (Exod 3.22), plundering the once-mighty empire of Egypt. The only explanation for such an impossible scenario is that the almighty God was with them. Seeing God's complete control over the superpower of the world should instill in us a courage and resilience which prevents us from being intimidated by political powers and the changes that they bring. If God can defeat and thoroughly humble a tyrant who ruled over the most powerful nation on earth, can he not also take care of us whatever happens in our political system?

In addition to having already experienced God's power, the Israelites had also seen the fulfillment of his promises. Exodus 13.19 refers to the fact that Moses took the bones of Joseph with him as he led the Israelites out of Egypt. Because Joseph believed the promises of God (Genesis15.13–14) he instructed his descendants to bring his

---

[1] Unless noted otherwise, all quotations of scripture are from the 1995 update to the NASB.

bones out of Egypt when it was time to leave for the Promised Land. The prophecy had now come true, and the promise made to Joseph on his deathbed was being kept. After years of slavery in a temporary land, they were homeward bound, carrying Joseph's bones and the promise of blessings to come. They had seen God's Word come true; not only in the matter of Joseph's bones, but also in the fact that in spite of all the obstacles and against all odds, they were no longer just a family, but a mighty nation. Exodus 12.37 says that there were about 600,000 men traveling on foot apart from the women and children. They were truly as numerous as the sand on the seashore. And finally, Exodus 12.40 states that the time they had lived in Egypt was 430 years. That is a reminder of the fact that in Genesis 15.13–14 God said, "Know for certain that your descendants will be strangers in a land that is not theirs, where they will be enslaved and oppressed four hundred years. But I will also judge the nation whom they will serve, and afterward they will come out with many possessions."[2] All of these prophecies were fulfilled before their eyes. God is not only a powerful God, but a promise-keeping one. Exodus13.19 says, "Moses took the bones of Joseph with him, for he had made the sons of Israel solemnly swear, saying, 'God will surely take care of you, and you shall carry my bones from here with you.'" Because Joseph believed that his God was a promise-keeping God, he said, "God will surely take care of you." If we, like Joseph, believe in the faithfulness of the God we serve, we will wait expectantly and prepare for the blessings to come.

Finally, before they experienced the astonishing demonstration at the parting of the Red Sea, the Israelites had already experienced the presence of God. Exodus 13.17–18 tells us that God led his peo-

---

[2] An alternate way to read Exodus 12.40–41 and Genesis 15.13–14 in that the total length of sojourning in Canaan and Egypt together was 430 years (as the Samaritan Pentateuch and Septuagint read) while the Egyptian portion was only 215 years (and the period of enslavement even shorter, somewhere between 80 and 144 years). A shorter Egyptian sojourn more easily fits Paul's argument that the Law was given 430 years after the promise to Abraham (Gal 3.17).

ple, but Exodus 13.21–22 tells us how he did it. Going before them as a pillar of cloud by day and a pillar of fire by night, he took them every step of the way. Notice two characteristics of his leading: First, his presence was always there. Exodus 13.22 says, "He did not take away the pillar of cloud by day, nor the pillar of fire by night, from before the people." His presence was constant. This calls to mind a similar promise made by Jesus to his disciples in Matthew 28.20 which says, "I am with you always, even to the end of the age." We serve a God who not only sets the captives free, but also continues with them on their journey.

Additionally, Exodus 13.17 tells us that God was mindful of the Israelites' weakness as he led them. He did not lead them through the quicker route through Philistine territory knowing that "the people might change their minds when they see war and return to Egypt" (Exod 13.17). God knew that these newly freed slaves were still fragile and not ready to fight, so he chose the long route for them. I imagine many were quietly wondering to themselves why the trip was taking so long, and likely expressed that this was not the way they would have taken. However, God knew what they could handle and when they could handle it. 1 Corinthians 10.13 says, "No temptation has overtaken you but such as is common to man; and God is faithful, who will not allow you to be tempted beyond what you are able, but with the temptation will provide the way of escape also, so that you will be able to endure it." How many times has God mercifully interceded in our lives in order to protect us from a trial we were not prepared to face? God is not just a powerful God who released his people from bondage, but a caring, invested God who continued with them on their journey and showed his presence and care in tangible ways.

What incredible things the Israelites had already experienced in seeing the power, the promise and the presence of God! We should not be surprised that Exodus 14.8 says the Israelites went out boldly! In the same way, Christians should not be characterized by fear, but boldness. When we see that our God is powerful, that he keeps his promises and that he is present in our lives, we should be motivated to have a type of confidence that those around us will never have. How do you live when there is political unrest? Are you afraid and nervous, or do you believe that the all-powerful God is in control? How do you walk when you are standing alone because of Jesus? Are you confident because you know God is with you? Are you filled with fear because no one else stands with you? May we always remember our powerful, ever-present, promise-keeping God and walk confidently in the way he leads us.

## The Chase (14.1–12)

Before we get into the details of the parting of the Red Sea, it is important to recognize its New Testament parallel in the cross of Christ. The cross is the place where God defeated our enemy and made a way for us to be saved. We can also compare the parting of the sea to that moment in which we are baptized into Christ and raised into newness of life, a life of freedom and no longer slavery (1 Cor 10.2; cf. Rom 6.3–6). The principle found in the story can also be applied to moments and events in our walk with Christ when we are personally delivered from a trial. For example, notice the parallels between Peter's deliverance and the Passover from Acts 12.1, 2, 7, 8, and 10. For the purpose of this essay, the primary comparison that I will be drawing is from the first example: God delivering us from slavery to sin through the cross of Jesus Christ.

After starting on the long route towards the Promised Land, the children of Israel were now officially on their way out of the land of Egypt. Contrary to customary military tactics, however, God told Moses to have the Israelites turn back and camp in front of Pi-ha-hiroth, between Migdol and the sea (Exod 14.2). This move would make Israel look leaderless and confused, as if they were wandering aimlessly around the land (Exod 14.3). God knew that this decision would cause Pharaoh to reconsider his freeing of the Israelites and set in motion a chain of events leading to a defining moment. It would be a moment in which he would display once and for all the vast scope of his power and would cause nations around the world to hear and shudder.

Israel proceeded to camp in the location God commanded and Pharaoh did exactly what God knew he would do. There are three important details to notice here: First, God made it appear to Pharaoh that he had no control of the situation, when the reality is that he was in full control. When Israel camped by the sea, Pharaoh concluded that the Israelites were leaderless, ill-equipped, and helpless. The reality is that nothing could have been further from the truth. It appeared to Pharaoh that the Israelites had committed a blunder, but the reality was that God was playing chess with Pharaoh, and he was about to checkmate him.

Not surprisingly, the Israelites also thought that God was no longer in control. When Pharaoh's army drew near, the Israelites become frightened (Exod14.10) and complained that it would have been better for them to have never left Egypt (Exod 14.12). From their perspective, God had made a mistake (or had no real plan at all) and he was no longer in control of the situation. The reality, however, was that God was in full control, and he was getting ready to defeat the enemy once and for all, as well as teach Israel a valuable lesson: God was, is, and always will be in control. Though such may not have appeared to be the case to Pharaoh and the Egyptians, or to Moses and the Israelites, he always was in control. This would still be true thousands of years later at the cross of Jesus Christ. After being betrayed by his closest friends, being arrested in the very place where he had been praying and finally being put to death on the cross, it appeared to the world that God was no longer sovereign. However, as believers know, the opposite was true. The cross was God's checkmate to Satan. While the Son of God was agonizing on a cross, nailed to it by human hands, he was forever saving and freeing his people. May we always remember and fully trust God's sovereignty in our own lives.

Why was God using this plan? Why did the Israelites need to use these tactics so that he would be honored through Pharaoh and his army, and so that the Egyptians would know that He is the LORD (Ex14.4)? God was creating a scenario in which he could display his great power and reveal his glory so that the Egyptians and Israelites would be compelled to see him for who he is. The crossing of the Red Sea was not only to save the Israelites, but also to display God's glory as he defeated his enemies. Similarly, the cross of Christ not only bestows salvation, but also displays God's ultimate power and glory as he defeats the enemy: Satan and his forces. Colossians 2.15 tells us that by means of the cross Jesus "disarmed the rulers and authorities and made a public display by triumphing over them." He stripped them of their power and made a public spectacle of them to be ridiculed. The reality is that God is willing to sacrifice our immediate comfort to show the world who he is and display his power and glory. As former slaves set free, we should have such gratitude for his intervention, that we willingly sacrifice our comfort for his honor.

Pharaoh was unwilling to let the Israelites leave without a fight. Pharaoh is the Old Testament representation of Satan. His mission was to enslave and kill the people of God (Exod 1), and he would not passively sit by and watch them leave. The text emphasizes that when Pharaoh began planning to chase down the Israelites, he intended to go himself. Exodus14.16 says that he (Pharaoh, according to the context) made his chariots ready and took his people with him. He wanted to personally oversee this mission of recapturing his former slaves and bringing them back to captivity. We should expect no less from Satan today.

There is another point of emphasis regarding the chariots in Exodus 14.7. The text says that he took six hundred "select" chariots along with all the other chariots of Egypt. It appears that there was a difference between the common chariot and the select ones chosen by Pharaoh. There is an allusion to this distinction in the Song of Moses when Moses mentions not only the chariots, but that the choicest of Pharaoh's officers accompanied him (Exod15.4). The point is that the best and most advanced army in the world, with the latest and greatest war technology, was advancing against the Israelites. As a result, when the Israelites saw Pharaoh and his army in the distance, they were frightened (14.10). However, the greater the army, the greater the salvation and deliverance. The greater the odds, the greater the God who overcomes them.

If we could see the same spiritual enemies coming against us that Jesus saw and faced on the cross, we would be as terrified as the Israelites. As pointed out previously, Jesus disarmed the rulers and authorities (Col 1.15). Ephesians 6.11–12 describes these enemies in more detail, mentioning the devil, rulers, powers, world forces of darkness and spiritual forces of wickedness. Ephesians 6.11–12 reveals two jarring truths: first, the magnitude of the power of the enemies working against us; and secondly, how much we desperately need help. Pharaoh's army was nothing in comparison to what is arrayed against us spiritually. But thanks be to God that when Jesus died and was raised from the dead, he disarmed these enemies and gave us the armor to defeat them (Col 2.15).

As the army drew near, the Israelites become terrified, and understandably so. The sea was on one side of them and the Egyptian army was on the other. They were trapped. Seeing this, they did the only thing they could do—they cried out to the LORD. This was and is always the right response when we are afraid or feel like we are trapped. Unfortunately, they did not stop there. According to Exodus14.11–12, they then accused Moses (and God) of not caring about them and making their situation go from bad to worse. They ended their tirade by declaring that it would have been better to serve the Egyptians than to die in the wilderness.

It is understandable that the Israelites were frightened. They were facing a trial that they had never experienced before, and they saw no way out of it. However, their conclusion that God did not care and their quick descent into despair show that they had not retained the faith that God had been trying to instill in them. They no longer saw his power, felt his presence, or trusted in his promises. Unfortunately, the same is often true of us today. When we forget who God is and what he has already done for us in moments of trial, despair sets in and all he has been trying to teach us begins to erode in our unbelief. It is understandable that we sometimes feel frightened when trials and challenges appear in our lives, but despair and dismay must never characterize true believers. When we find ourselves despairing, we must remind ourselves of the things we have forgotten, of all that God has already done. If the Israelites had in that moment called to mind all that had transpired in their recent lives—the innumerable signs which displayed God's immense power, constant presence, and enduring promises, they would have been able to respond with confidence when they heard the sound of Pharaoh's army approaching.

Not only did God's people make the mistake of forgetting, but they also failed to factor God into the equation. When the Israelites saw the chariots approaching, they said in essence, "everything we have experienced these past few months has been nice, but now we are back to reality." They began to think that their expectation of freedom was "too-good-to-be-true," a foolish hope rather that an actual possibility. For them, there had always been two choices in life: death or slavery. They could either serve the Egyptians or be killed. They did not believe in a third option. When we look at our lives and the trials that lay before us, we often see the same two possibilities: slavery to sin or imminent death. But God has intervened and made a third option: freedom and life. This is the option he made known to the Israelites on the day that he destroyed Pharaoh and his army, and it is the same option he extends to his people today. He made a new way when no other existed. When God parted the Red Sea and opened up a new world of possibility for the Israelites, he foreshadowed a greater parting and an even more momentous event to come—the death of Jesus on the cross. On the cross, Jesus made possible an existence never before feasible or imagined and ushered those who would trust in him into eternal life and true freedom—freedom from sin and death.

## The Parting (Exodus 14.13–31)

The first two words of Exodus 14.13 are, "But Moses." Can you imagine being in Moses' shoes at that moment? On one side was the sea, and on the other, the army of the most powerful country on earth. If that were not enough, the whole nation of Israel—bewildered, angry, and terrified, were crying out to you. Amid the mounting tension and dread, Moses held to his assurance that God would intervene in some way, though he did not know how (Exod14.4). He was surrounded by obstacles, doubt, and fear of the unknown. How did he respond? He first said, "Do not fear" (v. 13). Yes, it seemed to be a time to panic, but he believed that despite what appeared to be impending doom the Israelites had nothing to fear.

The next instruction of Moses was, "Stand by and see the salvation of the LORD which he will accomplish for you today" (v. 13). How did Moses know that God was about to bring salvation to the children of Israel? Why was he not drowning in fear and disbelief like his fellow Israelites? The reason was that Moses had become a true son of Abraham. He had learned to walk by faith and not by sight. The chariots in the distance had caused Israel to forget the truth, but Moses had not forgotten. Even as the army drew closer, he was aware of the presence of an all-powerful God, and his confidence would not be shaken. Moses was keeping his eyes on the Promise-keeper and waiting expectantly. Though he did not know exactly what God would do, he knew *who* he is and that was more than enough. He believed that he was more than able, and that this all-powerful God was not only able, but eager to protect and provide for His own. Moses was able to walk by faith because of what God had already done. In the same way, living by faith is a choice we make because of who he is and what he has already accomplished. This faith, produced in response to his faithfulness, enables those of us who believe to walk on water even while those around us are sinking.

Finally, Moses concluded with these words, "The Lord will fight for you while you keep silent" (v. 14). The idea that God himself would fight for his people is repeated several times (e.g., Exod 14.25; 15.3). God is powerful, and he uses that power on behalf of his people—both those in the past and those living here in the present. God showed that he would fight for his people by, among other things, causing the wheels of the chariots to swerve (v. 25). Our God showed us that he would fight for us when he waged war against sin and death, powers and principalities, and defeated them once and for all on the cross. Our God is a Warrior (Exod 15.3).

The need for silence on the part of the Israelites denotes full and complete trust. Notice that in Isaiah 30.15, silence equates to trust: "For thus the Lord GOD, the Holy One of Israel, has said, 'In repentance and rest you will be saved, in quietness and trust is your strength.' But you were not willing." We are also familiar with the passage "Be still and know that I am God" (Psa 46.10). So, are we silent and still? Or do we feel the need to plan and scheme? Are we characterized by anxiety or trust? In a world where people become increasingly anxious and rash to react, Christians should appear to people of the world as individuals who are remarkably calm and unfazed. We serve an undefeated God who fights for us. Let us fully trust him and be still.

Moses had exhorted the Israelites before the sea parted to "stand by and see the salvation of the LORD" (Exod 14.13), but what exactly was God going to do? How was he going to save a whole nation of dependent ex-slaves from this approaching army? Apparently, Moses did not know, and so he cried out to the LORD (v. 15). God stopped Moses in the middle of his prayer and told him to have the Israelites go forward and God would save Israel. He would fight for them, but he also required them to do something. Is that not how God always chooses to work? God continued to execute his plan by telling Moses to stretch out his hand over the sea to divide it (v. 16). Could not God have divided the Sea himself without the assistance of Moses' hand? Of course, we know that he could have carried out his plan without any action on Moses' part, but that is not his usual way of doing things. God has always wanted his people to act in faith before he begins his work. Moses did the small thing he could do before God began to do what only he can.

Notice how Exodus 15.12 connects to this idea. What happened when Moses stretched out his hand? The song of deliverance composed after the event says that God then stretched out his right hand and the earth swallowed up the Egyptians. When Moses acted in faith, he activated the great power of God. Is that not how prayer works? We stretch out our hands in prayer so that our great God will work mightily with his hands. We must act in faith and do the simple things that God has commanded, so that he will display the incredible power that only he possesses.

What happened when Moses stretched his hand out over the sea? "...The LORD swept the sea back by a strong east wind all night and turned the sea into dry land, so the waters were divided" (Exod14.21). How mind-boggling it must have been to witness that event! To see this astounding display of raw power would have been staggering, and yet, it should not have been surprising, because God had already done something even more formidable when he first created the heavens and the earth. There are striking similarities between God's power on display in both Genesis 1 and Exodus 14.20–21. First, there is the allusion to light and darkness. When the angel of God moved and stood between the camp of Israel and the camp of the Egyptians, there was light at night. There is also the allusion to wind. The Hebrew word here for "wind (*ruach*)" is the same word that is translated "Spirit" in Genesis 1.2. Just as the Spirit of God was hovering over the surface of the water before he created, God sent his wind over the water before parting it. Finally, the most obvious similarity is the idea that God separated the waters and caused dry land to appear in Genesis 1.9, just as he parted the waters of the Red Sea so that the Israelites could walk through on dry land (Exod 14.22).

The same God who created the heavens and the earth was now saving the Israelites. The God who makes light, who controls the wind and directs the sea, is fighting for Israel. The New Testament makes this point about Jesus in the stilling of the storm when his disciples ask in great fears, "Who then is this, that even the wind and the sea obey him?" (Mark 4.41). Jesus Christ is the Creator God of Genesis 1 and the one who saved Israel in Exodus 14. The writer of Exodus is making the point that God is creating again. Just as God created humanity in Genesis 1, he is now making a new nation and people. In the same way, when God parts the water when we are baptized, we become his people, a new creation.

The stretching out the hand of Moses was the first act of faith required; but the Israelites walking through the midst of the sea was the second. In obedience they stepped out into the sea (14.22), but the Egyptians also took up the pursuit and followed Israel into the gap in the water. Once again, we see Satan and his forces determined to keep God's people out of his grasp. Praise be to God that he fights the battle for us. Consider the emphasis on what the LORD does in Exodus 14.24–30. "The LORD looked down on the army of the Egyptians ...and brought them into confusion" (Exod 14.24). "He caused their chariots wheels to swerve, and He made them drive with difficulty," so the Egyptians saw that "the LORD was fighting against them" (Exod 14.25). "The LORD overthrew the Egyptians" (Exod 14.27). "Thus the LORD saved Israel that day from the hand of the Egyptians" (Exod 14.30).

Yes, Israel walked through the midst of the sea, but it was God who looked, brought, caused, and saved. God did the miraculous, but Israel had their own small part to play. Notice the dual nature of this salvation; God saved, but Israel had to walk by faith thought the midst of the sea. This is a great picture of how our salvation is attained in the New Testament. Jesus looked down from heaven and saw that humanity was outmatched by sin and Satan. Jesus overthrew Satan and his armies by dying on the cross and then rising from the tomb on the first day of the week at daybreak (John 20.1; Luke 24.1; Matt 28.1; cf. Exod 14.27). He saved us from the hand of the enemy. But what is our role? In faith, we must walk out into the midst of the sea—into the saving water of baptism (1Cor 10.1–2).

How did this salvation, with its grand manifestation of God's power, affect the Israelites? "When Israel saw the great power which the LORD had used against the Egyptians, the people feared the LORD and they believed in the LORD and his servant Moses" (Exod 14.31). Their immediate response was to fear the LORD. They went from being frightened by the Egyptians (14.10) to fearing God. Seeing the great power of God should lead us to be less fearful of the world, and more fearful of the One who holds it in His hands. As someone once said, "When we fear God, we realize there is nothing to fear."

Their next response was that they believed the LORD. Seeing how God parted the sea, or how Jesus died on the cross, should lead us to believe in the Lord, to trust him. We must learn to stop trusting in chariots and trust fully in the name of the Lord. We must make him our strength (Exod15.2). Our final reaction should be praise to the God of our salvation, just as "Moses and the sons of Israel sang this song to the LORD" (Exod 15.1). The people of Israel had gone from silence to song, and now God himself became their song (15.2). They praised God for saving them (15.2), for fighting for them (15.3), and for overthrowing their enemies (15.1). After God has delivered us from the hand of Satan and death, his name and his praise should be continually on our lips. As the old hymn says, "Redeeming love has been my theme and shall be 'til I die."

What a marvelous salvation God accomplished. One of the moments of deepest impact in this story must have been when the Israelites saw the dead bodies of the Egyptians washing up on the shore

(14.30). The Egyptians, who had oppressed them and enslaved them for so long were no more. One day, we will sit by the sea of glass, singing the Song of Moses and the Lamb (Rev 15.3). The enemies of sin and death who have oppressed and intimidated us will be no more. Praise God for his marvelous salvation.

# Conquest over the Kingdom of the World

## Mark Russell

The story of the Bible is both one and many. There is one overarching narrative telling us the lengths God goes to save us because of His infinite love and grace. Within this grand narrative, there are shorter stories telling us of the care and concern He has for His people through time. This grand narrative and the shorter stories within it set forth themes that point the reader to Jesus. Central to the unifying narrative of the Bible is the conflict between our God and our Adversary. The scriptures begin in the Garden with the conflict and the first declaration of God's intended victory (Gen 3.15); they end with the Adversary rendered powerless and defeated by our resurrected Lord in John's Apocalypse (Rev 12.17, 20.10). This conflict continues today as we live between its beginning in Genesis and its consummation in the New Jerusalem.

While our focus in this study is on Exodus, good Bible students see—or at least should endeavor to see—how this smaller story fits into and is repeatedly referred to again and again in the larger epoch of our salvation becoming a reality.

### The Conflict in Exodus

In one view, Exodus continues the story of the origins and history of God's people. It expands with the development of God's people as a defined nation and the laws that God intends for His people to follow. On another level, Exodus continues telling the story of the cosmic conflict between God and Satan played out on the Earth.

The kingdom of God is represented by Abraham's descendants who, at the beginning of the book, are living in Egypt due to a terrible famine at the end of Genesis. At the end of the book, we find a new nation with new laws on their way to a new land having been freed by the power of God. On the other side is Egypt representing the kingdom of man, a tool used by the Adversary to thwart God and His plans for mankind's benefit and ultimate salvation.

In Genesis, Satan shows his skill of tempting the kingdom of man with his deceitful ways. In Exodus, he hones his skills on a larger scale beguiling Egypt through their arrogance and self-importance. Pharaoh comes to believe that the only way they will survive and thrive is to act violently and oppress their neighbors (another continuing thread in human history). While most likely not the first such occurrence, Exodus records the first story in the scriptures of national interests used as a reason for violence against another group of people (and it is certainly not the last):

> Now there arose a new king over Egypt, who did not know Joseph. And he said to his people, "Behold, the people of Israel are too many and too mighty for us. Come, let us deal shrewdly with them, lest they multiply, and, if war breaks out, they join our enemies and fight against us and escape from the land." Therefore they set taskmasters over them to afflict them with heavy burdens. (Exod 1.8–11)[1]

Pharaoh arrogantly utilizes a political ploy to gain power and then dominion over the children of Israel. Pharaoh's plan starts with oppression and slavery:

> But the more they were oppressed, the more they multiplied and the more they spread abroad. And the Egyptians were in dread of the people of Israel. So they ruthlessly made the people of Israel work

---

[1] Unless noted otherwise, all quotations of scripture are from the ESV.

as slaves and made their lives bitter with hard service, in mortar and brick, and in all kinds of work in the field. In all their work they ruthlessly made them work as slaves. (Exod 1.12–14)

The machinations do not stop simply at slavery. No, Pharaoh's plan spirals into killing Israel's male babies to cull their growth. To make this policy national and effective, even the midwives are called to act in violence (Exod 1.10–22). The injustice and misuse of power by the kingdom of man stands against the backdrop of the creation account in Genesis that declares that all humanity is created in the image of God.[2] Like the initial sin in Genesis, Pharaoh's plans devolve into worse and worse indignities and abominations.

While this is abhorrent to modern readers, nations in the Ancient Near East considered the conquest, subjugation, and dominion of others not only as justifiable acts, but also as commendable. The kings who acted this way were imitating the stories told about their false gods or were themselves acting as gods on the Earth.[3] We can see that Egypt, like all of the kingdoms of men in the Hebrew Bible, ends up willing to do whatever it takes to achieve their goals. While the pagan superpowers see this brutality as part of doing business in a chaotic world, the one true God sees this as an arrogant abuse of His created order.

Many years before this particular conflict God made a promise to Abraham: "And I will make of you a great nation, and I will bless you and make your name great, so that you will be a blessing. I will bless those who bless you, and him who dishonors you I will curse, and in you all the families of the earth shall be blessed" (Gen 12.2–3). Even as the slavery and oppression continue, God is faithful in blessing Israel during their conflict with Pharaoh and his minions.

From one perspective, the early part of this story could be read as a bad run of "time and chance" for Abraham's descendants. On a

---

[2] J. Richard Middleton, *A New Heaven and a New Earth: Reclaiming Biblical Eschatology* (Grand Rapids: Baker Academic, 2014) 50.

[3] Ibid, 52.

spiritual level, we can see that the Adversary is behind Pharaoh's and Egypt's use of violence and oppression. This political power play is part of the playbook of Satan we see time and again in history. We also can see God, in His wisdom and love, finding men and women to carry out His plan in faith.

## Moses, An Unlikely Leader

The story of Moses' birth and his unlikely rescue serves as a transition showing the reader how God will use the conflict and be victorious. After being raised in the family of Pharaoh himself and nearing the end of his first forty years, Moses becomes aware of his heritage. For reasons that are not fully revealed to us, he attempts to help a fellow Israelite being abused by an Egyptian taskmaster. Moses kills the Egyptian and then flees as a fugitive for his crime and rebellion.

While Israel remains under cruel oppression, the next forty years of Moses' life present enormous changes. The narrative follows Moses into the desert and the land of Midian. We read of Moses adjusting to life as a shepherd, finding a wife, starting a family, and minding his own business until God interjects Himself into the story again.

God's plan for freeing Israel from their slavery and settling in Canaan takes many twists and turns. Who would have thought that God would have chosen as unlikely a character as a fugitive from Egypt to be His leader, prophet, and lawgiver?

## Conquest through the Plagues and the Red Sea

In one vein, the plagues are the story of God's judgment and punishment of Egypt for its corruption and mistreatment of other humans, specifically Abraham's descendants. The larger view of the conflict is the one true God versus the false gods of Egypt, with a step-by-step attack against the idol gods and goddesses in the Egyptian pantheon (Exod. 12.12).[4]

---

[4] Several resources are available in print and online that catalog the details. See Nahum Sarna, *Exploring Exodus: The Heritage of Biblical Israel*, (New York: Schocken Books, 1986) 75; Donnie S. Barnes, *The Ten Plagues: Jehovah vs. the Gods of Egypt*; www.biblecharts.org/ oldtestament/thetenplagues.pdf (accessed 8/15/2021); and J.

The battle at first simmers as the confrontation of Moses and Pharaoh bubbles up over whether Pharaoh will allow Israel to leave and worship the LORD. Pharaoh was not being coy when he said, "Who is the LORD, that I should obey his voice and let Israel go? I do not know the LORD, and moreover, I will not let Israel go" (Exod 5.2). Pharaoh initially had no reason to know about, much less believe in, a minor deity who seems to be no real threat to him or his people. As the confrontation becomes more pronounced through the plagues, Pharaoh, Egypt, and the forces of evil are shown time and again who wins.

The plagues and the sea crossing offer biblical scholars, historians, and even filmmakers a test. Readers are offered a sometimes maddening assortment of novel ideas about the plagues.[5] We are told by some that the plagues are simply natural events attributed to the God of Israel.[6] We are told by others that the plagues may have been historical events but more importantly are used as a polemic (a written attack) against Egypt for later Israelite generations to learn.[7] The Exodus narrative itself portrays the plagues inflicted on Egypt as both natural devastations and the miraculous working of God. While some may be blinded by their own philosophies seeing only naturalistic causes, there is no doubt the writer of Exodus credits God's power for their release and victory:

> And the LORD said to Moses, "See, I have made you like God to Pharaoh, and your brother Aaron shall be your prophet. You shall speak all that I command you, and your brother Aaron shall tell Pharaoh to let the people of Israel go out of his land. But I will

A. Dobelman, *Ten Egyptian Plagues for Ten Egyptian Gods and Goddesses*, http://www.stat.rice.edu/~dobelman/Dinotech/ 10_Eqyptian_gods_10_Plagues.pdf (accessed 8/15/2021).

[5] Ellen White, "Excruciating Exodus Movie Exudes Errors," *BAR* online review (December 18, 2014); https://www.biblicalarchaeology.org/daily/news/excruciating-exodus-movie-exudes-errors/ (accessed 8/15/2021).

[6] Ziony Zevit, "Three Ways to Look at the Ten Plagues," *BibRev 6.3* (June 1990): 16–23,42.

[7] John D. Currid, *Ancient Egypt and the Old Testament* (Grand Rapids: Baker, 1997) 109.

harden Pharaoh's heart, and though I multiply my signs and wonders in the land of Egypt, Pharaoh will not listen to you. Then I
will lay my hand on Egypt and bring my hosts, my people the children of Israel, out of the land of Egypt by great acts of judgment.
The Egyptians shall know that I am the LORD, when I stretch out
my hand against Egypt and bring out the people of Israel from
among them" (Exod 7.1–5).

The complete devastation of Egypt is recorded plague by plague as
God secures the victory for His people. As the LORD humbles and
conquers Egypt, we can see a contrast in Exodus set against the cre-
ation accounts in Genesis. A land that is regarded as on par with
Eden (Gen. 13.10) is decimated by God's de-creating judgment.[8] As
Egypt is left devastated, a lesson is left for Israel:

> Then Moses said to the people, "Remember this day in which you
> came out from Egypt, out of the house of slavery, for by a strong
> hand the LORD brought you out from this place. No leavened bread
> shall be eaten. Today, in the month of Abib, you are going out.
> And when the LORD brings you into the land of the Canaanites,
> the Hittites, the Amorites, the Hivites, and the Jebusites, which
> he swore to your fathers to give you, a land flowing with milk and
> honey, you shall keep this service in this month. Seven days you
> shall eat unleavened bread, and on the seventh day there shall be a
> feast to the LORD. Unleavened bread shall be eaten for seven days;
> no leavened bread shall be seen with you, and no leaven shall be
> seen with you in all your territory. You shall tell your son on that
> day, 'It is because of what the LORD did for me when I came out
> of Egypt.' And it shall be to you as a sign on your hand and as a
> memorial between your eyes, that the law of the LORD may be in
> your mouth. For with a strong hand the LORD has brought you out
> of Egypt. You shall therefore keep this statute at its appointed time
> from year to year" (Exod 13.3–10).

---

[8] Terrence E. Fretheim, "The Plagues as Ecological Signs of Historic Disaster,"
*JBL* 110 (1991): 385–396.

The history of the conquest of Egypt was written for Israel to remember. While it was God's plan to humble Egypt, it was also His plan to show Israel that Egypt's pantheon was powerless and subject to His judgment (Num 33.4). The conquest would be so lopsided that Egypt ends up begging Israel to leave (Exod 11.7–8, 12.33). The conquest was so profound some Egyptians even left with Israel in the exodus (Exod 12.38).

God's victory over Egypt is completed for Israel with no king, no army, no chariots or other cutting-edge technology, and no help from Israel. When the children of Israel pass through the sea as on dry land, it is only by God's awesome power: "Thus the Lord saved Israel that day from the hand of the Egyptians, and Israel saw the Egyptians dead on the seashore. Israel saw the great power that the Lord used against the Egyptians, so the people feared the Lord, and they believed in the Lord and in his servant Moses" (Exod 14.30–31).

It is patently clear that God intended both Egypt and Israel alike to know who was the Lord. What started with a staff being thrown down in front of Pharaoh ended with Egypt's chariots washing up on the shore. What started with Pharaoh wondering, "Who is the Lord?" ended with the full knowledge of who was the powerful One (Exod 5.2). The plagues serve as both a powerful show of force and a warning to any who would listen, even among the nations (Joshua 2.10), that the God of Israel will secure victory for His faithful people. Even more it was God's plan for Israel to learn and to know how He saved them from the kingdom of man.

## Real Power in the Exodus Conflict

In the larger narrative of the kingdom of God versus all who would rebel, we see patterns that recur throughout the story of God's redeeming His people. A challenging part of this conflict is seen in Pharaoh, as a representative of the evil forces of rebellion, being challenged by the truth. Half the time the writer tells us Pharaoh hardened his own heart (ten times) and half the time God hardens Pharaoh's heart (ten times).[9] We should miss neither his humanity, nor the part he plays in the larger spiritual view. Unlike Nebuchadnezzar later, Pharaoh sets aside any humility and charges ahead heedless, neither innocent nor blameless.

The Egyptian magicians, another example of evil forces afoot in Exodus, present a more challenging case to readers in Exodus. When the powers of the priests, as representatives of Egypt's gods, duplicate the same things done by Moses, the reader will undoubtedly have questions: How are they able to reproduce some of the same signs as Moses, admittedly on a lesser and weaker scale? How were they able to change their staffs into snakes (Exod 7.11)? How were they also able to change water into blood (Exod 7.22), and produce frogs (Exod 8.7)?

After the plague of the gnats, the magicians were not able to produce imitations of God's signs, and they warned Pharaoh that this was the power of God (Exod 8.18–19). But of course the damage was already done; regardless of what justification the magicians cite for their failure, Pharaoh will simply assume the other signs could be duplicated as well, given the right secrets or better magicians. The Egyptian magicians fail at reproducing any more of the signs and wonders of God as the plagues progress in the story.[10] After the plague of boils exposes the real powerlessness of the magicians (Exod 9.11), they are not heard from again. While there are parts of this story that leave us with unanswerable questions, the fact that they had this power is undeniable. What is also clear is that their power is no rival to the power and truth of God.[11]

There may be a temptation to dismiss these and other biblical accounts of battles with spiritual forces. However, it is clear from

---

[9] Sarna, *Exploring Exodus* 64.

[10] Ibid, 80.

[11] It is notable that Paul refers to these Egyptian magicians by their traditional names in Jewish literature, Jannes and Jambres (2 Tim 3.8–9), as he uses them as an object lesson to assure Christians that the foolishness of such false teachers is always eventually exposed. Indeed, the watchful and discerning Christian need not fear such spiritual forces, because they have been defeated by Christ (Eph 1.20–23; Col 2.15; 1 Pet 3.22).

the stories of Elisha asking for his servant's eyes to be opened (2 Kng 6.15–17) and the conversation about the messenger and Michael fighting against "the prince of the kingdom of Persia" (Dan 10.13) that evil spiritual forces are real and active. Even NT writers intimate that there are evil spiritual forces at work against the kingdom of God and His people (Eph 6.12). Paul again offers more proof of this battle when he warns the church in Thessalonica of false signs and wonders (2 Thes 2.9). The fortune-telling Pythoness in Acts 16.16–19 seemed to be able to predict the future legitimately because she was possessed by an evil spirit.

There is a temptation for modern readers steeped in science and technology to dismiss the existence of evil spiritual forces working on the Earth. Many are quick to dismiss the Egyptian examples, and others like them, as sleight of hand or ancient superstition. We should show humility and not dismiss the reality of evil power at work. We should accept that our enemy is real and remember the overarching lesson and truth from this story in faith - God wins every spiritual battle because He is a warrior for His people.

### God Is A Warrior

The story of Israel's exodus highlights a truth found throughout scripture: God is a warrior. In the explanation of the Passover remembrance to be told in succeeding generations is this important point: "For with a strong hand the LORD has brought you out of Egypt" (Exod 13.9). This is the first, but certainly not the last, battle and conquest in which God and Israel battle against the kingdom of man.

When God said, "You shall have no other gods before me" (Exod 20.3), He was declaring war on any potential rivals for Israel's attention and loyalty. After winning their freedom, providing for their every need, and granting them a magnificent law, Israel sadly does not remain loyal. Through their ingratitude they become more like the kingdom of man than the kingdom of God.

When Israel becomes enamored with lies of polytheism and the fleshly lusts it offers, God sends prophet after prophet pleading, wooing, and warning His own rebellious people. In His infinite love we see the fight He is having with evil forces and His desire to heal Israel. But His love for them does not keep God from the justice and the judgment Israel earns time and again, even using other evil nations as a rod of His anger (e.g., Isa 10.5).[12]

The warrior motif continues in the gospels. The battle front begins in the birth narratives where the child is attacked by the kingdom of men and the attack is foiled (Matt 2.1–16). A face-to-face battle is fought after a forty-day fast and the enemy fails again (Matt 4.1–11). When Jesus came healing the sick in profound ways, prophecy should have reminded them of the truth about the battle the Messiah would wage:

> The Spirit of the Lord GOD is upon me, because the LORD has anointed me to bring good news to the poor (afflicted); he has sent me to bind up the brokenhearted, to proclaim liberty to the captives, and the opening of the prison to those who are bound (blind, LXX); to proclaim the year of the LORD's favor, and the day of vengeance of our God; to comfort all who mourn" (Isa 61.1–2).

Mark gives an overview of the battle raging: "But no one can enter a strong man's house and plunder his goods, unless he first binds the strong man. Then indeed he may plunder his house" (Mark 3.27; cf. 1 John 3.8). Jesus entered the battlefield where Satan was dominating (the strong man) and conquered him. Similarly the casting out of demons gave many a cause for rejoicing and others a quandary they could not comprehend. In Mark many battles are fought by Jesus healing those who were possessed by demons. The first, oddly enough, is fought in a synagogue with Jesus showing Himself to be a warrior and restorer in Israel (Mark 1.21–27).[13]

---

[12] Gregory A. Boyd, *God at War: The Bible and Spiritual Conflict* (Downers Grove: IVP Academic, 1997) 135.

[13] Tremper Longman III and Daniel G. Reid, *God Is A Warrior,* Studies in Old

The symbol of Jesus as the conquering warrior reaches its climax in the Apocalypse. While suffering at the hands of the kingdom of men, John reminds the Christians in Asia, and all who will see and hear, that Jesus has won the victory and not without a great cost and sacrifice. Their task is to overcome the kingdom of men that is empowered by Satan, and they will do so in faith by the blood of the Lamb, by the word of their testimony, and not loving their earthly lives too much (Rev 12.11).

Leaving Pharaoh and Egypt behind, Israel continues on their journey toward their freedom and the land God promised Abraham. They begin an unlikely journey to become the kingdom of God in the midst of the kingdoms of men. They were blessed with His laws, justice, and righteousness as the cornerstone of their nation, not the normal foundations of the kingdom of men: violence and power. What started with a great victory by God's power devolves into a grasping for the evil fruit of earthly lusts, violence, and power of the kingdom of man. What Israel never truly appreciated is that whatever victory Israel gained was won by the power of God. Zechariah reminds us of this clear truth: "Not by might, nor by power, but by my Spirit, says the LORD of hosts" (Zech 4.6). Israel sadly becomes an object lesson of what happens to people who choose a path different from God's ways.

## Jesus, An Unlikely Conqueror

Jesus, like Moses, is an unlikely leader chosen by God as a warrior on Earth. Also like Moses, Jesus demonstrated the power of God to free His people without the people offering any real assistance. Unlike the story in Exodus, Jesus wins the war in a profound and eternal way. In Satan's confrontation with Jesus, the Adversary tries to woo Jesus with his shortcuts to earthly success (Matt. 4.1–11). This conflict, like the initial plagues, will move to a greater climax with these competing powers. As Jesus moves toward this climax, His followers

Testament Biblical Theology (Grand Rapids: Zondervan, 1995) 99.

remained confounded by the unlikely conclusion. Peter takes Jesus aside to correct his Lord's erring view and prophecy of what would happen in Jerusalem (Matt 16.21–23). The debate among the disciples about their pecking order in the new kingdom with Jesus as its head displays their complete misunderstanding (Matt 20.20–28, Mark 10.35–45). It is clear that no one understood that the kingdom of God would be different from the kingdoms of man.

The upside-down nature of the kingdom of God that Jesus proclaimed stands in stark contrast to the kingdom of man. Time after time, Jesus' teachings confront and contradict the established doctrine and ways of the two major Jewish factions. The Jews of Jesus' day who had any messianic expectation at all thought of a conquering king like David. However, Jesus and His followers after Him proclaimed that the power of the kingdom of God is shown vividly not in military might but in a myriad of instructive paradoxes. Jesus spoke of kingdom citizens being blessed by humbling themselves, by mourning over their sins, and by willing to be ridiculed and abused by the kingdom of men, all because they put their trust in the greater glory of the kingdom of God (Matt 5.3–12).[14]

The ways and power of Satan will always beguile and deceive those who set their mind on the kingdom of man rather than God. Considering this battle for our minds, is it any wonder why our Lord said, "For the gate is narrow and the way is hard that leads to life, and those who find it are few" (Matt 7.14)? Nowhere is the upside-down nature of the kingdom more evident than in the confrontation between Jesus and Pilate. Pilate, the Roman governor of Judea, is placed in the spotlight of the conflict between the kingdom of man on the one hand and the truth and goodness of the kingdom of God on the other hand. Like Pharaoh before him, Pilate has a difficult choice to make because even he recognizes that Jesus is innocent. In his conversation with Jesus, Pilate is be-

---

[14] For a broader and more detailed study of these unlikely and revolutionary ideals, a reader would be benefited to study Paul Earnhart, *Invitation To A Spiritual Revolution* (Chillicothe: DeWard Publishing, 1999).

wildered by the following unlikely pronouncement of God's king: "My kingdom is not of this world. If my kingdom were of this world, my servants would have been fighting, that I might not be delivered over to the Jews. But my kingdom is not from the world" (John 18.36). His wife even sends a message saying, "Have nothing to do with that righteous man, for I have suffered much because of him today in a dream" (Matt 27.19). When it looked like Pilate may relent, the other representatives of the kingdom of man challenge him to be faithful and loyal to Caesar:

> From then on Pilate sought to release him, but the Jews cried out, "If you release this man, you are not Caesar's friend. Everyone who makes himself a king opposes Caesar." So when Pilate heard these words, he brought Jesus out and sat down on the judgment seat at a place called the Stone Pavement, and in Aramaic Gabbatha. Now it was the day of Preparation of the Passover. It was about the sixth hour. He said to the Jews, "Behold your King!" They cried out, "Away with him, away with him, crucify him!" Pilate said to them, "Shall I crucify your King?" The chief priests answered, "We have no king but Caesar." So he delivered him over to them to be crucified (John 19.12–16a).

Pilate, following faithfully in the ways of the kingdom of men, disaffects himself of any responsibility and sends our Lord to be killed.

The startling and unlikely means by which God conquers the kingdom of men and the evil forces behind it through Jesus' death, burial, and resurrection are nothing like the conquests achieved by worldly powers. The cross of shame, death, and defeat becomes God's instrument of perfect glory, life, and victory. God uses the death of His son, a punishment meant for harm by the kingdom of man, as the means of victory and the undoing of the kingdom of man:

> Oh, the depth of the riches and wisdom and knowledge of God! How unsearchable are his judgments and how inscrutable his ways! 'For who has known the mind of the Lord, or who has been his counselor?' 'Or who has given a gift to him that he might be repaid?'

For from him and through him and to him are all things. To him be glory forever. Amen" (Rom 11.33–36).

## Conclusion

Exodus, like the rest of the scriptures, teaches all who will hear that God's values and the values of His kingdom are fundamentally different from the kingdom of man. The question that remains is which kingdom will we choose? The exodus from Egypt and the new exodus of the gospel illustrate that our God is a gracious God, inviting us into His victory over the kingdom of man. Time after time and century after century we see our God patient and compassionate toward Israel and all who will humble themselves before Him. Our God calls us to a better, albeit upside-down, way of living and loving in faith. All of this is for our benefit. Will we have faith to trust is His unlikely ways? Praise be to the God of our salvation who has triumphed over every evil and secured our victory in Jesus!

# God Leads and Provides for His People

## John Gibson

"When you have brought the people out of Egypt, you shall serve God on this mountain" (Exod 3.12b).[1] The exodus of Israel from Egypt and the events surrounding it are a vital part of the entire Bible story and referenced repeatedly in both the Old and New Testaments, thus making them more than worthy of the attention being given them in this year's lectures. I am honored to have a part in studying this critical period in the development of God's scheme of redemption and will be focusing on the time between Israel's crossing of the Red Sea and their arrival at Mt. Sinai. Though the exact route of the exodus is still debated, we know they did not take a direct route to Canaan and the path by which Yahweh led them involved more than avoiding the Philistines (Exod 13.17). When the LORD appeared to Moses in the burning bush, He told Moses then he would bring the people back to Mt. Sinai and this study will focus on how God led and provided for the people as they made their way to the mountain where they would enter into a covenant with the LORD.

### Overview of the Time Period

When we pick up the story with Israel on the eastern shore of the Red Sea, the LORD has shown both Israel and the Egypt who He is

---

[1] Unless noted otherwise, all quotations of scripture are from the NKJV.

and ransomed His people from bondage through a series of plagues and the parting of the Red Sea. As they made their way to Mt. Sinai the Almighty guided them by utilizing a pillar of cloud by day and a pillar of fire by night (Exod 13.21–22). While this study will not focus on the testing element of the journey, we must not lose sight of the fact that the Lord did not choose to lead them on an easy journey. As they journeyed south they went three days without water and then when they found water it was too bitter to drink, but the Lord showed Moses a tree with which the waters were made sweet (Exod 15.22–25). Having first led them to the bitter waters of Marah, the Lord then led them to the welcome rest of Elim and its twelve wells of water and seventy palm trees (Exod 15.27).

A month after their departure from Egypt, Israel reached the Wilderness of Sin and complained of a lack of food (Exod 16.1–3). That evening the Lord provided the people with meat in the form of quail, and the next morning He gave them the bread, the manna, which would sustain them for their remainder of their time in the wilderness (Josh 5.10–12).

As God continued to lead them to Mt. Sinai, through a sign witnessed by the elders of Israel, water was miraculously produced from a rock at Rephidim (Exod 17.1–7). Before they left Rephidim they had to face their first military conflict, but the Lord of hosts gave them victory and made certain they knew this victory was through His power by having Moses stand on top of a hill with the rod of God in his hand (Exod 17.8–16).

The transitional section between the Red Sea and Sinai ends with Exodus 18 where Jethro, Moses' father-in-law and priest of Midian, briefly joined Moses and the Israelites. While the main reason for his coming to Moses appears to have been to return his wife and two sons to him, it is difficult for me not to see the providential hand of God in this as Jethro helped Moses provide some early organization to the fledgling nation (Exod 18.13–27).

## The Cloud

Time will not permit a full exploration of the cloud concept as it is connected with the LORD's leading of Israel, but the glory of the LORD appeared in the cloud when they complained about a lack of food (Exod 16.10). The glory of God being seen or associated with clouds is a theme often repeated in scripture: at Mt. Sinai (Exod 19), the completion of the tabernacle (Exod 40), the dedication of the temple (1 Kng 8); the judgment against Egypt (Isa 19), the prophetic call of Ezekiel (Ezek 1), Daniel's vision (Dan 7), the transfiguration (Matt 17), the coming of the Son of Man (Matt 24), reaping the earth (Rev 14), and many of the psalms (e.g., Psa 18, 97). While the glory of the invisible God was often manifested in a cloud, may we all be determined to so live by faith that we can one day see Him without the cloud obscuring His glory (Rev 21.22–22.5).

## God's Leadership of Israel

As I consider the LORD's leadership of Israel while the ransomed slaves made their way to Mt. Sinai, I believe He led in three ways. First, they never had to doubt the path they were to travel because they were following the cloud by day and the fire by night (Exod 13.21–22). Later, we read that the cloud was over the tabernacle and they did not move from their campsite until the cloud lifted (Exod 40.34–38). Second, the LORD led them through the instructions He gave through His prophet Moses. Third, Jethro's arrival and advice regarding the establishment of a hierarchy of officials to assist Moses in judging the people (Exod 18) was providential. After all, Moses, Aaron, and the elders treated the priesthood of Jethro as legitimate (Exod 18.12) and Moses, the prophet of God, did follow the counsel given him by his father-in-law (Exod 18.25–26).

## God's Leadership Today

When I think of the cloud and its guidance of Israel one of the first things to come to mind is the need to wait upon and follow the LORD's guidance. Jesus demands of us that we do the Father's will

(Matt 7.21–23), and we cannot do His will if we act upon our own impulses and desires. We do not have the cloud Israel had, but we do have the Prophet like Moses (Acts 3.22–26) and His complete revelation to guide us (2 Tim 3.16–17; Jude 3). Rather than set out on our own, we must take the time necessary to study His word and find therein the path He has set for us. Having looked at the often difficult path He set before Israel, we should not be surprised when the Lord's word leads us to face our own difficult challenges. However, we can trust that the One who loved us enough to send His Son for us will lead us in the path that is best for us (John 3.16; Deut 6.24; 1 Cor 10.13).

While some might disagree that Jethro's counsel regarding the rulers of thousands, hundreds, fifties, and tens had was providential and part of God's leading of Israel, we do know the Lord's people today have local leaders who are part of the divinely revealed plan (Acts 14.23; 20.17, 28; Tit 1.5–9). These elders, overseers, and shepherds are important to the guidance of God's sheep, but if these shepherds ever seek to lead in a way contrary to the teachings of the Chief Shepherd, we must maintain our loyalty to the only Shepherd who can bestow upon us the unfading crown of glory (1 Pet 5.1–5).

When it comes to the providential leading of God I wish I knew and understood more. Because His providential guidance is nothing like the clarity of the cloud, my beginning point on this needs to be the realization that God's answer to prayer (Jam 1.5–8) or providential guidance will never contradict the concrete revelation of truth (John 8.31–32; 16.12–13; Jude 3). In fact, as Joseph learned in Egypt, providence is often seen best in hindsight (Gen 45.4–8; 50.19–20). We may not completely grasp all that is involved in God's providence at the time or even later, but we can live our lives in full assurance our God is in control and will so direct things that they will work for our eternal glory (Rom 8.28).

## Yahweh Provided for His People

When we begin to think about the Almighty providing for the people of Israel as they journeyed through the wilderness, one of the first questions that must be addressed deals with the number of people He was caring for. With the standard translations listing more than six hundred thousand soldiers, most estimates put the total number of Israelites at somewhere in excess of two million people when you include the women, children, and aged men. However, some argue the Hebrew *eleph* should not be rendered as "thousands" in the censuses of Israel. For example, Douglas Stuart suggests "platoon" or "squad" as better translations.[2] While good arguments can be made for the smaller count, I am hesitant to dismiss a rendering found in every major translation I am aware of. In addition, the total of half shekels collected in Exodus 38.25–28 seems to support the traditional count of more than six hundred thousand soldiers. So, while I still hold to the larger number, I would argue that even if there were "only" twenty to thirty thousand Israelites that left Egypt, it still took a mighty and merciful God to provide food and water for that many in a relatively barren wilderness.

## Water, Manna, and Quail

When it came to providing water for His thirsty (and oft complaining) people, it is interesting to note the three different ways God provided water in our text. God purified the bitter waters of Marah by showing Moses a tree he could cast into the water. He followed that by leading them to a natural oasis where twelve wells of water could be found. Finally, the same rod that had been used in so many other miracles before was used in bringing water from a rock. While

---

[2] Douglas K. Stuart, *Exodus*, NAC 2 (Nashville: B & H Publishing, 2006) 297–302. You may also wish to consult the online Faithlife Study Bible (Lexham Press 2016) for Exodus 12.37 with a hyperlink entitled *Large Numbers in the Exodus and Wilderness Journey*. Two other helpful sources are J. W. Wenham "Large Numbers in the Old Testament," *Tyndale Bulletin* 18 (1967): 19–53; and R. E. D. Clark, "The Large Numbers of the Old Testament – Especially in Connection with the Exodus," *Journal of the Transactions of the Victoria Institute 87* (1955): 82–92.

all of us have limitations, the LORD's power is unlimited and He is sovereign to bestow His blessings in any number of ways.

Though some have attempted to offer naturalistic explanations for the manna,[3] anything short of attributing it to the miraculous power of God falls short. We must not forget that a pot of the manna was to be kept as a memorial (Exod 16.32–34) to God's power and not a substance that naturally occurred in the wilderness.

> Yet He had commanded the clouds above,
> > And opened the doors of heaven,
> Had rained down manna on them to eat,
> > And given them of the bread of heaven.
> Men ate angels' food;
> > He sent them food to the full (Psa 78.23–25).

Six days a week for forty years, Yahweh made certain His people had the food necessary to sustain them and in doing so He did more than feed their bodies—He sought to teach them to trust Him and His word.

> Every commandment which I command you today you must be careful to observe, that you may live and multiply, and go in and possess the land of which the LORD swore to your fathers. And you shall remember that the LORD your God led you all the way these forty years in the wilderness, to humble you and test you, to know what was in your heart, whether you would keep His commandments or not. So He humbled you, allowed you to hunger, and fed you with manna which you did not know nor did your fathers know, that He might make you know that man shall not live by bread alone; but man lives by every word that proceeds from the mouth of the LORD (Deut 8.1–3).

---

[3] C. F. Keil and F. Delitzsch, *The Second Book of Moses (Exodus)*, Commentary on the Old Testament. Trans. by James Martin (Edinburgh: T&T Clark, 1866–91; rep. ed., Grand Rapids: Eerdmans, 1980) 69–74.

While we most often associate manna with the LORD's provision of food for Israel in the wilderness, we should not overlook the two times when He gave them quail (Exod 16; Num 11). Though the manna was sufficient to keep them alive and sustain them, on at least these two occasions Yahweh provided something extra, a blessing above and beyond what was necessary.

## Trusting God's Provisions Today

With both "Give us this day our daily bread" (Matt 6.11) and "Give us day by day our daily bread (Luke 11.3), Jesus seems to point us in the direction of Deuteronomy 8 and the entire wilderness experience of Israel as they were to learn to trust both God's willingness and ability to provide for them on a daily basis. When we come to the Sermon on the Mount and are told we can be freed from worry because the LORD will provide (Matt 6.25–34), the forty years of manna should be a great reassurance to us. Jesus wants us to focus on laying up treasure in heaven (Matt 6.19–24), and it becomes easier to make that our focus when our faith is strong enough to put anxiety aside and know that He will "give us day by day our daily bread." It is important for disciples to know that we are only promised "bread for tomorrow" (Matt 6.11; ESV margin) and not demand more, yet the reality is most of us enjoy "quail" on a regular basis. When we experience the LORD's provisions above and beyond the necessities, we must guard against a haughty arrogance which boasts of our accomplishments; instead, let us be sure we give genuine thanks to the God who has blessed us with extras.

> Command those who are rich in this present age not to be haughty, nor to trust in uncertain riches but in the living God, who gives us richly all things to enjoy. Let them do good, that they be rich in good works, ready to give, willing to share, storing up for themselves a good foundation for the time to come, that they may lay hold on eternal life (1 Tim 6.17–19).

## The Better Provisions

As essential to life as bread and water are, it is not surprising to find these frequently used to depict spiritual blessings or to be used as types and shadows of a reality only found in Jesus Christ. As the prophets spoke of the grace to come with the sending of the Messiah (1 Pet 1.10), they frequently used the language of food and drink. Consider for example these two Messianic passages from Isaiah:

> Therefore with joy you will draw water
>> From the wells of salvation (Isa 12.3)

> Ho! Everyone who thirsts,
>> Come to the waters;
> And you who have no money,
>> Come, buy and eat.
> Yes, come, buy wine and milk
>> Without money and without price.
> Why do you spend money for what is not bread,
>> And your wages for what does not satisfy?
> Listen carefully to Me, and eat what is good,
>> And let your soul delight itself in abundance.
> Incline your ear, and come to Me.
>> Hear, and your soul shall live;
> And I will make an everlasting covenant with you—
>> The sure mercies of David (Isa 55.1–3)

One does not need to have walked through a barren wilderness in order to have experienced a parched mouth and learned the joy that a drink of water can bring, so it is easy to appreciate the idea that the Root of Jesse (Isa 11.10) quenches our parched souls with salvation. The exhortation in Isaiah 55 still wrings true as mankind too often expends much time and effort searching for satisfaction in money, power, pleasure, alcohol, sexual immorality, philosophy, etc., while ignoring a spiritually satisfying feast that is laid out for them in Christ. Most of us from time to time find ourselves wanting something we cannot afford, but what we need most is given without price. "Amazing grace, how sweet the sound!"

We could look at several other passages from the prophets before we move to the New Testament, but the picture Ezekiel painted of God's people when they were reunited under the leadership of "David" is typical:

> I will make them and the places all around My hill a blessing; and I will cause showers to come down in their season; there shall be showers of blessing. Then the trees of the field shall yield their fruit, and the earth shall yield her increase. They shall be safe in their land; and they shall know that I am the LORD, when I have broken the bands of their yoke and delivered them from the hand of those who enslaved them (Ezek 34.26–27).

Do we fully appreciate the showers of blessings bestowed upon us? In Christ we are not eating literal fruit, but the joy we should derive from our great spiritual blessings is depicted in terms of things even those who have moved away from the agrarian lifestyle should be able to relate to and embrace.

These and other prophecies should have prepared the Jewish nation for the coming of the One who would call Himself the true Water and Bread and promise that He could satisfy a far greater hunger and thirst than that which Israel experienced in the wilderness. "Blessed are those who hunger and thirst for righteousness, for they shall be filled" (Matt 5.6).

Jesus performed many signs and wonders, all of them intended to produce faith (John 20.30–31), but His multiplication of the loaves and fish not only demonstrated His ability to provide the things we need for the body but pointed to Himself as the One to provide us with the food which endures to everlasting life (John 6.1–14, 26–27). The LORD who had provided water in a barren wilderness came in the flesh that we might have the water of life and become a source of blessing to others.

A woman of Samaria came to draw water. Jesus said to her, "Give Me a drink." For His disciples had gone away into the city to buy food. Then the woman of Samaria said to Him, "How is it that you, being a Jew, ask a drink from me, a Samaritan woman?" For Jews have no dealings with Samaritans. Jesus answered and said to her, "If you knew the gift of God, and who it is who says to you, 'Give Me a drink,' you would have asked Him, and He would have given you living water." The woman said to Him, "Sir, you have nothing to draw with, and the well is deep. Where then do you get that living water? Are you greater than our father Jacob, who gave us the well, and drank from it himself, as well as his sons and his livestock?" Jesus answered and said to her, "Whoever drinks of this water will thirst again, but whoever drinks of the water that I shall give him will never thirst. But the water that I shall give him will become in him a fountain of water springing up into everlasting life" (John 4.7–14).

On the last day, that great day of the feast, Jesus stood and cried out, saying, "If anyone thirsts, let him come to Me and drink. He who believes in Me, as the scripture has said, out of his heart will flow rivers of living water" (John 7.37–38).

Time will not permit a full exploration of John 6 and the Bread of Life discourse, but His words of eternal life (John 6.68) are for those who see in Him the only possible source of spiritual nourishment and are willing to gnaw His flesh and drink His blood. We often speak of devouring a meal when we are hungry and that is what we are to do with Jesus. Nibbling on spiritual hors d'oeuvres brings no satisfaction, but we must eat heartily. No, we are not called to literally eat and drink the Savior, but our lives become hidden with Christ in God because He is our life (Col 3.1–4). The old saying is that we are what we eat, so may we ever spiritually eat of the Savior and become more and more like Him.

## Conclusion

Because we are called to spend a number of years in these fleshly bodies, it is good to know our God is aware of our physical needs and has promised to provide for us. Yet, when we see this life as a time spent in exile or on a pilgrimage (e.g., 1 Pet 1.1, 17; 2.11), we are even more thankful to know we have a loving Father who will guide our footsteps to the true Promised Land and sustain us with the spiritual food and drink we need. How blessed we are in Christ, but we must heed the warning sounded in 1 Corinthians 10. Israel was blessed with this same great Leader and Provider, yet came up short because of unbelief. May we learn from their failure and one day enjoy the pure river of water of life and the fruit of the everbearing tree of life (Rev 22.1–2).

# God Tests His People

## Chris Huntley

In Genesis 22, one of the more difficult passages in the Bible, God calls upon Abraham to offer his child as a sacrifice. What could cause the God of Israel, who is so vehemently repulsed by child sacrifice,[1] to command it of the father of faith? This story is introduced by a simple phrase, "God tested Abraham."[2] This request is difficult for those who envision God as an all-loving benevolent deity who would never bring discomfort to his people through tests. Matthews connects this test to the story of Job who, in similar fashion, went through "testing that results in remarkable suffering."[3] We might be tempted to remove God from Job's suffering and insist that it was the diabolical Satan, not God, who caused Job's demise. But this view does not adequately represent Satan's place in Job. As Andersen points out, "the contribution of the Satan to the action of the book is minor. His place in its theology even less…. It is impossible to believe that the purpose of this tremendous book is to teach us…that human suffering is caused by the Devil."[4] Satan is not even a main character in the book considering he disappears from the story after

---

[1] Child sacrifice is condemned by God in numerous places (e.g., Lev 18.21; Deut 12.31; 18.10; 2 Kng 17.17; 21.6; 33.6; Psa 106.35–38; Jer 7.31; 19.4–5; 32.35; Ezek 16.20–21; 20.26; 20.31; 23.37).

[2] Unless noted otherwise, all quotations of scripture are from the ESV.

[3] Kenneth Matthews, *Genesis 1–11:26,* NAC 1A (Nashville: Broadman 1996) 289.

[4] Francis I. Andersen. *Job.* TOTC (Downers Grove: IVP, 1976) 83.

2.7. In fact, as Seow points out, Satan "is clearly subservient to God, indeed a mere functionary in the divine council."[5] When the story of Job concludes and Job's friends and family come to comfort him (Job 42.10), they do not comfort him concerning all that he suffered at Satan's hands. As Habel puts it, "the agency of Satan is now irrelevant. The 'evil' Job experienced is indeed the 'evil' he acknowledged from Yahweh's hands."[6] It was YHWH who was behind the suffering in Job. It was YHWH who told Abraham to offer his child as a sacrifice. As Brueggemann so aptly puts it, "Does God really test in this way? The premise of the story is that he does."[7]

Whether it is Abraham, Job or one of many other important characters in biblical history, God clearly tests his people. Perhaps the clearest demonstration of this testing begins in Exodus 15 as God tests the children of Israel numerous times after he has led them from slavery in Egypt. In this essay, I will demonstrate how God tested Israel in the wilderness and that they, summarily, failed those tests. Even so, I will show that Jesus steps in as the quintessential embodiment of God's people becoming the paragon of obedience in the face of testing. Leaning heavily on the Hebrews author, I will connect Jesus' triumph over Satan to the individual successes of many throughout Israelite history who persevered by faith when tested. Through this, we will discover the example to lead us through the tests we face in our wilderness experiences today.

## The Testing Narratives

In Exodus 15.25, just after the Red Sea crossing, when God delivered the children of Israel from the problem of too much water, God's people have travelled for three days without enough water. Stuart speculates that perhaps after three days of rationing the water, upon knowing that water was just ahead, "many of them drank their last

---

[5] C. L. Seow. *Job 1–21*. Illuminations (Grand Rapids: Eerdmans, 2013) 299.

[6] Norman Habel. *The Book of Job*. OTL (Philadelphia: Westminster, 1985) 585.

[7] Walter Brueggemann. *Genesis*. Interpretation. (Louisville: John Knox ,1982) 190.

water and/or gave it to their animals."[8] Imagine their elation as the water was seen in the distance only to turn to panic as they realized the water was undrinkable, creating a desperate situation for the children of Israel. It is here that for the first time, Israel "grumbled." "Grumbling" is a word often associated with this generation and is used multiple times through the testing narratives. For this exodus generation, when the going got tough, they all got going to Moses to complain.[9]

Even though this generation grumbled against Moses, God still delivered them from their predicament. He showed Moses a specific tree to toss into the water which would heal the water. In this way, God demonstrated that he was Israel's healer. This picture of YHWH as a healer is important for those who have come out of Egypt to see. So far, all they have seen of their God is death and destruction, exemplified in the Ten Plagues on Egypt and the destruction of Pharaoh's army in the Red Sea. Fretheim connects this test with the first plague against Egypt, noting that the result of the healing of the waters at Marah is that impotable water became useful, whereas in the first plague, the useful water became impotable.[10] God shows his people a different side of his power in that he not only uses that power to destroy, but also to heal. With this object lesson, YHWH implores them to hear and obey his commandments to avoid "the diseases that [he] put on the Egyptians" (Exod 15.26). In this, God "tested" his people.

---

[8] Douglas Stuart. *Exodus.* NAC 2. (Nashville: B&H Publishing, 2006) 365.

[9] There are some who suggest that Israel's grumbling in the wilderness is not viewed in a negative light until after the covenant was made and the Law was given. According to this line of thinking, grumbling is perfectly natural in the "initial period of testing." For example, see Thomas Dozeman, *Exodus,* ECC (Grand Rapids: Eerdmans, 2009) 368. According to this view, grumbling only becomes inexcusable after YHWH has demonstrated who he is and they are in covenant with one another, as in Numbers. Whereas there may be some merit to this perceived progression, it is not necessary. Even before these testing narratives they have already come to know YHWH by witnessing his power in Egypt and at the Red Sea, so they are without excuse. In addition, Numbers 14 will relate back to these testing narratives, indicating that the grumbling here is as inexcusable as it was at Kadesh.

[10] Terence Fretheim. *Exodus.* Interpretation. (Louisville: John Knox, 1991) 175.

This is only the second time the Bible explicitly states that God "tested" his people, the first being Genesis 22 when God tested Abraham.[11] Now that the next stage of God's promises to Abraham is soon to be accomplished, God again tests the line of Abraham. This generation does not fare as well as their father. There is debate concerning whether the test is to prove to God what is in man's heart or to prove to the people what is in their hearts.[12] Whichever is the case, or if there is a position in between, the test determines if man will, indeed, be faithful to the God he serves. These tests, as Garrett suggests, are done "to see if they look to him in time of need."[13]

As Exodus 15.26 shows, this testing is connected to a conditional proposition. That they have not yet received the "commandments" and "statutes" is immaterial, as God is taking them to the place where they will. For now, he is conditioning them to understand

---

[11] Perhaps we are to see some intertextuality in these accounts. The Israelites, as the new iteration of the line of Abraham, go three days out into the wilderness approaching a mountain in which God will appear to them and make covenantal statements, reminiscent of the events in Genesis 22.

[12] Alter puts this succinctly stating "either this is a God lacking absolute foreknowledge ascribed to deity by later theology, or the trial is essentially a means for man to show his mettle." Richard Alter, *The Five Books of Moses: A Translation and Commentary* (New York: Norton, 2004) 921. On the one hand, Gerhardsson among others provides a compelling argument that "when the Old Testament speaks of JHWH testing his covenant son, 'tempting' him (הִסָּנ, πειράζειν), it means that God arranges a test to find out if his son is true to the covenant...it is almost a formula that God tests 'that he may know' (תעדל) whether his chosen one is true or not." Birgir Gerhardsson. *The Testing of God's Son: (Matthew 4:1–11 &PAR) An Analysis of an Early Christian Midrash*. CBNTS 2 (Lund: Gleerup, 1966; rep. ed., Eugene: Wipf & Stock, 2009) 27–28). However, due to my own conception of God, I tend to agree with Sarna who, speaking of God testing Abraham, concludes, "when 'God put Abraham to the test' it was obviously not a trial, the outcome of which was meant to add to the sum of God's knowledge. Such an idea would obviously be incompatible with the biblical concept of the omniscience of God" (N. Sarna. *Exploring Exodus.* (Schocken 1986 Rev. 1996) 162). Perhaps there is a place between the two positions in which God, though fully omniscient, still gains data from these tests as he observes man's free-will choices while one has been through the testing can look back and observe what truly was in his heart.

[13] Duane Garrett, *Exodus,* Kregel Exegetical Library (Grand Rapids: Kregel, 2013) 414.

that his disposition as a healer or a destroyer is dependent upon
their obedience. Again, in the apodosis, God contrasts his work at
Marah with his works in Egypt to show their options. As Brueg-
gamann points out, whether YHWH treats them like the Egyptians
or not has to do with their ability to make "a deep and intentional
break with Egypt in order to be healed."[14] As we see moving forward, Israel does not make this break.

In Exodus 16, the children of Israel are tested again. After leading his people away from Marah, YHWH takes them to an oasis in
which there is plenty of water and some food. It is a decent place to
stop, but it is not a sufficient place to stay.[15] Judging by the response
of the people, they might have been content to settle in Elim and
forgo the land of promise altogether. As soon as they depart from
Elim, the grumbling begins anew.

Again in Exodus 16 God "tests" his people. In this instance, God
declares the test will determine "whether they will walk in my law or
not" (v. 4). After leaving Elim, which provided relative comfort, the
people begin to "grumble" again, this time about the lack of food.
For a Hebrew word first introduced in ch. 15, it is impressive that
the word "grumble" appears eight times in ch. 16. While repetition
is common within the Hebrew Bible, typically it is there to serve a
purpose. As Revell suggests, "the purpose of repetition is, in general,
to draw the item repeated to the attention of the hearer or reader,
to mark it as significant."[16] While repetition is common within the
Hebrew Bible, typically it is there to serve a purpose. Even then,
repetition on this scale is somewhat unusual, especially for a word

---

[14] Walter Brueggemann, "Exodus," in Leander Keck, ed., *The New Interpreter's
Bible Commentary* (Nashville: Abingdon, 1994.) 1:809.

[15] Enns suggests that Elim "foreshadows...entrance into the Promised Land"
which is "a glimpse of what is to come, the lush land of Canaan." Peter Enns, *Exodus,* NIVAC (Grand Rapids: Zondervan, 2000) 324. Though this is probably true, it
is important to remember that it is not a replacement for the promised land.

[16] E. J. Revell, "The Repetition of Introductions to Speech as a Feature of Biblical Hebrew," *VT* 47 (1997) 92.

which is hardly used outside the context of the exodus generation.[17] Thus, when we see this large-scale repetition, the significance is unmistakable. This is a group of people who, as they experience more demonstrations of God's deliverance and care, become less inclined to trust him.[18]

This lack of faith is illustrated by the test in this section. YHWH tells his people he will "rain down" bread from heaven for them, but they are only to collect enough for one day's worth and not to save any until morning. Considering their complaint concerns the lack of food in the wilderness, perhaps it is unsurprising some ration their manna, scared the food source would soon be just a memory like the oasis of Elim. This simple action demonstrates a lack of trust in God to provide what he promises. By noting the tents filled with outcries of disgust followed by people exiting their tents to remove the rotted refuse, it was probably obvious who had disobeyed by keeping manna overnight. Moses becomes angry with them, as they failed the test concerning whether the people listen to God's instructions or not.

Of course, there is one more test concerning God's law for the Israelites in Exodus 16. Though they are told not to save any overnight, and some try to do so with catastrophic results, on Fridays God tells them to save an extra omer's worth overnight so the Sabbath Day could be kept holy. Of course, the twenty-first century reader understands the significance of this command, but those receiving this command in the wilderness are hearing it for the first time as this is

---

[17] John Durham, *Exodus* WBC (Dallas: Word, 1987; rep. ed., Grand Rapids: Zondervan, 2015) 211. Here Durham states, "the verb is לון. It is used only of the 'murmuring' or 'grumbling' of Israel against their leaders, primarily in the period of Moses' leadership between Egypt and Canaan in Exod 15, 16, and 17, and in Num 14, 16, 17. The one additional context is Joshua's wars of conquest, Josh 9.18; Psa 59.16 appears to refer to the 'roving, prowling, scavenging' of wild dogs, another meaning of לון."

[18] While true that their "grumbling" was technically against Moses and Aaron, much of the repetition in this section is to signify that all of the grumbling is ultimately against God. Moses and Aaron deflect the complaints rightfully acknowledging that they do not have high enough authority or power to warrant such grumbling (vv. 7–8).

the first time "Sabbath" appears in the Hebrew Bible.[19] And just as "grumble" was significantly repeated numerous times, "Sabbath" is repeated four times in vv. 22–30, demonstrating how important it was to follow this command.[20]

Even so, Israel again fails the test.[21] Despite the command, some leave their tents on Saturday morning to gather manna and they find none. Again, Moses would easily have seen who disobeyed as they left their tents to gather, those whose lack of faith he found disturbing. This failure undoubtedly has greater consequences than leaving manna overnight to rot on the other days. In those instances, there was still manna to gather. Disobedience on this day means the family goes without.

Just as at the waters of Marah, this narrative comes with an "I Am" statement. God declares the miraculous nature of the manna in the wilderness is done "so you shall know that I am the LORD your God" (v. 12). Again, a testing narrative connects back to the plagues of Egypt as God is demonstrating how much differently he treats those who follow his laws and commandments. As Fretheim points out, "in the seventh plague, God 'rained' hail upon Egypt,

---

[19] Closely associated with the Sabbath, this is one of only three contexts in which the phrase "the seventh day" appears: (a) the creation narrative in Genesis 2; (b) the seven days of the Feast of Unleavened Bread and the Passover; and (c) here in connection with observing the Sabbath.

[20] Though the Sabbath is an important aspect of God's relationship with his people, it is not in the scope of this essay to discuss the specific nature of the Sabbath except as a test for Israel. The significance will be firmly established when Israel reaches Sinai and receives the Decalogue in Exodus 20. Until then, this narrative serves as a foreshadowing of what is to come. For a good treatment of the Sabbath, see David McClister, "The Promise of a Sabbath Rest," in Daniel Petty, ed., *Florida College Annual Lectures 2003* (Temple Terrace, FL: Florida College, 2003) 213–232.

[21] Interestingly, Moses does not simply call out the individuals who failed the tests. Because a portion of the group did not keep God's laws, all of Israel is at fault. When God confronts Moses about it, he says, "How long will you refuse to keep my commandments and my laws?" The "you" is a plural you which includes Moses and all of the people. Though it seems strange to our twenty-first century western minds, God's people were not characterized by rugged individualism, but by a corporate accountability. When a portion fails, they all fail.

which destroyed the food sources (9.18, 23), here God 'rains' bread from the heavens (16.4)."[22] Through the tests, YHWH not only places his people in positions which test their faith, but he also puts himself in a position to care for them and emphatically prove that he is worthy of their trust.

In the third testing narrative in Exodus 17, the Israelites again find themselves without water. Unlike at Marah, this time there is no water in sight that could be healed. The people who have continually displayed a lack of trust in God act as expected. Confronted with the scenario of stopping in a place with no water, they do what they have always done. However, a new word is introduced in this section: "quarreled" (v. 2). Stuart suggests this would be better translated as "protested" as "'quarreled with' tends to imply a heated argument back and forth between Moses and the people."[23] This indicates that the people are becoming more belligerent through these narratives.

The belligerent nature of Israel is also demonstrated in the nature of the "test" in this third of the testing narratives. In each of the previous two tests, it was YHWH who "tested" Israel. Though all the elements of a test are here, and Psalm 81.7 clearly shows that the Lord saw this narrative as a test, the text here does not explicitly say that God was testing his people as found in 15.25 and 16.4. Instead, Moses declares that it was Israel who tested YHWH (v. 2). This is later confirmed by the narrator in v. 7 who says Israel "tested the LORD by saying, 'Is the LORD among us or not?'"

The transition from God testing Israel to Israel testing God is significant. From our twenty-first century western perspective, it might seem proper that as God tests Israel, Israel has every right to test him in return. However, in most other societies, the folly would be apparent. God does not need to be tested. Lamprecht does not mince words, stating, "discontent with divine provision in the wilderness is characterized as unbelief, lack of trust and a violation of the basic

[22] Fretheim, *Exodus* 175.
[23] Stuart, *Exodus* 388.

obligation of the covenant."[24] God has already demonstrated he can be trusted. As Hamilton puts it, "testing God is demanding that he jump through our hoops and make himself answerable and accountable to us. Sovereignty passes to us."[25] Yet this is the response of those who face adversity without faith. The question becomes, "Is the Lord among us or not?" (v. 7). In essence, every instance of an improper response to God's testing is testing God in return. This is why the Lord states that Israel tested him "these ten times" when he condemned them to wander in the wilderness for forty years (Numbers 14.22), even though there is no explicit mention of ten times of testing. It is simply a statement concerning how often Israel failed God's tests by testing him in return.[26]

After the failure of the exodus generation at Kadesh in Numbers 14, there arose a new generation of Israelites. At the end of forty years, on the plains of Moab looking into the land of promise, as Moses provides the Law for a second time to the new generation, he reminds his hearers not only of God's miraculous help for them through their time in the wilderness, but also of God's continued testing. In Deuteronomy 8, Moses focuses on the events of the testing narratives and how God used the wilderness wandering as a test. Lohfink provides a chiastic structure for Deuteronomy 8 which centers around v. 11 in which Moses says, "Take care lest you forget the LORD your God by not keeping his commandments and his rules and his statutes, which I command you today."[27] This wording con-

---

[24] Liana Lamprecht, "Reading Matthew 6:13A ('Lead Us Not Into Temptation') Within the Massah-Matrix: Biblical and Historical Literary Evidence for a Further Consideration of the Sixth Petition in the Lord's Prayer," *Journal of Early Christian History* 6 (2016) 37.

[25] Victor Hamilton, *Exodus: An Exegetical Commentary* (Grand Rapids: Baker, 2011) 263.

[26] For a more thorough treatment of Numbers 14.22, see Reagan McClenny, "They Will Not Enter My Rest," in Thomas Hamilton, ed., *Florida College Annual Lectures 2022* (Temple Terrace: Florida College Press, 2022) xx-xx.

[27] Norbert Lohfink, *Höre Israel: Auslegung von Texten aus dem Buch Deuteronomium,* Die Welt der Bibel 18 (Düsseldorf: Patmos Verlag, 1965) 76, as quoted in R. O'Connell, *Vetus Testamentum* 40 (1990) 437.

nects directly to the purpose of the "tests" in Exodus 15.25–26 and 16.4. In fact, Deuteronomy 8 serves as the perfect summation to wilderness testing narratives as Moses tells them the purpose of their wandering was that God

> …might humble you, testing you to know what was in your heart, whether you would keep his commandments or not. And he humbled you and let you hunger and fed you with manna, which you did not know, nor did your fathers know, that he might make you know that man does not live by bread alone, but man lives by every word that comes from the mouth of the LORD…. Know then in your heart that, as a man disciplines his son, the Lord your God disciplines you (Deut 8.2–5).

In this way, Moses connects the tests in the wilderness with instruction and discipline so that after this new nation, the son of God, conquers the land, they would mature into a beacon of light that would draw all the nations to YHWH. Unfortunately, Israel's history does not follow this path.

## The Testing Narrative

Throughout the Old Testament, with few exceptions, Israel continues to follow in the steps of their forefathers as they fail the tests God provides. These failures not only show the inadequacy of God's people, they also setup the one who will step in as the Son of God *par excellence*. As Blomberg notes, Jesus' temptation narrative in the wilderness "recalls the wanderings of the Israelites in the wilderness. Jesus will succeed as the true representative and fulfillment of Israel where Israel had failed (Deut 8.2)."[28] The parallels between the gospel accounts of Jesus' temptations with the exodus generation are striking.[29]

---

[28] Craig Blomberg, *Matthew*, NAC 22 (Nashville: B & H Publishing, 1992) 83.

[29] For parallels between Jesus and the exodus generation, see Richard Patterson and Michael Travers, "Contours of the Exodus Motif in Jesus' Earthly Ministry" *WTJ* 66 (2004) 25–47. Though some of the connections seem contrived, overall they adequately connect parallels (or contrasts) from the exodus with Jesus.

Focusing on the narrative in Matthew 4, some connections stand out. Jesus going without food (and presumably water) in the wilderness (v. 2) hearkens back to Israel's lack of food and water. The forty days and nights Jesus fasts in the wilderness (v. 2) parallels the forty years that Israel wandered in the wilderness.[30] The temptation to turn stones into bread (v. 3) combines Israel's tests in which God rained bread from heaven for them and then provided water from a rock.[31] In response, Jesus quotes Deuteronomy 8.3 which, as previously noted, is directly connected with the wilderness testing narratives. When Satan calls upon Jesus to throw himself down from the pinnacle of the temple (vv. 5–6), Jesus compares the temptation with putting "the Lord your God to the test" (v. 7), that is, testing God to see if God was really with Jesus or not. The final test was a test to engage in idolatry and worship Satan (v. 9), a temptation which first became a snare in Israel's wilderness experience (Exod 32; Num 25) and remained one throughout the Old Testament.

As parallel as these narratives appear to be, Patterson and Travers argue that they should more properly be characterized as "contrasts."[32] Though the exodus generation constantly failed the tests by putting God to the test, Jesus successfully overcomes the temptations he encounters. He does not grumble over his lack of food and water, but instead focuses on the need to hunger and thirst for the word of God. Jesus does not demand a sign to demonstrate whether or not God is with him. Jesus does not bow down to or seek out refuge with one who promises to provide temporary relief but would turn out to be a horrible master. Where Israel fails, Jesus succeeds.

---

[30] The forty days and nights could also be connected with the time Moses spent on the mountain (Exod 24.18).

[31] Gerharddson, comparing the exodus narratives with Jesus' temptation narratives, observes that while "the differences…are too great for there to be any question of typological connection…it is interesting to note that the raw material for this presentation is also to be found in the wilderness narratives." Gerhardsson, *Testing* 53.

[32] Patterson and Travers, "Contours" 39.

In this, Jesus as the true Son of God provides the perfect embodiment of what it means to be part of the people of God. In Hebrews 4.15, the author argues for Jesus' credibility to serve as a priest, stating that Jesus "in every respect has been tempted as we are, yet without sin." This short statement speaks volumes concerning the testing of Jesus. Jesus passed every test, which included more than the three temptations found in this testing narrative. His entire life was lived as a human who did not sin. Doing so, he not only provides an example of how it can be done, but he becomes equipped to come to the aid of those who wish to follow him.

## Testing Narratives for the People of God

God's tests do not conclude with the temptations of Jesus. Just as Jesus was tempted, so are those who follow him. Lamprecht astutely notes:

> New Testament uses of the verb *peirazō* are, however, not limited to the temptation-of-Jesus narrative, but also refer to the testing of Christians (1 Pet. 1.6; 4.12 and Jas 1.2). Christians are warned to protect themselves with spiritual armour (Eph. 6.10–17) against the attacks of the 'prince of this world' and to stand firm and watchful in prayer (1 Pet. 5.8).... Humanity is in constant danger of falling into sin, because Satan can use all sorts of things to lead us into temptation (1 Cor. 7.5; 1 Thess. 3.5), to seduce us from the course which God has appointed for us.[33]

Gerhardsson suggests it is not enough to understand a "test" from God as simply challenging one's allegiance. A test is better thought of "as the paternal act of discipline and a part of a son's upbringing."[34] He

[33] Lamprecht, "Reading Matthew" 38.

[34] Gerhardsson, *Testing* 32. In this section, Gerhardsson shows how the Hebrew "*nâsâh*" is often connected with other Hebrew words regarding training. As he suggests, "since…the verb הסנ (πειράζειν) is used alongside other terms for discipline and education, it is enriched by their overtones; it has something of this meaning even when it occurs in Deuteronomy. In 8:2 ff, with which the accounts of Jesus' temptations are so clearly connected, the wandering in the wilderness and the feeding with manna are seen in terms of education and discipline." Ibid. 34. His connections

goes on to say, "The Rabbinic literature has many variations of the thought that JHWH tests, disciplines and chastens the son whom he loves, sometimes referring to the people of Israel and sometimes to the individual."[35] As seen previously in Deuteronomy 8.5, the conception of tests as "discipline" from a father is fully in force. Thus, in the New Testament, testing—which often came through the form of suffering—was seen as a demonstration of God's love as the heavenly father.

No New Testament author speaks more to this than the author of Hebrews. As noted earlier, the Hebrews author focuses on Jesus as the high priest and example for others to follow in 4.15. This theme carries through the entire letter and comes to a climax in chs. 11–12 where the author lists many who demonstrated faithfulness, culminating in Jesus.

As McClister points out, Hebrews 11 follows a form of rhetoric knows as "epideictic speech in which figures from the past were praised in order to strengthen the hearer's commitment to the values those figures embodied."[36] The question becomes, however, what are the values the Hebrews author praises? Hebrews 11 is often viewed, as Allen indicates, as a "Conviction to Live by Faith."[37] Whereas there is a sense in which this is accurate, there is also a sense in which this common assumption concerning Hebrews 11 is misleading. Hebrews 11 is not a Hall of Fame of people who lived faithful lives.[38] In

---

with instructional words in Exodus and Deuteronomy such as "that you may know" show this added level of meaning which shows that the "tests" are also about discipline.

[35] Ibid., 33.

[36] David McClister, *Hebrews* (Temple Terrace, FL: Florida College Press, 2010) 383–84.

[37] David L. Allen, *Hebrews,* NAC 35 (Nashville: B & H Publishing, 2010) 538.

[38] Halls of Fame recognize those who stand out as the greatest in their respective fields. This would suggest, as many have, that Hebrews 11 is focused on the people who lived faithful lives. While there are some listed, such as Abraham, Joseph, or Moses, who arguably lived faithful lives, it is difficult to use this as the criterion for inclusion. Consider that the exodus generation is included in Hebrews 11 as those who acted by faith (v. 29). As has been noted in this paper, as well as earlier in the letter to the Hebrews (3.16ff), that generation was most decidedly not faithful for their entire lives. It is also difficult to explain why Jephthah or Samson, solely based on the narratives from Judges, would be on a list of people who lived faithful lives to the Lord.

fact, there are only twenty people mentioned in Hebrews 11 as those who acted by faith. Comparatively, there are forty different actions which were performed by faith. If one were to suggest Hebrews 11 focuses on the people, he would have to admit, as does Alexander, "It is not only the patriarchs, the founding mothers and fathers of faith's family tree, who are held up as exemplars. The 'great cloud of witnesses' on which 12.1 looks back expands to include aunts and uncles, second cousins twice removed, named and unnamed, too many to number."[39] The emphasis is not on the people who live faithful lives to God; the emphasis is on faithful decisions. What is valued in epideictic fashion is not the character of individuals, but the perseverance in the face of adversity that many, including many unnamed in Hebrews 11, demonstrated by their actions.

Though the litany of deeds conducted by faith begins with explicit instances tied to individuals from the Old Testament scriptures, the intensity increases beginning in v. 32 where the author turns away from naming the individuals to naming only actions performed. The first series of examples in vv. 33–35 speak of those who acted by faith and were delivered from their suffering. However, lest one think the answer to prayer is earthly deliverance, vv. 36–38 speak of those who were not delivered from their earthly suffering. Sometimes God's people act by faith and are not rewarded with deliverance. Even so, the point the Hebrews author makes is that perseverance through the test, even if that perseverance leads to physical death, pleases God. These actions sometimes resulted in deliverance, sometimes did not, but were all done by faith and are a part of the great "catalogue of achievements"[40] which the Hebrews author lists.

---

[39] Loveday Alexander, "Prophets and Martyrs as Exemplars of Faith," in Richard Baukham et al., eds., *The Epistle to the Hebrews and Christian Theology*, (Grand Rapids: Eerdmans, 2009) 407. Alexander goes on to refer to vv. 32–38 as the "catalogue of faith's achievements" as the author does not explicitly connect these actions with any particular person. Ibid. 408. I view the entire litany as a catalogue of faith's achievements whether there is a name connected to it or not.

[40] Phrase taken from Alexander, "Faith" 408.

The list culminates in the example of Jesus who, as McClister shows, is "not just another example of faithful endurance for the readers to consider…He is *the* example by which their own conduct is to be measured and evaluated."[41] Again, it is not that Jesus lived faithfully his entire life, which he did, but that he made the decision to endure the cross despite the shame it would bring. The Hebrews author specifies this one event.[42]

This is the basis for the exhortation which the Hebrews author gives, "let us also lay aside every weight, and sin which clings so closely, and let us run with endurance the race that is set before us" (12.1). Though it seems the author suggests his readers are running a long endurance race, which would indicate a lifelong faithfulness, Lane sees the language differently. He suggests that the removal of weights and sin is comparable to "the usual preparation of stripping for a race."[43] This would indicate that the runner is about to face a trial which he will be going through and must prepare for it. The author has previously reminded them that they have been through such trials before (10.32ff). Now they need to prepare themselves for another test by focusing not only on the examples of all of those who have persevered through their tests in days of old, but also focusing on Jesus who persevered through the cross. As Kamell suggests, "If Christ, the divine Son of God, endured hardship, opposition and persecution to the point of death, the adopted children of God are fairly warned to expect hardships."[44]

---

[41] McClister, *Hebrews* 446.

[42] To be fair, "the Cross" may be metonymy for every instance in which Jesus lived "by faith" and did not give into temptation, including the previously discussed wilderness testing narrative.

[43] William Lane, *Hebrews*, WBC 47B (Dallas: Word, 1991; rep. ed., Grand Rapids: Zondervan, 2015) 408. To be fair, Lane does not suggest, as I have, that the language of starting a race dismisses the idea of the Hebrews author speaking of a lifetime race. Even so, his point is valid and lends weight to the idea of the author preparing his readers for the start of a new test.

[44] Mariam Kamell, "Reexamining Faith," in R. Bauckham et al., eds., *The Epistle to the Hebrews and Christian Theology* (Grand Rapids: Eerdmans, 2009) 427.

The Hebrews author then connects their hardships, or testing, with the discipline of God. Citing Proverbs 3.11–12, the author suggests that the suffering they will endure for the sake of Christ is a function of their relationship with God as their father. In fact, the author assumes that this suffering is a demonstration of God's love for them. Thus, as they stare into the oncoming tests in the form of persecution, they can understand it in the framework of God's love; a God who has not only left them with "a great cloud of witnesses," but who has also joined with their suffering and has demonstrated the value of perseverance through it.

## The Result of Perseverance in Testing

After encouraging his audience to practically prepare for the coming storm (Heb 12.12–17), the author then focuses on the eschaton. He reminds them of the eternal reward for this perseverance that is greater than any temporal suffering they might endure. By comparing two mountains, he makes it clear that the mountain for those who endure their testing "by faith" cannot be shaken. There is a hope that by following Jesus, they will have entry onto the holy mountain of God. This hope is reminiscent of a promised land given to the Israelites who came out of Egypt, a hope that did not motivate them properly. This hope is reminiscent of David who in Psalm 95, after looking at the failures of the exodus generation, encouraged his readers to not harden their hearts or put God to the test as he looked forward to a future rest. This hope is the hope we cling to as we contemplate eternity before us.

In a sense, we are also on our way to a "promised land." There is still a Sabbath rest that remains for the people of God (Heb 4.9).[45]

---

[45] In Deut 12.9–11, Moses connects the promise of land with the promise of rest. David connects this as well in Psalm 95 where, speaking for the Lord, he writes of the disobedient exodus generation, "I swore in my wrath, they shall not enter my rest." YHWH banned Israel from entering the "land" in Numbers 14.23. David calls it "rest." Commenting on Psalm 95, the Hebrews author says there is "a Sabbath rest for the people of God," referring to an eschatological hope of entering into God's eternal rest in the archetypal Sabbath that is still available for God's creation.

Like Israel on their way to Canaan, we live in a now-but-not-yet exis-tence. Though freed from Egyptian slavery, they were still wandering in the wilderness until the completion of the promises. Though they entered into a covenant with God in Exodus 24 and became a great nation as God had promised Abraham, they were a people of God without the fulfilment of the land promise. It was in that crucial time that God tested his people in various ways. We should expect the same kinds of tests today. In fact, though the letter to the Hebrews was written specifically for that audience about a testing they were about to endure, it serves as a timeless document for all generations who continue to face the tests of God in their own wilderness experi-ences. Every generation of God's people continues to face tests.

One of the greatest realizations from studying through Hebrews 11–12 is understanding our place in the great "catalogue of faith's achievements." The great cloud of witnesses does not end with those mentioned in Hebrews 11. Those first century Christians who read the exhortation and successfully persevered through their testing are now also part of that catalogue. All Christians who died as martyrs or were persecuted in the first few centuries are now a part of that catalogue. All Christians since then who have been persecuted for their faith are part of that catalogue. And as you and I face our own tests and moments of discipline from the Lord, if we also choose faith and persevere, our actions will be added to the catalogue of faith's achievements.

This discussion of perseverance in testing is reminiscent of a sec-tion of Theodore Roosevelt's "Man in the Arena" speech:

> It is not the critic who counts; not the man who points out how
> the strong man stumbles, or where the doer of deeds could have
> done them better. The credit belongs to the man who is actually
> in the arena, whose face is marred by dust and sweat and blood;

---

For more on this connection, see Caleb Churchill, "There Remains a Sabbath Rest," in Thomas Hamilton, ed., *Florida College Annual Lectures 2022* (Temple Terrace: Florida College Press, 2022) xx-xx.

who strives valiantly; who errs, who comes short again and again, because there is no effort without error and shortcoming; but who does actually strive to do the deeds; who knows great enthusiasms, the great devotions; who spends himself in a worthy cause; who at the best knows in the end the triumph of high achievement, and who at the worst, if he fails, at least fails while daring greatly, so that his place shall never be with those cold and timid souls who neither know victory nor defeat.[46]

God tests his people. He has always tested his people. As those who have been saved from the bondage of sin and are on our way to our own promised land, let us focus on the examples of those who have been in the arena, have been put to the test and have persevered. As we face our own tests, let us not test the Lord in return and ask, "Is God among us or not?" Let us look to Abraham and to Job who endured great tests from God but never gave in. Let us see the actions of all of those from Hebrews 11 who ran in the arena showing us that trust in God is never misplaced. Let us look to Jesus, the founder and perfector of our faith who endured the cross, despising the shame, and now sits at God's right hand. Let us remember we can always trust God as he has consistently proven himself by always keeping his promises. Let us run every race we face with endurance knowing that in the end, if we never shrink back to destruction, we will also have a place on that great mountain which can never be shaken, a place of rest with all the saints whom the Lord has tested and have persevered.

---

[46] Theodore Roosevelt, "Citizenship in a Republic," April 23, 1910, The Sorbonne, Paris, France. The speech may be accessed online at https://www.theodore-rooseveltcenter.org/Learn-About-TR/TR-Encyclopedia/Culture-and-Society/Man-in-the-Arena.aspx (accessed 8/15/2021).

# God Gives the Law

## John Weaver

Like the liberation from Egypt and the entrance into Canaan, the revelation of God's law at Mount Sinai in Exodus 19–24 was a gift. The value and identity of the gift of the law—its purpose in the life of Israel and its fulfillment in Christ and the Church—are the focus of this essay. My thesis is that the Mosaic law was the gift of God's wisdom for living in the divine presence under the old covenant, and that this law finds its final purpose and fulfillment in the law of Christ, which is the instruction and example of Jesus and his apostles as revealed in the new covenant writings.[1]

## The Law was a Gift

Contrary to a view of the law that sees it as a formulaic code for detailed and explicit direction of every aspect of an Israelite's life, the law is better understood as a type of wisdom for the life of the nation of Israel, giving principles for the type of life that should be learned and lived if the Israelites were to be God's people, living in God's presence, and representing God to the world.[2] The pedagog-

---

[1] The Mosaic law is no longer binding on the Christian's life, either in a ritualistic or moralistic sense, and so the view of this essay is distinct from the "theonomic" approach to Law and Gospel. For explication of a theonomic perspective, and arguments for the Mosaic law as God's gracious guidance for the promotion of holiness, and the new law as the fulfillment of the law of Moses, see Stanley N. Gundry (ed), *Five Views on Law and Gospel* (Grand Rapids: Zondervan Academic, 1996).

[2] The sapiential and non-juridical function of the Mosaic law in the life of ancient Israel is emphasized in recent scholarship comparing Exodus to literary cov-

ical value of the law as principles for living are seen in the description of the law in Exodus 24.12: "The LORD said to Moses, 'Come up to me on the mountain and wait there, that I may give you the tablets of stone, with the law and the commandment, which I have written for their instruction.'"[3]

It is crucial to see the law within the context of covenant. Exodus 19–24 is written in the form of an ancient covenant, and the historical prologue to this treaty between God and the people states that God has already saved them from Egypt by his grace (Exod 20.2). The law comes as another gift of God after their salvation from Egypt, and not as the initial basis for a relationship with God.[4] As with stipulations in ancient suzerainty treaties, the laws at Sinai are stipulations given by the king for the people to observe to maintain the king's presence and protection. If the laws are learned and maintained as wisdom for life, God's guidance and holy presence would continue with Israel, as during the escape from Egypt and at Sinai. This consequence of obedience was most focused on the conquest and the settlement of the promised land: "Now therefore, if you will indeed obey my voice and keep my covenant, you shall be my treasured possession among all peoples, for all the earth is mine; and you shall be to me a kingdom of priests and a holy nation" (Exod 19.5–6).

The primary purpose of the giving of the law, however, was not to give the Israelites the promised land, or to make the Israelites a moral people. As with ancient treaties, the stipulations of the law

---

enants in the Ancient Near Eastern context, e.g., Michael LeFebvre, *Collections, Codes, and Torah: The Re-characterization of Israel's Written Law*, LHBOTS (New York: T&T Clark, 2006), 47; Roy E. Gane, *Old Testament Law for Christians: Original Context and Enduring Application* (Grand Rapids: Baker Academic, 2017). Most recently, see John H. Walton & J. Harvey Walton, *The Lost World of the Torah: Law as Covenant and Wisdom in Ancient Context*, Lost World Series 6 (Downers Grove: IVP Academic, 2019), 25–45.

[3] Unless noted otherwise, all quotations of scripture are from the ESV.

[4] On the covenantal form of the text, see M. G. Kline, *Treaty of the Great King: The Covenant Structure of Deuteronomy* (Grand Rapids: Eerdmans, 1963).

were designed to exalt the authority of the lawgiver and, in the case of the Sinaitic covenant, to glorify God. This is seen in the Ten Commandments (Exod 20.3–17), which along with the "Book of the Covenant" (the name comes from Exod 24.7) was one of the two major parts of the law. For example, the instruction that the people have "no other god before me" is a requirement that God be held as the preeminent deity within their polytheistic culture. The glorifying role of God's law is evident in Moses' retelling of the giving of the law in Deuteronomy 4.7–8: "For what great nation is there that has a god so near to it as the LORD our God is to us, whenever we call upon him? And what great nation is there, that has statutes and rules so righteous as all this law that I set before you today?"

For readers today, the significance of such statements is in the recognition that the Mosaic law is more a specification of the holiness and highness of God—God's nature and authority—rather than primarily human-centered rules for everyday life. The law was relevant to Israel's life, but primarily as covenantal wisdom about who God is and how to maintain God's presence and obtain God's gifts. The law itself was a gift of knowledge for how to glorify God and to maintain the divine "lovingkindness" (i.e., God's generosity).

### The Law was a Gift of Life, but not Eternal Life

Within the ancient society of the Israelites, the life offered by the law (Lev 18.5; cf. Rom 10.5) was a physical existence of diving blessing and distinction from the other nations. This distinguishing blessing was due to the presence of God. The happy consequence of living according to the wisdom of the law is seen, for example, in the promise of the fifth commandment: "Honor your father and your mother, that your days may be long in the land that the LORD your God is giving you" (Exod 20.12). As stipulations for continuing relationship with God, therefore, the laws given by Moses are preconditions for the enduring presence of God in this life. The relationship between law and God's presence is underscored by the climatic nature of the laws concerning the construction of the tabernacle for the dwelling of God's presence in Exodus 25–40. In addition to the law leading to God's dwelling place, the causal relationship between the law and the divine presence is evidenced by mention of God's presence and blessing in the promised land throughout the scenes at Sinai, including the clear statement at Deuteronomy 30.16: "If you obey the commandments of the LORD your God…, then you shall live and multiply, and the LORD your God will bless you in the land that you are entering to take possession of it" (cf. Deut 28.58–62). The blessings and curses that result from relationship to God's law are, therefore, this-worldly in nature, and the sin offerings made are limited to maintaining of physical proximity to God within the geographical boundaries of holiness, whether the tabernacle in the wilderness or the promised land of Canaan.

If we step outside the Ancient Near Eastern context of Exodus and view the law from the first-century AD perspective of the New Testament writings, the Sinaitic law was recognized as limited to a this-worldly relationship with God. The apostle Paul especially emphasizes that the law of Moses did not offer enduring spiritual life, eternal life: "for if a law had been given that could give life, then righteousness would indeed be by the law" (Gal 3.21). A similar Christian perspective is echoed in other NT scriptures. The account of Paul's sermon at Antioch Pisidia in Acts 13.28–39 distinguishes between, 1) the forgiveness of sins and freedom from everything through Jesus Christ, and 2) "everything from which you could not be freed by the law of Moses." It is a qualitative difference between the two covenants elaborated also throughout the book of Hebrews, reaching a crescendo of comparison with the blood of the Mosaic law: "…the law has but a shadow of the good things to come…. For it is impossible for the blood of bulls and goats to take away sins" (Heb 10.1–4). The this-worldly focus of the Sinaitic covenant and law is not described as a fault of the covenant or lawgiver, but as its intended purpose—a limitation of a law that was "good" (e.g.., Rom 7.12), but that was designed for a planned transition to a new covenant.

## The Gift of the Law Would be Replaced

The persistence of the Mosaic covenant and its laws was dependent on the allegiance of the Israelites. From its start at Sinai, the breaking of the law and covenant was predictable (e.g., Deut 31.20), and maintenance of the relationship to God, as with its initiation, would continue to be entirely dependent upon divine grace. Despite this divine longsuffering, the Hebrew prophets are replete with oracles of God's displeasure with the people's breach of contract. For example, Israel's breaking of the covenant is represented as an act against God: "But like Adam they transgressed the covenant; there they dealt faithlessly with me" (Hos 6.7). The prophets' persistence in announcing Israel and Judah's failure to keep the law is often accompanied by divine promises of mercy and renewed relationship if Israel repents. But it is important to note that God's overtures were beyond the bounds of a Mosaic covenant, which was already broken. As a result, God's repeated offers of salvation were displays of divine grace and mercy, and not indications of Israel's worthiness to return to God.

This cycle of establishment, exile, and restoration leads to the revelation that God would give a new covenant. The promise of a new covenant and its connection to the giving and breaking of the Mosaic Law is most clearly and fully stated in Jeremiah 31.31–34. Here the declaration of a "new covenant" follows upon recollection of the covenant given during the exodus, "my covenant that they broke." Three qualities distinguish the new from the old covenant: 1) its interiority on the heart; 2) its equity in access to and knowledge of God ("they shall all know me, from the least of them to the greatest"); and 3) the enduring, even eternal forgiveness of sin: "I will forgive their iniquity, and I will remember their sin no more" (Jer 31.34).

Beyond a new law, the prophets predict a transformation of the hearts and spirits of those to whom the law would be given. Particularly in Ezekiel, a renewed keeping of the law is accomplished by a giving of the divine Spirit, which gives a power to obey the law through transformation of the heart: "And I will give you a new heart, and a new spirit I will put within you. And I will remove the heart of stone from your flesh and give you a heart of flesh. And I will put my Spirit within you and cause you to walk in my statutes and be careful to obey my rules" (Ezek 36.26–27).

So, while Israel was continually commanded to remember the law given to Moses (e.g., Mal 4.4), the ongoing observance of the law and gift of God's presence is connected to a future giving of a new law and a new ability both to know and to keep it. The giving of the Mosaic Law is, therefore, portrayed in the prophets as a precursor to a subsequent gift of new instruction and renewed inspiration to know and follow the law.

## Christ is the Completion and Goal of the Law of Moses

Moving outside the context of the Ancient Near East into the cultural expectations of "law" within Hellenistic Judaism and the Greco-Roman world of the first-century AD, early Christian literature presents Jesus as God's new lawgiver, teaching with authority, revising, and deepening the law of Moses. Among the Gospels, this vision of Jesus as a new Moses is most pronounced in the Gospel of Matthew, and particularly in the Sermon on the Mount, where the literary echoes of the Sinai event are most clearly sounded in Jesus' self-revelation: "Do not think that I have come to abolish the Law or the Prophets; I have not come to abolish them but to fulfill them "(Matt 5.17; cf. John 13.34). The nature of this fulfillment is not just an interiorizing and intensification of the Mosaic Law or its traditional interpretation—e.g., "you have heard it said…, but I say to you…." (e.g., Matt 5.21–22, etc.), but is also the introduction of Jesus' authority and his replacement of the law's authority in areas as diverse as anger, marriage, oaths, charity, and prayer. Jesus' fulfillment of the law is therefore seen both in his reinterpretation of the Mosaic law and his re-presentation of it as Christ's law in the kingdom God.

This two-way fulfillment as both a finalizing and new expression of the Mosaic law is evident in the apostle Paul's description of the relationship between Jesus and the law in Romans 10.4: "For Christ is the end (*telos*) of the law for righteousness to everyone who believes." In this verse and in the immediate context of Romans 10, the principles and the purpose of the law are seen to conclude and culminate with a "righteousness based on faith" that believes in Jesus (Rom 10.6–13), but also in an obedience of faith that comes in response to "the word of Christ" (Rom 10.17). This is one of several Pauline texts that point to a new word or commandment, which is not given from Sinai, but by Jesus and his apostles (e.g., Phil 2.16; Col 3.16; 1 Tim 4.6; 6.3, 14). This new word is the object of faith in the sense of allegiance to King Jesus: "everyone who calls on the name of the Lord will be saved" (Rom 10.13).[5]

What does this mean? Is the word of Christ limited to the message that God raised him from the dead and there is salvation in this? Some commentators limit the "word of Christ" to the "kerygma," that is, the basic message of the identity of Jesus and the salvation in this. Beyond this concept of a saving word or salvific message, Paul in Romans expands the expression(s) of faith to the concept of a "law of faith" that stipulates what God considers and makes right or righteous: "Then what becomes of our boasting? It is excluded. By what kind of law? By a law of works? No, but by the law of faith" (Rom 3.27). This concept of a law of faith is opposed to a "law of works," and so it remains to be seen in what sense this opposition

---

[5] For a helpful investigation of "faith" in the New Testament as including allegiance to Jesus as Lord, including works of obedience, see Matthew W. Bates, *Salvation by Allegiance Alone: Rethinking Faith, Works, and the Gospel of Jesus the King* (Grand Rapids: Baker, 2017). See especially his treatment of the law of Christ: "The 'law of Christ' (and the like) is spoken of in a positive fashion because *pistis* is not fundamentally opposed to all law but involves enacted obedience to the wise rule that Jesus the king both embodies and institutes" (86–87). I am in general agreement with this interpretation.

exists. Does "law of works" signify the Mosaic law as a whole and so all efforts to obey law? Or is it only those boundary requirements of the Mosaic law that most distinguish the Jews as a people from others (e.g., circumcision)? This latter viewpoint is the position taken by proponents of "The New Perspective on Paul," which is a modern school of thought that restores at least some second-century Christian understandings of the law and works in the scheme of God's offer of salvation.[6] Although the exact identity of the "law of works" is debated, the connection of the new "law of faith" to the power of God through Jesus is evidence of a new law operative in the lives of Christians under a new covenant. This is seen in other Pauline references to law: "For the law of the Spirit of life has set you free in Christ Jesus from the law of sin and death" (Rom 8.2). Here, akin to Ezekiel's prophetic promise of a new spirit and freedom from a heart of stone, Paul correlates the giving of a "law of the Spirit" to faith in Christ and to freedom from the old law. In what sense then have Christians been given a new law?

## Like Paul, we are Free from Law, but under Law

It seems clear that this new law goes beyond the "basic message" of the gospel to define the life lived as a Christian. One of the most insightful contrasts in the New Testament between the new and old laws is seen in Paul's self-description of his protean approach to evan-

---

[6] The classic exposition of this perspective, which varies significantly across its main representatives, is E. P. Sanders, *Paul and Palestinian Judaism: A Comparison of Patterns of Religion* (Philadelphia: Fortress Press, 1977). Common among most expounders of this "New Perspective" is a delimited understanding of what is meant by Paul when he refers to works of the law. Sanders, for example, tends to limit it to circumcision, rules governing eating, and observance of the sabbath. Other major scholars holding this view (e.g., James Dunn and N.T. Wright) agree with Sanders, in contrast to the "Old View of Paul" (e.g., held by Luther, Bultmann, and Moo) that Paul does not generally oppose good works of the law to faith in Jesus Christ, but rather opposes only those works of the Mosaic Law that signified one's membership in God's chosen people, the Jews. An argument that this is the primary viewpoint of Christians in the second century is made by Matthew J. Thomas, *Paul's "Works of the Law" in the Perspective of Second-Century Reception* (Downers Grove: IVP Academic, 2020).

gelism, in which he adapts himself to the needs and demands of his audiences, so that they might hear and accept the gospel:

> To the Jews I became as a Jew, in order to win Jews. To those under the law I became as one under the law (though not being myself under the law) that I might win those under the law. To those outside the law I became as one outside the law (not being outside the law of God but under the law of Christ) that I might win those outside the law (1 Cor 9.20–21).

Here is there is clear contrast between Paul not being under the law of Jews, but being under the law of God, which is the law of Christ. Paul does not elaborate on the meaning of "the law of Christ" in the immediate context of 1 Corinthians 9, but the parallelism of the passage above indicates that living as a Jew under the law of Moses is comparable to a Christian living under the law of Christ. The one is a law not applicable to the Christian but of importance to those who might become Christians (hence Paul's willingness to "become as a Jew"). The other, the law of Christ, is applicable to the Christian, but a significant enough barrier to the gospel among Gentiles that Paul became as one not under this law of God in Christ. Whatever its content, this law of Christ replaces the law of Moses in the life of Paul and constitutes "the law of God" for the Christian.

## The Law of Christ is a Law of Love, and More

This "law of Christ" is described elsewhere in the New Testament but never with clear definition of its content.[7] Most similar to 1 Corinthians 9 is Galatians 6.2. In the preceding verse the "spiritual" Christian is instructed to restore the one caught in sin and to do it with a spirit of gentleness (Gal 6.1). This leads to the instruction, "Bear one another's burdens, and so fulfill the law of Christ" (Gal 6.2). How does bearing burdens fulfill the law of Christ? Bearing

---

[7] One limited, but suggestive, effort to define the "law of Christ" along the lines that I identify here is Brian S. Rosner, *Paul and the Law: Keeping the Commandments of God*, NSBT 31 (Downers Grove: Intervarsity, 2013), 111–134.

burdens may be seen as a loving act that fulfills the law that "You shall love your neighbor as yourself" (Lev 19.18), which earlier in the letter Paul describes as fulfilling the whole law (Gal 4.14) and connects to serving one another (4.13). Though the command in Leviticus 19.18 is not identified as the law of Christ, it is cited by Jesus as one of the greatest commandments (Mark 12.31, etc.), and is like the "new command... that you love one another: just as I have loved you, you also are to love one another" (John 13.34; cf. 1 John 4.21). This association of love with fulfillment of the Mosaic law and the command of Christ is seen again in Paul's command to "Owe no one anything, except to love each other, for the one who loves another has fulfilled the law" (Rom 13.8).

This close association of the law of Christ with the command to love neighbor and one another leads commentators to focus the identity of the law of Christ on the love injunction. This is an association that seems to be strengthened by the use of the term "law" in the book of James, where references to "the royal law" associated with Leviticus 19.18 are seemingly applicable to Christians: "If you really fulfill the royal law according to the Scripture, 'You shall love your neighbor as yourself,' you are doing well" (Jam 2.8). As in Paul, this law applicable to Christians is contrasted to the law of Moses, termed "the whole law":

> But if you show partiality, you are committing sin and are convicted by the law as transgressors. For whoever keeps the whole law but fails in one point has become guilty of all of it. For he who said, "Do not commit adultery," also said, "Do not murder." If you do not commit adultery but do murder, you have become a transgressor of the law. So speak and so act as those who are to be judged under the law of liberty. For judgment is without mercy to one who has shown no mercy. Mercy triumphs over judgment (Jam 2.9–13).

Here, in contrast to the impossibly judgmental and guilt-laden "whole law" of Moses, there is a "law of liberty" applicable to

Christians and governing their lives, a law that shows mercy, including the impartiality towards the poor that is the issue throughout the first half of the second chapter of James. The "law of liberty" in James therefore extends the love commands from the Mosaic Law and from Jesus' teaching to a broader set of stipulations in the New Testament. James' phrase "law of liberty" (1.25; 2.12) not only applies to a broader injunction to be impartial to the poor, but is used more broadly in the first chapter in a series of ethical injunctions to know and obey "the implanted word that is able to save your souls" (1.21). In James 1.22–25, this saving word and its reading and doing is directly connected to looking at and doing "the perfect law (*teleion nomon*), the law of liberty" (v. 25), which is extended to such actions as self-control in speech, care for the widows and orphans, and abstinence from worldly pursuit (vv. 26–27). Here and elsewhere in James (e.g., 4.11–12), obedience to the law is a positive action accompanying and effecting the Christian's salvation and includes more than "love" in even a general sense.[8] Rather, it more broadly describes a rule for Christian faithfulness that is inclusive of vices to avoid (e.g., evil speaking, 4.11), but also virtues to enact (e.g., good speech, 1.26).

The book of James opens for us the broader sense of "the law" that God has given to Christians to obey through faith in Jesus. Whether termed the "law of faith," "the law of Christ," or "the perfect law, the law of liberty," this set of norms describes moral and ethical stipulations that are centered on, but not exclusive to, the love commands. What emerges from these "law" passages in the New Testament is the portrait of commands and examples that together constitute a pattern of precepts for Christians to obey in faithful allegiance to Jesus Christ. As such, the law of Christ concludes, but also fulfills and continues the law of Moses in providing instructions for how to maintain God's presence in the life of his people, both individually

---

[8] For a similar interpretation of these passages on law in James, see Douglas J. Moo, *The Letter of James*, PNTC (Grand Rapids: Eerdmans, 2000), 94, 112.

and collectively. Of course, the life- and law-changing difference is the man Jesus Christ, who is himself both the law—himself the pattern of good works—and the deliverer of this law through his teachings and those of his apostles by revelation through the Holy Spirit.

Although not explicitly terming it "law," the writings of Paul describe a set of apostolic instructions that were consistently taught as replacement for the Mosiac law. The Greek word used for these instructions is *typos*, which conveys the idea of a standard or pattern of teaching. The relationship of this normative Christian instruction to the Mosaic Law is stated in Romans 6.15–17: "What then? Are we to sin because we are not under law but under grace? By no means! ... thanks be to God, that you who were once slaves of sin have become obedient from the heart to the standard of teaching *(typon didachēs)* to which you were committed." This standard of teaching is not primarily about works of the law, but about servitude to God through faith in his son and the power of God's Spirit, which nevertheless manifests itself in obedience to a type of teaching, which later in the letter is termed "the law of the Spirit of life" (Rom 8.2).

Elsewhere in Paul's letters a similar phrase is used to describe the apostolic teachings that express and enact faith in Jesus and the power of the Holy Spirit: "Follow the pattern of the sound words *(hypotypōsin hygiainontōn logōn)* that you have heard from me, in the faith and love that are in Christ Jesus. By the Holy Spirit who dwells within us, guard the good deposit entrusted to you" (2 Tim 1.13–14). Like his own life, which Paul later describes as a pattern or "example" *(hypotypōsis)* of God's salvation in Christ for everyone else (v. 16), Paul's instruction to Timothy provides for healthy teaching that is to be preserved and taught to others. Understood in this way as a spoken and written standard for "faith and love in Christ Jesus" (v. 13), the words of Paul serve as normative instruction that is a type of law for Christians. The pattern of his words is a regulative wisdom for spiritual health and soundness coming both through "faith and love in Christ Jesus" (v. 13), and "by the Holy Spirit" (v. 14). This "pattern" therefore should be understood as a law of Christ, a law of faith, a law of the Spirit, and a perfect law of liberty leading to love and life. Paul's description of the pattern of faith communicated through his example and instructions is, therefore, a reference to the norms of Christian life that are elsewhere described as "law" with various qualifiers (Christ, Spirit, faith, liberty, etc.,) all of which indicates this new law's place in the new covenant.

There is then a progressive development in the giving and application of God's law across the Mosaic and Christian covenants. The law at Sinai, though distinctive to its ancient context in form and function, both points forward to and is fulfilled in the new covenant law of Jesus Christ. Predicted by Jeremiah, Ezekiel, and other Old Testament prophets, the new covenant is not distinguished by the precedence of divine grace. Both the Mosaic and Christian laws and covenants—and their different relationships to God—were gifts of divine love. Nor are the two laws distinguished by the presence of written instructions as conditions of divine presence within chosen individuals and communities, whether Israel or the Church. Both laws contain written words to be examined, remembered, and obeyed both for blessing, and for avoidance of divine punishment.

The difference between the two covenants and their corresponding laws is Jesus Christ. Because of God's loving justice in Jesus, it is our faith's obedience by the Spirit working in us for loving allegiance to Christ our Lord that brings a salvation springing up into eternity. This is the new, spiritual covenant through Christ's blood, and the law of faith by which we live in Christ. This law of Christ is centered on love, but has a circumference extending to every word of the new covenant as revealed by the Spirit through Jesus and his apostles. This revelation is the Word of God in His Son and the writings of the new covenant. The scope of the law of the Spirit, therefore, is the scripture inspired by God.

The line running from Sinai to the Son is, therefore, marked by both continuity and discontinuity, fulfillment, and finality. The giving of the law at Sinai was a wisdom for maintaining a pattern of worship and life that led to God's presence and glory in this life. Moses' law was superseded by a law of Christ empowered by His love and Spirit. Now the law and the covenant find their highest goal not only in this life's praise of the divine glory, but also as our blessed part in the life of divine glory to come.

# God Declares a New Name for Himself

## Marc Hinds

"They beheld God, and they ate and drank" (Exod 24.11). On Mount Sinai, the leaders of Israel—Moses, Aaron, Nadab and Abihu, and seventy elders—gazed upon "the God of Israel." He stood before them on a resplendent pavement of blue sapphire atop the mountain. The surface beneath him shined like a dazzlingly bright blue sky. These seventy-four men prostrated themselves before God's presence. Then they participated in a ceremonial meal with God, ratifying the covenant he had made with them (Exod 24.9–11).

Soon after this covenant ceremony, Moses ascended the mountain again. Over a period of forty days, he received detailed instructions for the construction of a tabernacle, a portable temple-like structure which would facilitate God's presence among his covenant people (Exod 24.12–31.17). At the end of the forty days, God gave Moses two stone tablets (Exod 31.18). The Ten Commandments, which were written on these tablets by "the finger of God" (cf. Deut 9.10; see also Exod 34.28), were intended to be placed inside the tabernacle (cf. Deut 10.5), solidifying the covenant between God and his people. But the tablets never made it. Instead, after coming down the mountain, Moses in a fit of anger threw them down, shattering them into pieces (Exod 32.19).

### Israel Worships the Golden Calf (Exod 32.1–6)

Prior to ascending Mount Sinai to receive God's instructions and the tablets of stone, Moses had designated Aaron as the people's temporary leader in his absence (Exod 24.14). But the longer Moses stayed away, the more anxious this nation of freed slaves must have grown. They turned to Aaron, demanding that he assist them in the construction of an idol:

> "Make us some gods who can lead us. As for this Moses, the man who brought us up out of the land of Egypt, we do not know what has become of him." So Aaron said to them, "Take off the rings of gold that are in the ears of your wives, your sons, and your daughters, and bring them to me" (Exod 32.1–2).[1]

He used the gold to fashion a golden calf. When the idol was completed, the people declared, "These are your gods, Israel, who brought you up out of the land of Egypt" (Exod 32.4).[2] Aaron also built an altar and, on the following day, used it to lead the nation in sacrifices to the golden calf. In some perverted way, Aaron wanted the worship of the golden calf to honor God. And yet, the celebratory feast that ensued did not resemble worship at all: "The people sat down to eat and drink and rose up to play" (Exod 32.6).

The apostle Paul quotes these words and clearly identifies this decadent charade of "worship" for the idolatry it really is: "Do not be idolaters as some of them were; as it is written, 'The people sat down to eat and drink and rose up to play'" (1 Cor 10.7). Similarly, Psalm 106 affirms in its historical commentary that ancient Israel's worship of the golden calf caused their inherent glory of being created in God's image to be swapped for "the image of an ox that eats grass:"

> They made a calf in Horeb [Mount Sinai]
>> and worshiped a metal image.
> They exchanged the glory of God
>> for the image of an ox that eats grass.

---

[1] Unless noted otherwise, all quotations of scripture are from the ESV.

[2] Both the terms "these" and "gods (Heb. *'elohim*)" could be examples of an honorific plural, translated as a singular (e.g., NASB), lending itself to the interpretation that the idol was only intended as a representation of the LORD. In addition, it is clear that Aaron consecrated a feast to the LORD in Exodus 32.5 and Nehemiah's quotation of Exodus 32.4 makes it singular (9.18).

> They forgot God, their Savior,
>> who had done great things in Egypt (Psa 106.19–20)

God's people had broken the covenant they had just made with him (cf. Exod 19.8). In fact, by building this golden calf, they blatantly broke the first several commandments of the Decalogue (cf. Exod 20.1–6). The entire scene degraded as the people sang, danced, and lost control of themselves (see Exod 32.18–19, 25).

## God Reacts to Israel's Sin (Exod 32.7–14)

While conversing with Moses on the mountain, God knew what the people were doing in the camp. "Get down there," he command-ed Moses, "for *your* people have corrupted themselves" (v. 7, empha-sis added).[3] He then labeled Israel as "a stiff-necked people," a bovine trait of the cow they now worshiped (see also Exod 33.3, 5; 34.9). Like wild calves, they had "turned aside quickly out of the way [God] commanded them" (Exod 32.8), "broken loose" (Exod 32.25), and needed to be "gathered" (Exod 32.26).[4]

Immediately, Moses pleaded with God to relent, providing several reasons rooted in his divine character and eternal purposes for Israel.[5]

1. God was the true deliverer (v. 11). It was not Moses who had delivered the nation from Egyptian bondage, but God.

2. Egypt will ridicule God (v. 12). The world's superpower, Egypt, had been thoroughly embarrassed by the unleashing of the ten plagues. Moses will not hear of God giving the Egyptians an opportunity to blaspheme his great name (cf. Num 14.13–16).

3. The promises would be annulled (v. 13). This was not an idle threat on God's part. He had every right to disregard his covenant

---

[3] When God says to Moses, "For your people …" (Exod 32.7), he is reflecting the people's derision of Moses when they said, "As for this Moses …" (Exod 32.1). See also the derogatory uses of "these people" by both God and Moses in Exod 32.9, 21, 31; and 33.12.

[4] G. K. Beale, *We Become What We Worship: A Biblical Theology of Idolatry* (Downers Grove: InterVarsity Press, 2008) 78.

[5] R. W. L. Moberly, *At the Mountain of God: Story and Theology in Exodus 32–34*, JSOT Supplement Series 22 (Sheffield: JSOT Press, 1983) 50.

with Israel, since the nation had so quickly broken it (see Exod 32.8). But Moses appealed to God's covenantal love and loyalty by invoking the names of "Abraham, Isaac, and Israel."

As the nation of Israel's intercessor, Moses averted its annihilation by successfully persuading God to relent (v. 14). The ungrateful Israelites had no idea how close they came to being destroyed.

## Moses Reacts to Israel's Sin (Exod 32.15–29)

Carrying the two stone tablets, Moses made his way toward the base of the mountain. Meeting him along his descent was his loyal assistant Joshua, who exclaimed, "It sounds like war in the camp" (32.17), not knowing the true source of the sounds. But Moses already did. "No," he replied. "It is not the sound of shouting for victory, or the sound of the cry of defeat, but the sound of singing that I hear" (v. 18). Their hearts must have been filled with dread as they anticipated seeing the calamitous chaos in the camp.

After Moses descended the mountain and witnessed firsthand the debauchery of the people by their "worship" of the golden calf, he became incensed. He threw the stone tablets to the ground, smashing them into pieces. On them had been written the Ten Commandments, which represented God's covenant with Israel. But that relationship was now severed by sin, broken and in shambles, just like the stone tablets.

Moses then destroyed the golden calf by burning it, grinding it into powder, and throwing its ashes into a mountain stream. He then forced the people to drink the contaminated water (Exod 32.20). Afterwards, he turned his attention to his brother, Aaron. When confronted by Moses, Aaron blamed the people. He preposterously proposed that, when he tossed the people's gold earrings into the furnace, the calf somehow had emerged on its own (Exod 32.24). But despite his protestations, Aaron was responsible for assisting the people with "a great sin" (Exod 32.21). Without Moses' intercession on his brother's behalf, God would have destroyed Aaron also (see Deut 9.20).

Moses, speaking on God's behalf, said, "Who is on the LORD's side? Come to me" (Exod 32.26). All the Levites answered the call. This was the tribe designated by God to maintain and care for the future tabernacle (Num 1.50). Their task here was to systematically survey the camp and perform a "controlled execution of those clearly guilty."[6] As a result, three thousand Israelites lost their lives.

### Moses Intercedes on Israel's Behalf (Exod 32.30–35)

The worship of the golden calf was "a great sin" and thus entailed serious consequences (Exod 32.21, 30–31).[7] Moses was the only person who could possibly "make atonement for [their] sin" (32.30). He had already persuaded God to relent from destroying the nation completely, but their forgiveness was another matter entirely.

Moses had to be the people's intercessor. There was not, after all, a tabernacle or an ark of the covenant in existence yet. Plans for its construction had been provided (Exod 25.10–22), but it had yet to be produced. (Only later would the high priest be able to offer sacrifices at the tabernacle for the sins of the entire nation.) Additionally, the priesthood itself was in jeopardy since Aaron, with his moral failings, had been chosen by God to be the first high priest (Exod 28.1–4).[8] In his heart, Moses must have feared that the people might not be forgiven. As a result, they would be forever severed from God.

In an emotional appeal, Moses seemingly choked on his words as he appealed to God on Israel's behalf. "But now if you will forgive their sin...," he started to say, but failed to finish his thought (Exod 32.32). Contemplating the possibility that God might not forgive

---

[6] Christopher J. H. Wright, *Exodus*, The Story of God Bible Commentary (Grand Rapids: Zondervan Academic, 2021) 557.

[7] The term "sin" (as both a verb and a noun) occurs eight times in Exod 32.30–34 (vv. 30[3x], 31[2x]; 32, 33, 34).

[8] Similarly, Aaron's sons, Nadab and Abihu, faced God's wrath as well. These two men had accompanied Moses and Aaron when they met with God atop Mount Sinai (Exod 24.9). But that honor did not exempt them from God's future judgment. Nadab and Abihu were consumed with fire because they offered "unauthorized fire" on the altar during the tabernacle's dedication ceremony (Lev 10.1–2).

them proved too much for Moses, causing him to pause before completing his intercessory request. When he resumed, Moses then made a remarkable demand. "But if not, erase my name out of your book you have written!" By saying this, he was "not offering to die *for* the people but asking to die *with* the people."[9] For us as Christians, we can readily see a contrast between Moses and our intercessor Jesus. We know that as an imperfect human Moses could not possibly have removed the people's guilt. Thankfully Jesus the sinless Son of God was able to die for our sins, and he did so willingly (Rom 5.6–11). Jesus our Savior "bore the sin of many, and [made] intercession for the transgressors" (Isaiah 53.12).

The severity of God's anger over the construction and worship of the golden calf cannot be overestimated. It was mentioned again in the last verse of Exodus 32, along with Aaron's role in its construction (v. 35). At the start of ch. 33, God again labeled the people with the bovine moniker—"a stiff-necked people"[10]—as he told them more devastating news: his plans about the tabernacle had now changed.

Ancient Israel failed to learn from the golden calf disaster. Five hundred years later, King Jeroboam I of the Northern Kingdom of Israel set up two golden calves at Dan and Bethel, the northernmost and southernmost points of his kingdom. Mirroring the same language of the exodus generation, Jeroboam exhorted the people to worship these golden calves: "Behold your gods, Israel, who brought you up out of the land of Egypt" (1 Kings 12.28; cf. Exod 32.4). Now almost three millennia later, we as 21st century Christians are in just as much danger as ancient Israel. We would like to think that we are far too sophisticated and would never worship an idol, but anytime we "[exchange] the truth about God for a lie and [worship]

---

[9] Wright 559, emphasis in the original.

[10] In Exod 32–34, this expression "stiff-necked people" is applied to the nation four times (Exod 32.9; 33.3, 5; 34.9). It is used similarly throughout the Old Testament, describing Israel's rebelliousness and stubbornness (Deut 9.6, 13; 31.27; 2 Kng 17.14; 2 Chr 36.13; Jer 17.23; 19.15; Neh 9.16–17, 29; see also Acts 7.51). It is often translated as "stubborn."

and [serve] the creature rather than the Creator," we find ourselves just as guilty (Rom 1.25). The more we let the world into our lives, the less we will resemble Jesus.

## God's Presence Will Not Travel with Israel (Exod 33.1–6)

When Israel first arrived at Mount Sinai, God had intended for Israel to build the tabernacle "that I may dwell in their midst" (Exod 25.8). After the sin of the golden calf, however, he no longer planned to travel in their midst:[11] "I will not go up among you, lest I consume you on the way, for you are a stiff-necked people" (Exod 33.3). The detailed blueprints provided in Exod 25–31 apparently would no longer be necessary. God was not able to dwell among a people so rebellious and bent on sin. In his holiness, he would be unable to constrain himself from destroying them. When the people heard this, however, they mourned and showed genuine signs of repentance (Exod 33.4, 6).

God's words at the end of Exod 33.5 make us wonder what will happen next. Not on speaking terms with Israel, God commanded the people through Moses to "Take off your ornaments, that I may know what to do with you." The narrative leaves us hanging, wondering what God will do with his rebellious people, Israel.

## God's Presence Will Travel with Israel (Exod 33.7–17)

Thus far through the narrative, the detailed events have happened quickly (Exod 32.1–33.6). Beginning in Exod 33.7, the narrative slows down. This is achieved by providing a flashback to an earlier time when Moses had erected a tent outside the Israelite camp that served as a makeshift tabernacle called "the tent of meeting."[12] With

---

[11] John N. Oswalt, "Exodus," in Philip W. Comfort, ed., *Genesis and Exodus*, Cornerstone Biblical Commentary 1 (Carol Stream: Tyndale House, 2008) 529. See also John H. Sailhamer, *The Pentateuch as Narrative: A Biblical-Theological Commentary*, Library of Biblical Interpretation (Grand Rapids: Zondervan, 1992) 314.

[12] Later, the actual tabernacle will also be referred to as "the tent of meeting" (e.g., Exod 40.2; Lev 1.1). But this is not the same structure for two reasons: (a)

many of the Israelites looking on, he would enter the tent and "the LORD used to speak to Moses face to face, as a man speaks to his friend" (Exod 33.11).[13] Obviously, this language is figurative, since no human being can survive seeing God's essence (see Exod 33.20, 23). Rather, this is an expression that denotes the closeness of Moses' relationship with God.

But this time, while sitting inside this tent, Moses was not feeling like he was God's friend. That is because Moses did not feel particularly close to him at that moment. Instead, he was bewildered and confused:

> Moses said to the LORD, "See, you say to me, 'Bring up this people,' but you have not let me know whom you will send with me. Yet you have said, 'I know you by name, and you have also found favor in my sight.' Now therefore, if I have found favor in your sight, please show me now your ways, that I may know you in order to find favor in your sight. Consider too that this nation is your people" (Exod 33.12–13).

Moses asked God, "Show me your ways." In other words, "If I am really the chosen leader of your people, then you must let me know who will travel with us." In his response, God uses the term "presence," which is also used in v. 11 and is the normal Hebrew word for "face:" "My presence (or "face") will go with you, and I will give you rest" (Exod 33.14). In Exod 32.15–16, Moses expanded on this request by repeating the term again: "If your presence (or "face") will not go with me, do not bring us up from here." Moses insisted that God's presence must go with them, otherwise "do not make us leave from here." What made Israel unique as a nation is God's presence. Without it, Israel was no different from any other nation "on the

---

the tabernacle is not built until later in Exodus 35–40; and (b) this first "tent of meeting" is pitched outside the camp rather than its center, as the later tabernacle would be (Num 2.2).

[13] The noun "face" is used several times in Exod 33.11–23. In many English translations, "face" is translated as "presence" in vv. 14–15. Daniel I. Block, *Covenant: The Framework of God's Grand Plan of Redemption* (Grand Rapids: Baker Academic, 2021) 176.

presence (or "face") of the earth" (Exod 33.16). In his response, God assures Moses that he had listened to him and was responding to his request by repeating the very words used by Moses in his request: "This very thing that you have spoken I will do, for you have found favor in my sight, and I know you by name" (Exod 33.17).

| The Requests of Moses in Exodus 32–34 | | | |
|---|---|---|---|
| Moses' request | Citation | God's Response | Citation |
| 1. "Relent from this disaster" | Exod 32.11–13 | He relents | Exod 32.14 |
| 2. "Forgive their sin" | Exod 32.30–32 | He punishes only the guilty with a plague | Exod 32.33–35 |
| 3. "Show me now your ways" | Exod 33.12–13 | "My presence will go with you" | Exod 33.14 |
| 4. "If your face/ presence will not go with me, do not bring us up from here" | Exod 33.15–16 | "[Everything you ask] I will do" | Exod 33.17 |
| 5. "Show me your glory" | Exod 33.18 | "The LORD, The LORD, merciful and gracious ..." | Exod 34.6–7 |
| 6. "Let the Lord go in the midst of us" | Exod 34.8–9 | He reestablishes the covenant | Exod 34.10–28 |

Table 1

This was now the fourth time God had acquiesced to Moses' pleadings (see Table 1). First, God promised not to destroy the nation and start over with Moses (Exod 32.14). Then, he agreed to forgive the nation and only punish the guilty (Exod 32.33–35). And finally, he promised that his "presence" will be with Israel and do everything Moses has asked of him (Exod 33.14, 17). God has patiently interacted with Israel's intercessor, speaking with Moses "as a man speaks to his friend" (see Exod 33.11).

### God Shows Moses His Glory (Exod 33.18–34.7)

But Moses was not finished yet and makes another request: "Please show me your glory" (Exod 33.18). By asking to see God's glory, Moses went a step beyond requesting forgiveness for Israel. Moses wants God to dwell among Israel, just like he promised earlier in Exod 29.43–46. While Moses was receiving the instructions for the construction of the tabernacle prior to the golden calf incident, God had told Moses that he would "meet with the people of Israel" and "[the tabernacle] shall be sanctified by my *glory*" (Exod 29.43; emphasis added). He made this promise, too: "I will dwell among the people of Israel and will be their God" (Exod 29.45).

After the disastrous worship of the golden calf, the covenant was broken; and this promise's fulfillment was in jeopardy. Moses knew Israel did not deserve this second chance. Even after the covenant was renewed, it would not be possible for Israel to keep the covenant perfectly. Despite the danger of future sinful acts provoking God's righteous anger against Israel, Moses wanted God to keep his promise that his glory would dwell among his people.

Israel's entrance into the Promised Land will not be the result of sinless obedience to the covenant. In his answer to Moses' request, God acknowledges that his relationship with Israel will only be possible by his grace and mercy: "I will make all my goodness pass before you and will proclaim before you my name 'The LORD.' And I will be gracious to whom I will be gracious, and will show mercy on whom I will show mercy" (Exod 33.19).

But what is God's "glory" (33.18) and what does God's answer have to do with his glory (33.19)? God's words imply that his glory is defined as his divine attributes, particularly his "goodness, graciousness, and compassion."[14] God will further define his character in Exod 34.6–7 as "merciful and gracious, slow to anger, and abounding in steadfast love and faithfulness." He will also describe his "goodness" in terms of forgiveness of sin without nullifying punishment for sin. All these qualities are on full display in Exod 32–34 as God deals with the sin of his wayward people with righteous judgment and love. He condemns them for the sinful idolatry and punishes the guilty, but lavishes his grace, mercy, and compassion on his people, despite their shortcomings and failures.

In addition to hearing this sublime description of God's goodness, Moses is also permitted to see it. Although God will make all his "goodness" pass right in front of Moses, he will not permit him to see his "presence/face," because no human being can see God's "face" and live (Exod 33.20). Instead, in this enigmatic and beautiful scene, God promised to place Moses in a cleft of a rock atop Mount Sinai and to cover him with the palm of his "hand." Only after God's presence had passed would he remove his "hand," allowing Moses to see his "back" (Exod 33.23).[15]

In Exod 34.1–4, the two stone tablets are remade. Like other ancient covenants of the 15th century B.C., the ruling king who authored a covenant required that the agreement between both parties be permanently represented in written form. These two stone tablets represented the covenant between God and Israel. No longer smashed and crumbled, both the covenant and the tablets are whole again.

In Exod 34.5–9, as God's presence descends upon Mount Sinai, the climax of the narrative unfolds. This is now the third time in Ex-

---

[14] Beale 89.

[15] "Hand" denotes the palm of a person's hand. This is an affectionate description of God gently covering Moses to protect him. The term "back" is not the usual word for a person's back, but rather refers to someone's (or something's) backside (e.g., the tabernacle's backside, Exod 26.12). This is anthropomorphic language being used to depict God's glorious presence passing before Moses.

odus that God has descended and spoken with Moses at this mountain (see Table 2). At the base of the mountain, God had appeared to Moses in a burning bush. He spoke to him from the bush and revealed his covenantal name, "the Lord" (Exod 3.13–15). Now, he calls it out again: "The Lord descended in the cloud and stood with him there, and proclaimed the name of the Lord" (Exod 34.5). Moses' extended intercession of Exod 32–34 has now taken us back to when he was initially commissioned in Exod 3–4, just several months prior. Standing before the burning bush, Moses had made numerous excuses to deflect God's command to represent Israel in Egypt (Exod 3.11, 13; 4.1, 10, 13). Now, the roles have been reversed. Having grown exponentially in his relationship with God, Moses finds himself convincing God to take back his "excuses" for rejecting Israel.

Before Israel worshiped the golden calf, God had called them "my people." After the golden calf, Moses pled with God to accept them again as his own covenant people.[16] In his answer, he made it clear that he had, by his grace and mercy, renewed his relationship with Israel:

> The Lord passed before him and proclaimed, "The Lord, the Lord, a God merciful and gracious, slow to anger, and abounding in steadfast love and faithfulness, keeping steadfast love for thousands, forgiving iniquity and transgression and sin, but who will by no means clear the guilty, visiting the iniquity of the fathers on the children and the children's children, to the third and the fourth generation" (Exod 34.6–7).

In Exod 34.6, he revealed his glory by describing his divine character, starting with his divine name: the Lord. Repeated for emphasis the name is then described by several sublime terms contained in three verbless clauses.

---

[16] "This nation is your people," Moses had just said (Exod 33.13). Prior to Exod 32–34, God had referred to Israel frequently as "my people" (Exod 3.7, 10; 5.1; 6.7; 7.4, 16; 8.1, 8, 20–23; 9.1, 13, 17, 27; 10.3–4; 12.31; 22.25). He never does again in Exodus, however; and he only refers to them as "your people" twice (Exod 32.7; 34.10).

| Three Theophanies at Mount Sinai in Exodus | | | |
|---|---|---|---|
| Occasion | Witness | Description | Citation |
| 1. The burning bush | Moses | "I have come down to deliver [Israel] out of the hand of the Egyptians" | Exod 3.8; cf. Gen 46.4 |
| 2. The establishment of the covenant with Israel | Moses and all Israel | "The LORD will come down on Mount Sinai in the sight of all the people" | Exod 19.11, 18, 20; see also Exod 24.9–11; cf. Neh 9.13 |
| 3. The renewal of the covenant with Israel | Moses | The LORD descended in the cloud and stood with [Moses] there | Exod 34.5 |

Table 2

"A God merciful and gracious." These adjectives are near synonyms and describe God's compassion. Because they sound rhythmically similar to each other (*raḥûm* and *ḥannûn*), they add a poetic flare to God's self-description. They often appear together in the Old Testament and are always describing God.[17]

"Slow to anger." This expression describes God's patience.[18] It was also used earlier to describe both God's loss of patience with Israel (Exod 32.10–12) as well as Moses' (Exod 32.19, 22). Although God is compassionate and slow to anger, he obviously can lose patience with sinful humanity.

---

[17] "Gracious and merciful" are used together in eleven verses across the Old Testament (Exod 34.6; 2 Chron 30.9; Neh 9.17, 31; Pss 86.15; 103.8; 111.4; 112.4; 145.8; Joel 2.13; Jonah 4.2). Each of these references is alluding to Exod 34.6. See also James 5.11, which alludes to this pair of terms as well.

[18] The Septuagint translated this phrase using the Greek term *makrothumos*,

"And abounding in steadfast love and faithfulness." A pair of additional nouns describe God's character. The first, "steadfast love," is a theologically rich term that is variously translated by our English versions.[19] Its companion noun, "faithfulness," denotes trustworthiness and reliability. These two terms often appear as a pair in the Old Testament.[20]

Three participial phrases—which start with "keeping," "forgiving," and "visiting"—further define his character in Exod 34.7:

1. "Keeping steadfast love for thousands." The term "steadfast love" (see Exod 34.6) is repeated and applied to "thousands." Most likely, this is not referring to thousands of individuals, but generations (cf. Exod 20.5–6), as reflected in our English versions.

2. "Forgiving iniquity and transgression and sin." The participle "forgiving" appeared earlier in Exod 32.32. Literally, it denotes "carrying" the sins of the people. This is the verb used to describe the "scapegoat" that would "bear" the sins of the people outside the camp on the Day of Atonement (Lev 16.22). These three nouns—"iniquity," "transgression," and "sin"—are virtually synonymous.

3. "Visiting the iniquity of the fathers on the children …" This final phrase shares similar language with the Second Commandment (Exod 20.5–6; see also Num 14.18; Deut 5.9). As a retribution formula, it specifies the seriousness of sinful behavior. The consequences of sin can affect several generations. This is certainly true of the southern kingdom of Judah, who suffered Babylonian captivity for a period of 70 years, which would be roughly equivalent to three or four generations. But the three or four generations pales in comparison with the thousands of generations that are the beneficiaries of

whose cognate is often translated in the New Testament as "long-suffering" or "patience" (e.g., Rom 2.4; 9.22; 1 Cor 13.4; Gal 5.22; Eph 4.2; Col 1.11; 3.12).

[19] In Exod 34.6, the Hebrew term *ḥesed* is translated in numerous ways: "goodness" (KJV, NKJV), "lovingkindness" (ASV, NASB95), "faithfulness" (NASB20) "faithful love" (CSB), "love" (NIV), "steadfast love" (RSV, NRSV, ESV), "loyal love" (NET), "unfailing love" (NLT).

[20] King David was fond of this word pair, using it in several of his psalms (Pss 25.10; 26.3; 40.10–11; 57.3, 10; 61.7; 69.13; 86.15; 108.4; 138.2).

God's compassion and mercy. In addition, it is by God's mercy that he places a limit upon the devastating effects of our sin.

| Repeated Elements of the Covenant Renewal | | |
|---|---|---|
| Description | First Covenant Citation | Second Covenant Citation |
| 1. God gave Moses instructions for the people to obey. | Exod 20–23 | Exod 34.10–26 |
| 2. God's glory appeared with the leader(s) of Israel. | Exod 24.1–17 | Exod 34.28; cf. Exod 34.31 |
| 3. Moses was with the LORD for "forty days and forty nights" atop Mount Sinai. | Exod 24.18 | Exod 34.28 |
| 4. The two stone tablets with the Ten Commandments written on them were restored. | Exod 31.18 | Exod 34.28 |
| 5. The Sabbath was consecrated. | Exod 31.12–17 | Exod 35.1–3 |

Table 3

## God Renews the Covenant (Exod 34.8–28)

What would you do in the face of such a magnificent display of God's power and love? Moses responded with humility and awe. He bowed his head and worshiped (Ex 34.8; cf. Exod 4.31; 12.27). Moses then made one final request: "If now I have found favor in your sight, O Lord, please let the Lord go in the midst of us, for it is a stiff-necked people, and pardon our iniquity and our sin, and take us for your inheritance" (Exod 34.9). Moses used two phrases that appeared earlier in Exod 33: (a) he prefaced his request with the phrase "if I have found favor in your sight," as he had previously (v. 16); and (b) he applied the metaphor "stiff-necked people" to Israel, which God had used three times previously to deride Israel's resemblance to the golden calf they worshiped (Exod 32.9; 33.5, 9). However, Moses' use of this bovine metaphor is the opposite of God's original use of it. God used it to explain why he could no longer dwell among his people, but Moses turned its original purpose around when he asked God to dwell among his people *because* they were "a stiff-necked people."

In Exod 34.10–28, God answered Moses in the affirmative by renewing the covenant. Several elements of the previous covenant ratification were repeated, including the stone tablets (see Table 3). As Israel's intercessor, Moses was successful. Without their great leader, the nation of Israel would not have been able to be corralled and redirected on the path leading to God's love and mercy.

## The Shining Face of Moses (Exod 34.29–35)

After spending another forty days with God atop Mount Sinai, Moses finally returned to the Israelite camp. This time, however, something was different about him: Moses' face radiated brightly.[21] This apparently did not happen after his first forty-day visit with God. What caused this change in his appearance was spending time with the LORD and being shown his glory.

"Show me your glory," Moses had asked God (Exod 33.18), because he wanted all Israel to witness God's glorious presence again. They did not get to see it, though, except as a reflection on the face of Moses.[22] When they saw Moses' face, they were afraid to come near him (Exod 34.30), even having him cover his face with a veil to obscure God's glory reflected on his face. Thus, this rebellious generation of Israelites saw only a reflection of God's glory on Moses' face.

---

[21] The term "face," which was used prominently in Exod 33.11–23 of God's face, is used six times in Exod 34.29–35 of Moses' face (Exod 34.29, 30, 33, 35[3x]).

[22] Sailhamer 314–315.

This closing section of the golden calf narrative makes a brilliant play on the verb "to shine." This word appears commonly in the Old Testament as a noun and means "horn." Over 70 times in the Old Testament, this noun refers to literal horns of animals or is used symbolically to denote power or authority. In this rare instance when it is used as a verb, it means "to shine."[23] This play on words in Exod 34.29–35 is intentional, of course. As a bovine feature, it reminds us of the golden calf and the stiff-necked Israelites who resembled what they worshiped with their stubbornness and rebelliousness. In contrast with them, God's leader resembled God with his "horned" face that glowed with God's glory.

## Two New Testament Uses of Exodus 32–34

It is impossible to underestimate the importance of Exodus 32–34. They are quoted and alluded to throughout both the Old and New Testaments. As we close, we will briefly consider two New Testament passages that apply them to Jesus our Lord: Stephen's speech in Acts 7 and the Gospel of John.[24]

### Jesus, the New Moses (Acts 7.39–53)

In the closing verses of Deuteronomy, Moses is described as the only leader "whom the LORD knew face to face" (Deut 34.10; Num 12.7–8; cf. Exod 33.11). Moses predicted, however, that one day there would be another prophet who would eclipse him (Deut 18.15–18). During Stephen's defense before the Sanhedrin Council, Stephen

---

[23] The connection between "a horn" (noun) and "to shine" (verb) can be illustrated by 1 Chron 25.5, in which the literal phrase "to lift up the horn [of someone]" (KJV) is paraphrased as "to exalt his horn" (NKJV) or "to exalt him" (ESV, NASB, NIV).

In the Latin Vulgate Jerome (d. A.D. 420) translated the Hebrew verb "to shine" as "to horn," indicating that Moses' face grew horns. Influenced by the Latin Vulgate's rendering of Exod 34.29–30, the Italian sculptor Michelangelo (1475–1564) created his famous marble statue of Moses with horns projecting out of his head.

[24] Another significant use of Exodus 32–34 in the New Testament is Paul's application of Exodus 34.29–35 in 2 Corinthians 3.7–16, where he laments the unbelief of Jews in his day who refused to accept Jesus as Messiah.

clearly identified Jesus as the fulfillment of Moses' prediction. Jesus is this future prophet who was greater than Moses. Jesus not only knew God "face to face," but was himself God (cf. 2 Cor 4.4; Col 1.15; Heb 1.3). As the new Moses, Jesus was also the mediator of a new covenant in his blood (Luke 22.20; 1 Cor 11.25; Heb 12.24).

To disabuse his audience of their revisionist and romanticized notions of how much more popular the Messiah would have to be than Moses, Stephen quoted Exod 32.1 to remind his audience of the ancient Israelites' *rejection* of Moses as God's chosen leader:

> Our fathers refused to obey [Moses], but thrust him aside, and in their hearts they turned to Egypt, saying to Aaron, "Make for us gods who will go before us. As for this Moses who led us out from the land of Egypt, we do not know what has become of him" (Acts 7.39–40).

Indeed, the Jewish people who were expecting a Prophet like Moses should have been watching for a despised and rejected prophet, just like Jesus. Stephen was martyred because he applied the bovine language of Exod 32.9 to the Jewish leaders who had killed the new Moses, Jesus: "You stiff-necked people, uncircumcised in heart and ears, you always resist the Holy Spirit. As your fathers did, so do you. … [T]he Righteous One … you have now betrayed and murdered" (Acts 7.51–52).

### The Manifested Glory of God (John 1.14–18)

The language of Exodus 32–34 permeates the Gospel of John as it describes Jesus and his ministry. For example, John 1.14 declares he is "the only Son from the Father, *full of grace and truth*" (emphasis added). This is John's own paraphrase of God's self-declaration made in Exod 34.6.[25] Even as God is "abounding in steadfast love and faithfulness,"

---

[25] C. John Collins, "How the New Testament Quotes and Interprets the Old Testament," in Wayne Grudem et al., eds., *Understanding Scripture: An Overview of the Bible's Origin, Reliability, and Meaning* (Wheaton: Crossway, 2012) 183.

so also Jesus is "full of grace and truth" (John 1.14).[26] At the beginning of Jesus' ministry, he "revealed his glory" by turning water to wine (John 2.11). This first of his miracles ("signs," as John consistently calls them) "also forms the opening act of John's story of *how Jesus reveals his glory*, and as such is the foundational pattern for everything else that follows."[27] All the "signs" of Jesus recorded in the Gospel of John are intended to produce faith in our hearts, enabling us to see Jesus' glory for ourselves: "Now Jesus did many other signs in the presence of the disciples, which are not written in this book; but these are written so that you may believe that Jesus is the Christ, the Son of God, and that by believing you may have life in his name" (John 20.30–31). After the completion of his ministry and shortly before his death on the cross, Jesus prayed these words in the Garden of Gethsemane: "Father, the hour has come; glorify your Son that the Son may glorify you" (John 17.1). By dying on the cross and being raised from the dead, Jesus provided the world with the ultimate manifestation of God's glory.

According to Exod 33–34, only Moses was permitted to see God's glory, and that but a pale shadow of what we can see in Jesus. Those who have read the gospel accounts and have come to "believe that Jesus is the Christ" have thus "seen his glory" (John 1.14), the glory of a crucified Christ overflowing with grace enough to forgive every sin. As John says in 1.18, "No one has ever seen God," including Moses most notably, but "the only God, who is at the Father's side, he has made him known," that is, revealing God's character to be one of mercy, patience, grace, and forgiveness, which could only fully be realized after the crucifixion. Later in the Gospel of John, when Philip asked Jesus to reveal the Father to the disciples, Jesus chided him for his failure to understand that he had already seen the glory

---

[26] It is important to note that the sublime description of the Lord's glory in Exod 34.6–7 is now applied to God the Son, Jesus. In other words, Jesus is the embodiment of the fullness of deity (Col 2.9).

[27] Karen H. Jobes, *John through Old Testament Eyes: A Background and Application Commentary*, in Andrew T. Le Peau, ed., Through Old Testament Eyes: New Testament Commentaries (Grand Rapids: Kregel Academic, 2021) 61, emphasis in the original.

of God at work: "Have I been with you so long, and you still do not know me, Philip? Whoever has seen me has seen the Father. How can you say, 'Show us the Father'?" (John 14.9).

Here is yet another reference to Exod 32–34 in the Gospel of John. Jesus said to his apostles: "No longer do I call you servants, for the servant does not know what his master is doing; but I have called you friends, for all that I have heard from my Father I have made known to you" (John 15.15). Do you remember when Moses had felt slighted, believing that he was not privy to God's complete plan for Israel (Exod 33.12–13)? Yet in the previous verse, we were told that "the LORD used to speak to Moses face to face, as a man speaks to his friend" (Exod 33.11). Jesus lifted up his disciples to the same status as Moses by calling them his "friends" (John 15.15).[28] But note also that, in the previous verse, Jesus told us how we too can be his friends: "You are my friends, if you do what I command you" (v. 14). Like Moses, we may feel confused and discouraged, not understanding God's plans. We should take comfort in Jesus' words, who calls us his "friends" and his "brothers" (cf. John 20.17; Heb 2.11–12).

## Conclusion

At the beginning of Exodus, God told Moses, "I am the LORD" (Exod 3.14–15). Near the end, he further defined his name as "the LORD, the LORD, a God gracious and merciful" (Exod 34.6–7). As Christians, this is the name that we carry with us every day (cf. Acts 9.15). We are the light of the world, reflecting the glory of God by how we live our lives and represent him (Matt 5.14–16). Some of us might hide our light, as did ancient Israel. We want to worship what pleases us, not realizing that the sin of this world will blind us to the glory of Jesus. At other times in our lives, we are more like Moses, getting discouraged as we witness the rotting of our culture, watching it sag deeper into the mire of sinful behavior.

---

[28] See Craig S. Keener, "Friendship," in Craig A. Evans et al., eds., *Dictionary of New Testament Background* (Downers Grove: InterVarsity Press, 2000) 385.

Paul admonishes us to be like Jesus. We are to be transformed into his image (Rom 8.29). Despite the change and decay all around us and within us, we should let "our inner self [be] renewed day by day" by the power of God's word (2 Cor 4.16):

> For this light momentary affliction is preparing for us an eternal weight of glory beyond all comparison, as we look not to the things that are seen but to the things that are unseen. For the things that are seen are transient, but the things that are unseen are eternal (2 Cor 4.17–18).

"Show me your glory," Moses had said. If we ever find ourselves saying that to God, then we should listen carefully for the gentle answer he whispers in our ear: "I already have."

# God with His People
## *The Tabernacle*

### Gianni Berdini

The encounter between God and man is a fundamental fact of our faith as Christians and has always been fixed within human history. The term "religion" itself comes from the Latin *religare*, that is "to unite together, put in relationship," it expresses God's will to re-establish a strong and lasting bond with man. Paul emphasizes how man has never been able to find God by himself. It was therefore God who sought man to establish this bond with him: "For since, in the wisdom of God, the world through wisdom did not know God, it pleased God through the foolishness of the message preached to save those who believe" (1 Cor 1.21).[1]

The first relationship that God establishes with man is a creative relationship. God creates man and reveals himself to him. The Bible is the history of God's revelations. The word "reveal" is traced back by some to the expression *retro velum dare*, which in Latin means "to give what is behind the veil," that is to make known what is not immediately understandable by finite and limited human reason. Therefore, God is a God who speaks, who reveals himself, who cares about his creature.

Sacred scripture continues God's revelation over time, making it accessible also to subsequent ages. While in the Old Testament peri-

---

[1] Unless noted otherwise, all quotations of scripture are from the NKJV.

od the recipient of all this was primarily limited to the one nation Israel, in the New Testament universal accessibility is realized: all men of the world can enter into the church, the summit of the Lord's plan of redemption. Christianity sees in Jesus Christ the greatest revelation of God in history:

> God, who at various times and in various ways spoke in time past to the fathers by the prophets, has in these last days spoken to us by His Son, whom He has appointed heir of all things, through whom also He made the worlds; who being the brightness of His glory and the express image of His person, and upholding all things by the word of His power, when He had by Himself purged our sins, sat down at the right hand of the Majesty on high (Heb 1.1–3).

The truth brought by Jesus is a truth that saves men. The history of God is the history of salvation. The discovery of a God who saves is the most joyful testimony in the whole Bible. Faith is not simply believing something to be true, but trusting in God who saves man from sin. Already in the Garden of Eden, the first dwelling place of God with humanity, the LORD establishes an intimate relationship with his creature. He walks, talks, and interacts with his creature to whom he provides everything necessary for his happiness. Unfortunately, Adam and Eve did not know how to appreciate what God had given them, nor did they remain faithful to his commands, and we all know how it ended.

God, however, does not abandon his creature, he wants to bring his people to him. He speaks to the patriarchs, guides them, protects them, and creates a relationship of trust and love with them. Through Abraham he gives birth to a nation, hearing their cry and lament when they became slaves of the Egyptians, and so delivering them from Egypt. The Lord brings the Hebrews to Mt. Sinai where the covenant is ratified and once again God is dwelling with humanity in a special way. This mountain is even divided into the same three degrees of holiness that both the later tabernacle and temples would symbolize: (a) the common people could gather around the center of God's presence; (b) some special representatives could enter into the holy area forbidden to the commoners; and (c) only the one specially designated could enter all the way to where the LORD dwelt.

As part of God's covenant with Israel, the LORD provides a special place to meet with Israel to be worshiped. This "tabernacle" (Hebr. *mishkān* "dwelling, abode") was God's first artificially constructed dwelling place among his people, a holy place exclusively owned by him and specially designated for the people have visible and tangible access to his presence.

With their offerings as a symbol of their desire for God to dwell among them, they build the tabernacle, an established and used place to have their intimate relationship with God and offer him their worship. It is the "Holy Place" that indicates the majesty and holiness of God, a place where only priests have access: "This shall be a continual burnt offering throughout your generations at the door of the tabernacle of meeting before the LORD, where I will meet you to speak with you. And there I will meet with the children of Israel, and the tabernacle shall be sanctified by My glory" (Exod 29.42–43). When it was completed, God descended in a cloud covering the tabernacle entirely with his own glory to symbolize his presence with his people (Exod 40.34–38).

This "tabernacle" or "tent" is a prominent symbolic and typological plan of the Old Testament and is linked to the religious convictions of the Jews during their pilgrimage in the desert. Many provisions and laws of the Old Testament period "are a shadow of things to come, but the substance is of Christ" (Col 2.17). The tabernacle contains many illustrations of the work of Christ and constitutes an important link between the Old Testament and the New Testament, as the New Testament is hidden in the Old Testament, and the Old is revealed in the New. In fact, the Hebrew writer argues that one reason the Hebrews were to be so careful to follow the divine pattern revealed to Moses is that this tabernacle was to be a type or model of the "true tabernacle," heaven itself (Heb 8.1–5; 9.11–28; cf. Exod 25.40).[2]

As a typological plan the tabernacle embodies the plan of salvation that will develop with Christ by highlighting the relationship between Israel and the grace and redemptive nature of divine revelation: "He established a testimony in Jacob, and appointed a law in Israel, which He commanded our fathers, that they should make them known to their children" (Psa 78.5). The tabernacle is the bridge between God and his people; it is the means to reestablish the communion interrupted by the disobedience of Adam and Eve in the Garden of Eden. The tabernacle with its furnishings and rites is the largest concentration of typology in the Old Testament:

> For if He were on earth, He would not be a priest, since there are priests who offer the gifts according to the law; who serve the copy and shadow of the heavenly things, as Moses was divinely instructed when he was about to make the tabernacle. For He said, "See that you make all things according to the pattern (Gr. *typon*) shown you on the mountain" (Heb 8.4–5).

> For the law, having a shadow of the good things to come, and not the very image of the things, can never with these same sacrifices, which they offer continually year by year, make those who approach perfect" (Heb 10.1).

> Now all these things happened to them as examples, and they were written for our admonition (Gr. *typikōs*), upon whom the ends of the ages have come" (1 Cor 10.11).

The primary function of the tabernacle was the covering of transgressions and filth so that man could be reconciled with God. Sin necessarily demands a sanction that cannot be anything other than

---

[2] A "type" (Gr. *typos;* "blow" or "impression left by a blow"; "mark" or "mold") is a double representation in action, in which the literal is understood and conceived to represent the spiritual. A type can be a person, an event, an institution, an office, or an action. The fulfillment of the prophecy conveyed by the type is called the "antitype."

death, that is, separation from God (Gen 2.17; Rom 3.23; 5.12; 6.23). Therefore, the Jew offered an animal sacrifice to atone for his sins. This animal had to be immolated to God since according to the Law, sin had to be washed with blood (Heb 9.22). Several biblical references reveal the importance that God gives to the shedding of blood for the atonement of sins and salvation: the sacrifices of Abel (Gen 4.4), the blood of the lamb placed on the door jambs and lintels of the doors of the houses that allowed the exit from Egypt (Exod 12.7), and above all else the perfect sacrifice of the Lord Jesus Christ on the cross (John 1.29).

## The Courtyard

There are several Hebrew terms by which the tabernacle is identified: e.g., *'ōhel* ("tent"), *'ohel mô'ēd* ("gathering tent"), *ōhel ha'ēdûth* ("testimony tent"), *mishkān* ("dwelling"), and *miqdāš* ("sanctuary"). It was 30 cubits long and 10 cubits wide, and consisted of a solid frame of forty-eight boards of acacia wood coated with gold, covered with fine veils and goat, ram and dolphin skins.[3] It was separated into two unequal sections by a veil: (a) the first section (20 cubits long) was twice the size of the second section and was called the "Holy Place" that contained the table of loaves, the seven-branched golden candlestick, and the altar of incense; an (b) the second section (10 cubits long) was called the "Most Holy Place" (or "Holy of Holies") and was the innermost part of the tent where the ark of the covenant was kept. Entrance into the Most Holy Place was limited to one day out of the year (the Day of Atonement) and one person, Aaron as the high priest or his later descendants who became the high priest.

The sanctuary tent was enclosed by a fabric fence, creating a courtyard about 150 feet long and 75 feet wide (45 m by 22.5 m). Outside in the courtyard in front of the sanctuary tent was

---

[3] If the standard cubit is intended (approximately 45 cm or 18 inches), the dimensions of the tabernacle sanctuary would be about 45 feet by 15 feet (or 13.5 m by 4.5 m).

the altar of burnt offering for sacrifices and the copper basin for water to be used by the priests for washing. Sinners could enter the courtyard to present unblemished male animals to be sacrificed for their sins. They could bring large livestock (calves), small livestock (sheep or goats) or birds (turtledoves or young pigeons). The sacrifice consisted, on the part of the sinner, in laying his hands on the animal in the courtyard and confessing his sins (Lev 1.4); then the priest proceeded, once the animal had been slaughtered, to shed the blood on the altar.

As the first piece of sacred furniture to be encountered in the courtyard, let us consider the altar of burnt offering. In our language the term "altar" derives from the Latin *altaris* and means "high, elevated place." But in Hebrew it derives from *mizbeah* which refers to the verb "kill, slaughter, sacrifice." This immediately makes us think of the important relationship that exists between this furniture and the sacrifice of Christ. For the people of Israel there could not be an altar without a sacrifice with blood (Heb 9.22). Christ represents the unique, definitive and unrepeatable sacrifice that brings to fulfillment the limits and imperfections of the Mosaic Law:

> But Christ came as high priest of the good things to come, with the greater and more perfect tabernacle not made with hands, that is, not of this creation. Not with the blood of goats and calves, but with His own blood He entered the Most Holy Place once for all, having obtained eternal redemption. For if the blood of bulls and goats and the ashes of a heifer, sprinkling the unclean, sanctifies for the purifying of the flesh, how much more shall the blood of Christ, who through the eternal Spirit offered Himself without spot to God, cleanse your conscience from dead works to serve the living God? (Heb 9.11–14).

The altar was made of acacia wood covered with bronze or copper, a symbol of stability and power (Dan 10.6; Rev 1.15). Acacia wood was light, easy enough to come by, strong, not easily affected by insects, and therefore durable. The four horns placed in the corners, on which the priest shed the blood of the sacrifice, also represented strength and power, as well as serving the practical function of helping to hold the sacrificial offering in place. The priests used the copper altar for burnt offerings to the LORD according to the ordinances received from God. On the altar they burned different animals such as bulls, goats, lambs, cows, etc. The priests shed the blood of some of these animals on the various objects of the tabernacle.

The sacrifices were burnt offerings, oblations, thanksgiving, and sin sacrifices. When the copper altar had to be transported, it had to be cleaned of the ashes and wrapped in a scarlet cloth. The ashes tell of a consummated offering, a finished work, and a victim who has suffered.

Next in order is the bronze or copper laver. The basin (Heb. *kîyôr*) was probably semicircular in shape and stood on a pedestal or base. It contained the water needed by the priests for their purification rituals. The basin was cast with bronze (Exod 38.8) like ancient mirrors, so that it had a lustrous sheen that made its surface shiny in which the priests could see their own image. It was located between the altar and the front of the sanctuary. To build the copper basin, some faithful Jewish women donated their mirrors to render a service to God. At that time, the mirrors were made of worked and polished copper (Exod 38.8). The bronze laver was used only by the priests to wash themselves before entering the tabernacle to perform the various services (Exod 40.30–33). If the priests tried to enter the tabernacle without washing, they died there.

It is only in the New Testament that water becomes the symbol of the complete and perfect purification of sinful man. The apostle Peter assures us of this when he compares Christians who pass through the baptismal waters to Noah and his family who passed through the flood unscathed because they were enclosed in the ark: "There is also an antitype which now saves us—baptism (not the removal of the filth of the flesh, but the answer of a good conscience toward God), through the resurrection of Jesus Christ" (1 Pet 3.21). John expresses the same concept with the term "born again" when he reports the dialogue between Jesus and the Pharisee Nicodemus:

> Jesus answered and said to him, "Most assuredly, I say to you, unless one is born again, he cannot see the kingdom of God." Nicodemus said to Him, "How can a man be born when he is old? Can he enter a second time into his mother's womb and be born?" Jesus answered, "Most assuredly, I say to you, unless one is born of water and the Spirit, he cannot enter the kingdom of God" (John 3.3–5).

The affirmation of Jesus on the need to be born of water and spirit echoes the account of his own baptism. There are two components: (a) water as the physical element, a purifier that symbolizes the tomb of Christ; and (b) the spirit as the divine element that indicates the interior change that the Holy Spirit works in the heart of man through the Word of Christ (1 Pet 1.23).

Baptism (or "immersion" or "submersion" or "burial" in water, as these are the meanings of the Greek word *baptisma*) symbolizes death and resurrection: first, the burial of the "old man" who was living according to the desires of the flesh; and then resurrection, the escape from the water to a new life in which Jesus becomes the point of reference (Rom 6.3–7). As Christ died and was buried, only to rise again triumphing over death and sin, likewise those who are buried with him in baptism rise from the water cleansed of their sins to take on a new life in Christ:

> Buried with Him in baptism, in which you also were raised with Him through faith in the working of God, who raised Him from the dead. And you, being dead in your trespasses and the uncircumcision of your flesh, He has made alive together with Him, having forgiven you all trespasses (Col 2.12–13).

> As newborn babes, desire the pure milk of the word, that you may grow thereby, if indeed you have tasted that the Lord is gracious (1 Pet 2.2).

## The Holy Place

The table of showbread was fundamental in the tabernacle. The golden table always had twelve cakes of unleavened bread on it (Lev 24.5), equal to the number of the tribes of Israel and perhaps foreshadowing the twelve disciples at the Last Supper with Jesus. Twelve is a highly symbolic number in the culture of Israel which indicated a complete and perfect organization willed by God. Twelve are the tribes of Israel and twelve are the apostles chosen by Christ. In the book of Revelation, the apostle John symbolizes the perfection of the church by multiplying the number of tribes (12) by the number of the apostles (12) and one thousand (the three-fold multiple of 10, signifying human completeness). This results in the total 144,000 that indicates the totality of God's people, the militant church in its strength and completeness (Revelation 7 and 14).

Only the priests had the right to eat the bread of the presentation. In fact, all those who were outside the tabernacle, the Levites included, could not even see the table inside. However, all Christians, men and women who are God's elect, are true priests in the new dispensation in Christ and have the right to reign with Christ and sit at his table. This priestly condition of the Christian, so simple and intuitive, has been widely misinterpreted over the centuries. The churches of the first century, as established by the Lord, had their elders, bishops, pastors (different definitions of the same office) whose primary task was and still is today, to watch over the behavior of the faithful and the integrity of the divine message: "Therefore take heed to yourselves and to all the flock, among which the Holy Spirit has made you overseers, to shepherd the church of God which He purchased with His own blood" (Acts 20.28). However, due to the influence of the pagan and Jewish systems, precisely those who should have defended the truth began to claim sacred powers unavailable to other Christians, something that had been prophesied: "For I know this, that after my departure savage wolves will come in among you, not sparing the flock" (Acts 20.29). The influence of the Jewish priesthood was decisive. Clement of Rome in his epistle to the Corinthians at the end of the first century (1 Clem 40.1–5) assimilated the Jewish priesthood precisely to the one of Christ by writing that Christ represented the high priest, the bishops replaced the priests, the deacons the Levites. Soon the simple acts of worship were transformed into sacrificial acts. The bread and wine of the Lord's Supper were transformed into the consecration of the host and the wine, making the celebrant become a priest. The idea of the priesthood entrusted to a particular caste slowly but definitively advanced in the centuries that followed, increasing the power of the Catholic Church and its control over the mass.

History had to wait for Martin Luther (1483–1546) to reaffirm the idea of the priesthood of all the faithful, an idea that would be condemned by the Council of Trent (1545–1563). Instead the council strongly affirmed the Catholic priesthood as the true priesthood and clarified that ordination gives to priests alone the power to "consecrate, offer and to dispense his body and blood, the power to forgive and retain sins."[4] The priesthood of all Christians was understood only in the metaphorical sense, while a particular ordination of ministers, also admitted by historical Protestant churches, confers official representation in the liturgy of the church.

Most religions have a priestly caste that mediates between God and man. The people of Israel were no exception. From the Mosaic age, they chose priests from the house of Aaron. Under Solomon the Jewish priesthood passed from the line of Abiathar to the family of Zadok (1 Kng 2.27–35) who exercised its functions until the second century BC. With Josiah's reform (621 BC), the temple in Jerusalem became the only place of legitimate worship and the Levites were used for the humblest religious services (Ezek 44.10–31).

Although God had instituted for Israel a very specific priestly order with limited access, already in the Old Testament God had foretold the new system that would be completed with the birth of

---

[4] Council of Trent, Session 23, "Sacrament of Orders, 15 July 1563," chap. 1.

the church: "But you shall be named the priests of the LORD; they shall call you the servants of our God" (Isa 61.6). The apostle Peter explicitly states: "…you also, as living stones, are being built up a spiritual house, a holy priesthood, to offer up spiritual sacrifices acceptable to God through Jesus Christ (1 Pet 2.4–5); and "you are a chosen generation, a royal priesthood, a holy nation, His own special people, that you may proclaim the praises of Him who called you out of darkness into His marvelous light" (1 Pet 2.9). Christ, in fact, allows us to enter the *sanctuary*, that is, he allows us to be in contact and have a tender communion with the Father:

> Therefore, brethren, having boldness to enter the Holiest by the blood of Jesus, by a new and living way which He consecrated for us, through the veil, that is, His flesh, and having a high priest over the house of God, let us draw near with a true heart in full assurance of faith, having our hearts sprinkled from an evil conscience and our bodies washed with pure water (Heb 10.19–22).

The priesthood of all Christians is also remembered by John in the book of Revelation:

> …and from Jesus Christ, the faithful witness, the firstborn from the dead, and the ruler over the kings of the earth. To Him who loved us and washed us from our sins in His own blood and has made us kings and priests to His God and Father, to Him be glory and dominion forever and ever. Amen (Rev 1.5–6).

> And they sang a new song, saying: "You are worthy to take the scroll, and to open its seals; for You were slain, and have redeemed us to God by Your blood Out of every tribe and tongue and people and nation, and have made us kings and priests to our God; and we shall reign on the earth" (Rev 5.9–10).

The priestly task of Christians is to offer a spiritual sacrifice with one's own obedience, one's fidelity, one's dedication to the Lord. Sacrifices are called spiritual not because they have something metaphorical and unreal, but only because they must be in harmony with the Word revealed by the Spirit.

The life of the Christian in every moment and in every circumstance must be lived according to the teaching of Jesus representing the practice of his priestly work: "I beseech you therefore, brethren, by the mercies of God, that you present your bodies a living sacrifice, holy, acceptable to God, which is your reasonable service" (Rom 12.1). The Christian does not follow the trend of the world but fixes his gaze on Jesus and in every action tries to understand what God wants from him. The writer of the letter to the Hebrews admonishes: "Fixing our gaze on Jesus, he who creates faith and makes it perfect. For the joy that was placed before him he bore the cross, despising the infamy, and sat at the right hand of the throne of God" (Heb 12.2). As the apostle Paul exhorts, Christians must crucify their own flesh with all vices and lusts (Galatians 5.24) and look at the example of Jesus, grasping his humility, sacrifice and love, as Zechariah had prophesied in his song of praise for the birth of his son John: "To perform the mercy promised to our fathers And to remember His holy covenant, The oath which He swore to our father Abraham: To grant us that we, Being delivered from the hand of our enemies, Might serve Him without fear, In holiness and righteousness before Him all the days of our life. (Luke 1.72–75). Every day the Lord calls us to be priests, even if necessary for the sacrifice of our life, without ever being discouraged, like Paul taking his ministry as an example: "Always carrying about in the body the dying of the Lord Jesus, that the life of Jesus also may be manifested in our body. For we who live are always delivered to death for Jesus' sake, that the life of Jesus also may be manifested in our mortal flesh" (2 Cor 4.10–11).

The candlestick is the most representative symbol of the nation of Israel, and it is no coincidence that it is represented in Rome on the arch erected in honor of Titus, as evidence of the repression he conducted against the Jewish revolt, which culminated with the destruction of the temple of Jerusalem in AD 70. However, in the letter to the church of Ephesus (Rev 2.1–7) Christ presents himself as the one who watches over the church, who holds her hand, who supports, encourages, helps, and if necessary, exhorts and reproaches her. Christ has in his right hand the seven stars, that is the active spirit of every community of faith, and it is Christ Himself who walks in the midst of the seven golden candlesticks, the one who is constantly in the midst of His church: "For where two or three are gathered together in My name, I am there in the midst of them" (Matt 18.20). Removing the candlestick would mean the cancellation of belonging to the Lord. A local church can write outside the meeting place "Church of Christ" and yet may already have lost their spirit of fidelity to the Lord. It is not a name that makes us belong to Christ, but it is love and respect for his will.

The altar of incense provided a pleasing aroma that was always being offered to God and symbolized the prayers and petitions of God's people. The tabernacle had a gold altar in the Holy Place, a few meters from the table and the candlestick before the veil that separated the Holy Place from the Most Holy Place. Every morning and evening the high priest offered incense on the altar with burning coals from the external courtyard. The incense flowed beyond the veil into the Most Holy Place, where the presence of the glory of God was found. No one except the priests had the right to burn incense to the LORD, and when King Uzziah arrogantly considered himself to be more than he was because of his prosperity and success, and he presumed to usurp the burning of the incense from the priests, God punished Uzziah with leprosy (2 Chr 26.16–21).

The priest burned pure aromatic incense in the morning when he rearranged the candlestick and at sunset when he relit the candles (Exod 30.7–8). On the altar of incense, it was forbidden to burn "profane incense" or to offer burnt animal sacrifices, alms, and libations; only pure incense was to be used. This wooden altar was covered with gold, not only to prevent it from being burned by the fire that consumed the offerings, but also to indicate the holiness of God. It had four transport rings and four horns at the corners, still a symbol of the power of God, on which the high priest made atonement once a year.

Incense in scripture is associated with sacrifice, with prayer: "Let my prayer be set before You as incense, the lifting up of my hands as the evening sacrifice" (Psa 141.2). Christians raise their heart, their thanksgiving, and their sacrifice to God who accepts it as a sweet perfume: "Then another angel, having a golden censer, came and stood at the altar. He was given much incense, that he should offer it with the prayers of all the saints upon the golden altar which was before the throne. And the smoke of the incense, with the prayers of the saints, ascended before God from the angel's hand" (Rev 8.3–4). Perhaps we are to envision that our prayers are the incense that mingles with and adorns the sin offering of Christ: "And walk in love, as Christ also has loved us and given Himself for us, an offering and a sacrifice to God for a sweet-smelling aroma" (Eph 5.2).

## The Most Holy Place

The Most Holy Place was separated from the Holy Place by a curtain, a thick curtain of five meters on each side. It was the same cloth that wrapped the ark whenever the encampment of Israel had to relocate. Behind this curtain was the ark of the covenant, which was really two distinct pieces of furniture: (a) the solid gold lid adorned with the two cherubim was called the "mercy seat" because it represented the very throne of God (1 Sam 4.4; 2 Sam 6.2; 2 Kng 19.15); and (b) a wood box overlaid with gold inside and out, representing God's footstool (1 Chr 28.2; Psa 99.5; 132.7). Because this represented the very throne room of God, heaven itself where God dwells, only the high priest could enter the Most Holy Place once a year on the Day of Atonement (*Yom Kippur*). Before entering, he had to wash and put on special all-white priestly garments (Lev 16.4), then he had to burn incense so that the thick smoke prevented him from seeing, and then he had to sprinkle the "mercy seat" with the blood of the sacrificial animal (Lev 16.12–15).

The tabernacle is clearly the anticipation of God's will to reunite every man with himself. Once the tabernacle had been built, it accompanied the people of Israel on their journey until it was surpassed by a permanent temple, a point of reference, a place where the Jews had to go during the Jewish holidays of *Pesach* (Passover), *Sukkot* (Feast of Tabernacles or Feast of Ingathering) and *Shavuot* (Feast of Weeks or Pentecost). These were called the feasts of pilgrimages, precisely because the people went on pilgrimage to the Temple to meet God.

The earthly Jerusalem thus becomes the type of the heavenly one, prefiguring the new relationship of sonship that every man could have had with the Father through the blood of Christ:

> Jesus answered and said to them, "Destroy this temple, and in three days I will raise it up." Then the Jews said, "It has taken forty-six years to build this temple, and will You raise it up in three days?" But He was speaking of the temple of His body. Therefore, when He had risen from the dead, His disciples remembered that He had said this to them; and they believed the scripture and the word which Jesus had said (John 2.19–22).

The tabernacle and the temple are types of the church, the new house where God dwells and where every man can enter by obeying His Word: "In whom the whole building, being joined together, grows into a holy temple in the Lord, in whom you also are being built together for a dwelling place of God in the Spirit" (Eph 2. 21–22). The church is the new tabernacle, it is his dwelling with us: "But if I am delayed, I write so that you may know how you ought to conduct yourself in the house of God, which is the church of the living God, the pillar and ground of the truth" (1 Tim 3.15); "But Christ as a Son over His own house, whose house we are if we hold fast the confidence and the rejoicing of the hope firm to the end" (Heb 3.6).

After Jesus' death, the temple veil was torn in two from top to bottom. It was the divine testimony of the end of the Jewish system and the beginning of the era of Christianity: "And Jesus cried out again with a loud voice and yielded up His spirit. Then, behold, the veil of the temple was torn in two from top to bottom; and the earth quaked, and the rocks were split" (Matt 27.50–51). Now Jesus leads us directly to God: "Therefore, brethren, having boldness to enter the Holiest by the blood of Jesus, by a new and living way which He consecrated for us, through the veil, that is, His flesh" (Heb 10.19–20). The Most Holy Place indicated the presence of God with the nation of Israel, while the veil protected the sinful people of Israel from God's holiness. Jesus' death put an end to this method of worship, opening access to God to all who would believe and obey the Word of the Lord (Rom 10.17). Whereas under the old law there was an inaccessible barrier guarded by cherubs (both on the ark and embroidered on the veil), just like in the Garden of Eden, God has now opened a way through the blood shed by his Son, a way where not even a fool will be able to get lost: "A highway shall be there, and a road, and it shall be called the Highway of Holiness. The unclean shall not pass over it, but it shall be for others. Whoever walks the road, although a fool, shall not go astray" (Isa 35.8).

Jesus is the head of the body which is his church (Col 1.18; 1 Cor 12.12–13; Eph 4.4–6). The body of Christ is purely spiritual and is made up of innumerable members. We who will inherit the glory are united in Christ in the Spirit so that we can become one Spirit with Him (1 Cor 6.17) and consequently we are with Him one body of a spiritual and non-earthly nature. With the wisdom which He provides us with His Word, we will grow more and more in spiritual stature, and we will look with joy and living hope at the "house not made with hands, eternal, in the heavens" (2 Cor 5.1) that Christ went to prepare to welcome us to Himself. The church is the new tabernacle, the house of God, the temple where every Christian meets the Father and where every Christian becomes a priest and every Christian is offering himself (his own life) as a living sacrifice.

In addition to the *earthly* Jerusalem, which was a symbol of the Jewish nation and of the Mosaic law, and in addition to the *heavenly* Jerusalem, which is a symbol of the church designed and built in Christ (Heb 12.18–24), there is the *future* Jerusalem, the one that descends from heaven as a symbol of the afterlife and of the glorified church, the final dwelling that Christians aspire to reach, and the place that Jesus went to prepare for his own (John 14.1–4). John in the Apocalypse sees Jerusalem in its perfection: the holy city, the new city of my God, descending from heaven, the betrothed, the wife of the Lamb, and the bride of Christ. But the most astounding thing about what John sees is Jerusalem without a temple, because "the Lord God Almighty and the Lamb are its temple (Rev 21.22). Instead, "the tabernacle of God is with men, and He will dwell with them, and they shall be His people. God Himself will be with them and be their God" (Rev 21.3).

Our hope and our goal are to come to know Jesus in a serious and spiritual way, and to feel his love and mercy through his Word. For this reason, we try to please him and obey him, knowing that as Christians, we live spiritually in his tabernacle, yearning for the day when he will deliver us out of the tomb, taking us into his glory in the middle of his final tabernacle, where there will be eternal delights and where there will be no more death, no grief, no sorrow, and no pain (Rev 21.4). The Christian is no longer tied to the earthly Jerusalem; that is, he is free from all the Mosaic Law. The Christian instead is living in the heavenly Jerusalem; that is, he lives in the church under the law of Christ. The Christian confidently awaits the Jerusalem which descends from heaven so that he may be with God forever:

> Then one of the seven angels who had the seven bowls filled with the seven last plagues came to me and talked with me, saying, "Come, I will show you the bride, the Lamb's wife." And he carried me away in the Spirit to a great and high mountain, and showed me the great city, the holy Jerusalem, descending out of heaven from God (Rev 21. 9–10).

# "They Will Not Enter My Rest"

## Reagan McClenny

It can sometimes be hard to find urgency for immediate, present action when considering events of a different people, in a different time, under a different covenant. However, nothing should startle us awake from our drowsy detachment faster than to hear application made to "Today!" and "You!":

> Therefore, as the Holy Spirit says: "Today, if you will hear His voice, do not harden your hearts as in the rebellion, in the day of trial in the wilderness, where your fathers tested me, tried me, and saw my works forty years. therefore I was angry with that generation, and said, 'They always go astray in their heart, and they have not known my ways.' **So I swore in my wrath, 'They shall not enter my rest'**" (Heb 3.7–11; emphasis added).[1]

The Hebrew writer's words, taken from the pen of the psalmist and twice-inspired by the Holy Spirit, should be both spoken and heard by all Christians—in the first or twenty-first centuries. "Beware, brethren, lest there be in any of you an evil heart of unbelief in departing from the living God; but exhort one another daily, while it is called "Today," lest any of you be hardened through the deceitfulness of sin" (Heb 3.12–13). The unbelief and apostasy of the exodus generation is an exhortation and warning to *all* who would follow God and His Son out of slavery and into rest. In taking their example seriously, we are

---

[1] Unless noted otherwise, all quotations of scripture are from the NKJV.

forced to ask important questions of the text: What did God swear? Why did He swear it? And what does it mean for the Hebrews and us?

## "I Swore"—God's Faithfulness to His Oaths

The Exodus account really begins with God remembering his promise to Abraham. "So God heard their groaning, and God remembered His covenant with Abraham, with Isaac, and with Jacob" (Exod 2.24). This promise, made to Abram in Genesis 12 and expanded in Genesis 15, 17, and 22, is the basic outline for the entire biblical narrative and a foundational proof of the covenant faithfulness of God. However, God did not "just" promise, He swore an oath to Abraham and his descendants. This oath was remembered and recalled by God and His people on many occasions (Gen 24.7; 26.3; 50.24; Exod 6.8; 13.5, 11; 32.13; 33.1; Num 11.12; 14.16, 30; Deut 7.8–9; etc.) and provides a basis for confidence in all other oaths of God.

God taking an oath is, in some ways, superior to God merely promising. Not that anything God says is unreliable or uncertain ("…it is impossible for God to lie;" Heb 6.18), but from the perspective of the ones about whom or to whom the oath is taken, it emphasizes the magnitude of what God is saying and reassures the hearer of the confidence one can have in what has been promised. This is suggested in Hebrews 7.20–22 concerning Jesus' priesthood:

> And it was not without an oath. For those who formerly became priests were made such without an oath, but this one was made a priest with an oath by the one who said to him: "The Lord has sworn and will not change his mind, 'You are a priest forever.'" *This makes Jesus the guarantor of a better covenant* (ESV; emphasis added).

One thing that makes Jesus' priesthood superior is that He was "made a priest with an oath."

Likewise, the Hebrew writer reminds his readers that the promises to Abraham were confirmed and guaranteed with an oath by God:

For when God made a promise to Abraham, since he had no one greater by whom to swear, he swore by himself, saying, "Surely I will bless you and multiply you." And thus Abraham, having patiently waited, obtained the promise. For people swear by something greater than themselves, and *in all their disputes an oath is final for confirmation. So when God desired to show more convincingly to the heirs of the promise the unchangeable character of his purpose, he guaranteed it with an oath,* so that by two unchangeable things, in which it is impossible for God to lie, we who have fled for refuge might have strong encouragement to hold fast to the hope set before us (Heb 6.13–18 ESV; emphasis added).

What are the "two unchangeable things" to which the Hebrew writer refers? "Nearly all interpreters have understood these 'two immutable things' as God's promise and God's oath."[2] While Worley compellingly argues that "the author of Hebrews had something quite different in mind—that, in fact, he was thinking of God's double role as oath-taker and oath-witness,"[3] this interpretation does not have the same contextual support as the former. The "two unchangeable things" that can be found immediately prior in verse 17 are "the promise" and "oath" made by God to Abraham.

Even more importantly for the purposes of our study, God's oath in Hebrews 3.11 and 4.3, 5 that "They shall not enter my rest" follows the same pattern of his oath to Abraham in Hebrews 6.13: a promise (Num 14.22–23), followed by an oath (Num 14.28–29; 32.10–11), that are both proven true in fulfillment (Deut 1.34–36). Thus, these same "two immutable things" (NKJV), the promise and oath of the God who cannot lie, are found in this "oriental negative"[4] oath against the children of Israel as well.

---

[2] David R. Worley, "Fleeing to Two Immutable Things, God's Oath-Taking and Oath-Witnessing: The Use of Litigant Oath in Hebrews 6.12–20," *ResQ* 36 (1994) 223.

[3] Ibid.

[4] Walter Kaiser, "The Promise Theme and the Theology of Rest," *BibSac* 130 (1973) 143.

God's nature as an oath-keeper does not change with the nature of the oath. He is faithful to oaths whether they are positive or negative in their consequences. Paul confirms this truth in 2 Timothy 2.11–13, when he says:

> This is a faithful saying: For if we died with Him, We shall also live with Him. If we endure, We shall also reign with Him. If we deny Him, He also will deny us. If we are faithless, He remains faithful; He cannot deny Himself.

These sayings are true (Gr. *pistos,* "trustworthy, faithful, dependable, inspiring trust/faith"[5]—used in v. 11 of the saying and v. 13 of God), for our good or for our bad. Though v. 13 is sometimes crossstitched into pillows or framed and put on a wall, the full context of this song of God's faithfulness is darker than some realize. "If we are faithless, He remains faithful" does not mean that God will overlook our faithlessness and break His covenant to save us—just the opposite. "If we deny Him, He also will deny us. If we are faithless, He remains faithful" and will give us the punishment due us eternally. Anything less would be to "deny Himself" and His nature. This is who God is: God cannot lie (Num 23.19; Heb 6.18; Tit 1.2). He is faithful to His word, faithful to His promises, and faithful to His oaths.

## "In My Wrath"—God's Anger with His People

What would cause God to take such an unchangeable oath against His own people? He was relentlessly provoked to anger by them. God is often described in the Old Testament as slow to anger (Psa 30.5; 103.9–10; Isaiah 54.7–8; 57.16; Nah 1.3) and abounding in steadfast love (Exod 15.13; 20.6; Num 14.19; Deut 5.10; 7.9, 12; 1 Chr 16.34, 41; Neh 1.5; Psa 136)—often in the same verse (Exod 34.6; Num 14.18; Neh 9.17; Psa 86.15; 103.8; 145.8; Joel 2.13; Jon 4.2). At the same time, "God is a just judge, and God is angry with the wicked every day" (Psa 7.11). God's wrath is not petty and selfish, as ours often is, but righteous—a result of His "just" nature.

---

[5] BDAG 820.

God's anger toward wickedness of all kinds does not dull because of exposure, it burns brighter as his lovingkindness, longsuffering, and grace is rejected in further sin. The people of Israel provoked God's anger by repeatedly putting Him to the test long after He had proven his goodness and glory:

> …because all these men who have seen My glory and the signs which I did in Egypt and in the wilderness, and have put Me to the test now these ten times, and have not heeded My voice, they certainly shall not see the land of which I swore to their fathers, nor shall any of those who rejected Me see it (Num 14.22–23).

"These ten times" is probably not intended to be taken literally, though one can count the events to this point in the exodus in such a way to make them ten occasions of testing God.[6] The use of this number is more likely symbolic of a complete testing of God by the people, that "God's anger…was not aroused by a single incident but by a persistent tendency to refuse his direction."[7] It highlights the extreme and consistent rebellion of the children of Israel for God to be forced to make this vow as well as the wrath He had in making it.

## "They Shall Not Enter My Rest"—God's Justified Oath Against His People

The children of Israel who were brought out of Egypt are characterized by their dissatisfaction with the mercy, grace, and blessings of God. The Hebrew men in Exodus 2 are emblematic of the rebellious, ungrateful spirit of the people of Israel. Moses saves a Hebrew man from the hand of an Egyptian by striking down the oppressor. The very next day there is a fight between two Hebrew brethren and "the one who was in the wrong" (Exod 2.13 NRSV) coldly says to Moses when he tries to intervene, "Who made you a prince and a judge over us? Do

---

[6] For example, numbers 2–8, 10–11, and 13 listed below add up to 10 by limiting occasions of "testing" to congregational rebellion after leaving Egypt.

[7] Daniel H. King, *The Book of Hebrews,* Truth Commentaries (Bowling Green: Guardian of Truth Foundation, 2008) 114–115.

you intend to kill me as you killed the Egyptian?" (Exod 2.14). In Acts 7, Stephen tells us that Moses "supposed that his brethren would have understood that God would deliver them by his hand, but they did not understand" (Acts 7.25). God's blessings, salvation, and leader are rejected by the very ones whom God desires to save. This pattern would continue to Christ Himself (Acts 7.51–53)—but it is seen clearly in all the ways the people of Israel doubted God and rejected His salvation and blessings in the exodus. These are well-known accounts, but they are staggering when listed one after another:

1. The children of Israel "did not heed Moses" in his call for continued faith after Pharaoh required them to make bricks without straw (Exod 6.9).

2. At the Red Sea, they cry out to Moses and say, "It would have been better for us to serve the Egyptians than we should die in the wilderness" (Exod 14.10–12).

3. At Marah, "the people complained against Moses, saying, 'What shall we drink?'" (Exod 15.24).

4. When they came to the "Wilderness of Sin," the "whole congregation of the children of Israel complained against Moses and Aaron in the wilderness" saying they would die of hunger (Exod 16.1–3).

5. Upon receiving manna from heaven, they were told not to leave any that they collected until the morning, but "they did not listen to Moses" and the manna they laid up overnight "bred worms and stank" (Exod 16.19–20).

6. They were also told to gather twice as much on the sixth day and lay it up for the Sabbath, but "some of the people went out on the seventh day to gather, but they found none" (Exod 16.22–29).

7. At Rephidim, "the people complained against Moses, and said, "Why is it you have brought us up out of Egypt, to kill us and our children and our livestock with thirst?" (Exod 17.1–3). It was

here that the children of Israel had the audacity to ask, "Is the LORD among us or not?" (Exod 17.7). This occasion, referenced in Psalm 95, is when Moses names the place "Massah" and "Meribah," meaning "tempted" and "contention."[8]

8. Moses was delayed in coming down from Mount Sinai while receiving the law, so "the people gathered together to Aaron and said to him, 'Come, make us gods that shall go before us; for as for this Moses, the man who brought us up out of the land of Egypt, we do not know what has become of him'" (Exod 32.1). So, Aaron makes them a golden calf which they worship as the god who brought them out of the land of Egypt (Exod 32.2–4).

9. After receiving detailed instructions from God on offerings and seeing fire from God come out and consume the first offerings on the altar, Nadab and Abihu, the sons of Aaron, almost immediately "offered unauthorized fire before the LORD, which he had not commanded them" (Exod 10.1 ESV).

10. Three days after leaving the Wilderness of Sinai, the people complain again. The text does not even specify what the complaining was about (Num 11.1–3).

11. Soon thereafter, the multitude "yielded to intense craving; so the children of Israel also wept again and said: Who will give us meat to eat?" (Num 11.4). They reminisce about how good things were for them in Egypt, and how bad things are with only the manna from the LORD (Num 11.5–6). So extreme was their ingratitude, the text says they "despised the LORD" (Num 11.20).

12. At Hazeroth, Miriam and Aaron spoke against Moses in jealousy and said, "Has the LORD indeed spoken only through Moses? Has He not spoken through us also?" (Num 12.2).

---

[8] "The Septuagint translators (later quoted in Hebrews 3.8) rendered the Hebrew 'Meribah' by the Greek word, 'Embitterment.' These rebellious people made God's life bitter throughout that period." Jay Bowman, "The Rest that Remaineth," in Melvin Currey, ed., *Hebrews for Every Man*, Florida College Annual Lectures 1988 (Temple Terrace: Florida College Bookstore, 1988) 89.

13. At Kadesh, twelve spies were sent into the land of Canaan for forty days. Ten returned with a bad report and said, "We are not able to go up against the people, for they are stronger than we" (Num 13.31). The reaction of the people was predictable:

> Then all the congregation raised a loud cry, and the people wept that night. And all the people of Israel grumbled against Moses and Aaron. The whole congregation said to them, "Would that we had died in the land of Egypt! Or would that we had died in this wilderness! Why is the LORD bringing us into this land, to fall by the sword? Our wives and our little ones will become a prey. Would it not be better for us to go back to Egypt?" And they said to one another, "Let us choose a leader and go back to Egypt" (Num 14.1–4).

14. When Joshua and Caleb spoke up in opposition to this bad report, admonishing the people to have faith and not rebel against the LORD, "all the congregation said to stone them with stones" (Num 14.10).

All these events occurred *before* God swore that they would not enter His rest. Over and over the people ask some version of the question, "Would it not be better for us to return to Egypt?" (Num 14.3). Slavery in Egypt is described vividly in Exodus 1.8–14, 22. It is difficult to imagine a life characterized by such cruelty: former allies enslave you, beat you, drive you in your work like animals, and kill your children by throwing them into the river when you grow so numerous that you become a threat. Such was the lot of the Hebrews in their Egyptian slavery. Egypt is described in the Bible as the "house of bondage" (Exod 13.3, 14; 20.2; Deut 5.6; 6.12; 7.8; 8.14; 13.5, 10; Josh 24.17; Jdg 6.8; Jer 34.13; Mic 6.4) and slavery in Egypt is called the "iron furnace" (Deut 4.20; 1 Kng 8.51; Jer 11.4). Yet, the people seemingly yearned to "shrink back" into that slavery. If everything did not go exactly the way they wanted, on exactly their schedule, they were going to complain about it.

God heard their every complaint, and He fulfilled their every need with a blessing. His love, longsuffering, mercy, and grace are astounding. Despite their complaints and unfaithfulness, God sent the plagues on the Egypt but spared Israel from them as a sign that they were His people.[9] He brought them out of Egypt with a mighty hand, and He showered them with gifts from the Egyptians. He led them in a pillar of cloud by day and a pillar of fire by night and parted the Red Sea so they could walk across on dry ground (but destroyed the Egyptian army behind them). He gave them sweet water from bitter, He gave them quail and manna, and He brought water from a rock struck by Moses. He gave them miraculous victory over the army of Amalek. He spoke to them and gave them the Law at Sinai, and He offered them perfect health (no sickness, miscarriages, or barrenness) and victory over their enemies if they would keep His Law. God relented from destroying them when Moses stood in the gap before Him, He made a covenant with them, and His presence entered the tabernacle in a cloud. He organized them, numbered them, and gave their elders His Spirit so they prophesied. He brought them to the edge of the land of Canaan that He had promised to give into their hand and showed them how wonderful a land it was. Again, all these blessings were given before He swore they would not enter His rest.

In all this, they did not learn to have faith and they were not satisfied with God's gifts. At what point were God's blessings sufficient to prove His power, love, and faithfulness to the children of Israel? Yet, their response was to put Him to the test, again and again, in unbelief. They refused to believe God, His word, and His promises, despite the signs and wonders He had performed for them. So, He promises and then swears in His wrath that they will not enter the promised land:

> …because all these men who have seen My glory and the signs
> which I did in Egypt and in the wilderness, and have put Me to

---

[9] The text of Exodus is specific in saying that the Hebrews were spared from plagues 4. lice (Exod 8.22-23), 5. death of the livestock (Exod 9.4, 7), 7. hail (Exod 9.26), 9. darkness (Exod 10.23), and 10. death of the firstborn (Exod 11.7). It is reasonable to infer that the Hebrews were also spared from some or all of the other plagues—a clear sign of God's favor and protection of His people.

the test now these ten times, and have not heeded My voice, they
certainly shall not see the land of which I swore to their fathers,
nor shall any of those who rejected Me see it…. And the LORD
spoke to Moses and Aaron, saying, "How long shall I bear with
this evil congregation who complain against Me? I have heard the
complaints which the children of Israel make against Me. Say to
them, 'As I live,' says the LORD, 'just as you have spoken in My
hearing, so I will do to you: The carcasses of you who have complained against Me shall fall in this wilderness, all of you who were
numbered, according to your entire number, from twenty years old
and above (Num 14.22–23, 26–29).

The example of the exodus generation is a sad one—not just in
their failure to enter the "rest" of the promised land, but in their
failure of faith to receive the greater promises of God in Christ as
did the men and women of Hebrews 11. Kaiser calls the children
of Israel who fell in the wilderness, "twice the losers: temporally and
spiritually"[10] having no part in the physical promised land of Canaan
and no part in the rest of which the Hebrew writer speaks.

## Application to the First-Century "Hebrews"

The readers of the Hebrew letter would have believed God to be
justified in His wrath, His oath, and this fulfillment of that oath in
denying entrance into the promised land to those who fell in the
wilderness. What the Hebrew writer seeks to emphasize in chapters
three and four is that if that is true, then God is *much more justified* in
denying His "rest" to the Hebrew Christians. Any who "turn back"
from the gift of grace in Jesus will be denied access to the remaining
"rest" that could be theirs if they were faithful. He begins this section
by comparing Moses and Jesus:

Therefore, holy brothers, you who share in a heavenly calling, consider Jesus, the apostle and high priest of our confession, who was
faithful to him who appointed him, just as Moses also was faithful

[10] Kaiser, "Rest," 143.

in all God's house. For Jesus has been counted worthy of more glory than Moses—as much more glory as the builder of a house has more honor than the house itself. (For every house is built by someone, but the builder of all things is God.) Now Moses was faithful in all God's house as a servant, to testify to the things that were to be spoken later, but Christ is faithful over God's house as a son. And we are his house, if indeed we hold fast our confidence and our boasting in our hope (Heb 3.1–6a ESV).

Arguments from the "lesser" to the "greater," such as this one comparing aspects of the old covenant (the lesser) to the new covenant (the greater), are not exclusive to the book of Hebrews,[11] but they are especially common in this epistle, in part no doubt because of the familiarity of the writer's audience with the Old Testament, but also because this style of argumentation aligned with the Jewish methods of interpretation among the rabbis. As Guthrie states, "the author of Hebrews especially uses methods of interpretation and argumentation found in the Rabbis."[12] Specifically, this device is a method of interpretation attributed to Rabbi Hillel in the early first century. Hillel's seven exegetical rules "were, according to later rabbinic tradition, expounded by the great teacher Hillel († c. AD

---

[11] A clear example from the writings of Paul is 2 Cor 3.4–18. Paul describes the covenant of Moses as "old" (vv. 6, 14), "of the letter" (v. 6), "the ministry of death" (v. 7), "the ministry of condemnation" (v. 9), and "what is passing away" (v. 11). In contrast, he describes the covenant of Christ as "new" (v. 6), "of the spirit" (v. 6), giving "life" (v. 6), "the ministry of righteousness" and "the spirit" (vv. 8–9), and "what remains" (v. 11). He then argues that if Moses' ministry of death was "glorious" (vv. 7, 11), how much more glorious must Jesus' ministry of life be (v. 11)? It is as if the Law of Moses "had no glory in this respect, because of the glory of that which excels" in the covenant of Christ (v. 10). There are several practical applications of this truth in the context, including that if the gospel we proclaim is so glorious, we (like the apostles) should proclaim it everywhere (2.12–17), and should remember that the sufficiency is not of us (3.5–6), but that we are just imperfect vessels for that perfect gospel of the glory of Christ" (4.3–7). For an excellent treatment of these verses, see Melvin Curry, *Second Corinthians,* Truth Commentaries (Bowling Green: Guardian of Truth Foundation, 2008) 133–148.

[12] George H. Guthrie, *The Structure of Hebrews: A Text-Linguistic Analysis,* NovTSup 73. (Leiden: E. J. Brill, 1994) 45.

10). They represent general hermeneutical principles of inference, analogy and context that were probably in use before that time."[13]

The first of these rules is especially relevant to the book of Hebrews: "1. An inference drawn from a minor premise to a major and vice versa (*Kal wa-homer* = 'light and heavy')."[14] Argumentation from the "lesser" to the "greater" would have been a readily accepted method of interpretation among the Jews and was even used by Jesus himself (see Matt 7.11; 12.11; Luke 12.28, etc.). McClister suggests, "Hebrews employs [this kind of reasoning] in several passages (see 2.1–3; 3.2–6; 7.4–10; 9.13f; 10.28f; 12.9). There is a very real sense in which this kind of argument is the foundation of the argument of Hebrews."[15]

It is noteworthy in 3.1–6 that the Hebrew writer did not bring up the obvious negatives about Moses and his life when establishing him as the "lesser," but talks about him in the most positive way he is presented in scripture, using an allusion to Numbers 12.7. This reference to Moses being called "faithful in all the house of God" was a repetitive theme in the work of the Jewish philosopher Philo (c. 20

---

[13] E. Earle Ellis, *The Old Testament in Early Christianity: Canon and Interpretation in the Light of Modern Research*, WUZNT 54 (Tübingen: Mohr Siebeck, 1991; rep. ed., Eugene: Wipf and Stock, 2003) 87.

[14] The other rules, some of which are used by the Hebrew writer, are:

2. An inference drawn from analogy of expressions, that is, from similar words and phrases elsewhere (*Gezera Shawa* = 'an equivalent regulation').
3. A general principle established on the basis of a teaching contained in one verse (*Binyan 'ab mi-katub 'ehad* = 'constructing a leading rule from one passage').
4. A general principle established on the basis of a teaching contained in two verses (*Binyan 'ab mi-shenei ketubim* = 'constructing a leading rule from two passages').
5. An inference drawn from a general principle in the text to a specific example and vice versa (*Kelal u-ferat* = 'general and particular').
6. An inference drawn from an analogous passage elsewhere (*Kayotse' bo mi-makom 'aher* = 'something similar in another passage').
7. An interpretation of a word or passage from its context (*Dabar halamed me-'inyano* = 'explanation from the context'). Ibid. 87–88.

[15] David McClister, *Hebrews* (Temple Terrace: Florida College Press, 2010) 50.

BC – c. AD 50) and in early Christian writing.[16] Again, the Hebrew writer is using the accepted and familiar arguments of the Jews of the first century to make the case of Christ to Christians from a Jewish background. He uses it here and proceeds to show how Jesus is even "greater" than this "glorified" version of Moses.

A wider contextual look at Numbers 12.5–8, an occasion where Moses is described by God in one of his highest levels of glory and communion, makes this point even stronger. In the text, Miriam and Aaron's jealousy of Moses caused them to speak out against him and exalt their own status as prophets. God responds this way:

> Suddenly the LORD said to Moses, Aaron, and Miriam, "Come out, you three, to the tabernacle of meeting!" So the three came out. Then the LORD came down in the pillar of cloud and stood in the door of the tabernacle, and called Aaron and Miriam. And they both went forward. Then He said, "Hear now My words: If there is a prophet among you, I, the LORD, make Myself known to him in a vision; I speak to him in a dream. Not so with My servant Moses; He is faithful in all My house. I speak with him face to face, even plainly, and not in dark sayings; and he sees the form of the LORD…" (Num 12.4–8).

God draws a sharp distinction between Moses and other prophets (including Miriam and Aaron). God speaks to Moses "face to face" ("mouth to mouth, clearly, and not in riddles" ESV), and he even has the honor of seeing "the form of the LORD." All this emphasizes Moses' superiority to the rest of God's prophets. However, as great as Moses was, he was still "only" a faithful *servant in* the house of God. Jesus by comparison is the *Builder* of the house and *Son over* the house of God! "Christ's superiority to Moses aims not at disqualifying the latter as a servant within God's house, but rather at enhancing the honor of the former as Son over God's house (Heb

---

[16] Gert J. Steyn "An Overview of the Extent and Diversity of Methods Utilised by the Author of Hebrews When Using the Old Testament," *Neotestamencia* 42 (2008) 342.

3.5)."[17] The Hebrew writer makes the application, "whose house we are if we hold fast the confidence and the rejoicing of the hope firm to the end." (Heb 3.6b) We are the very house of God, overseen by the Son and superior to the children of Israel, if we "hold fast" and "firm" to the end. These Hebrew brethren, tempted to give up the blessings of Christ in a return to the laws and community of Moses, would be persuaded to hold fast their confidence and hope in Christ if they could see Christ as far "greater" than Moses.

While the "lesser" to "greater" is not as overt as some of the other examples in the epistle, the Hebrew writer then employs a connected, similar argument:

> Therefore, as the Holy Spirit says: "Today, if you will hear His voice, do not harden your hearts as in the rebellion, in the day of trial in the wilderness, where your fathers tested me, tried me, and saw my works forty years. therefore I was angry with that generation, and said, 'They always go astray in their heart, and they have not known my ways.' So I swore in my wrath, 'They shall not enter my rest'" " Beware, brethren, lest there be in any of you an evil heart of unbelief in departing from the living God; but exhort one another daily, while it is called "Today," lest any of you be hardened through the deceitfulness of sin (Heb 3.7–13).

The Hebrew writer is quoting from Psalm 95.7b-11 (taken from the LXX). This psalm begins with a familiar call to worship God because He is both our creator and savior. The first seven verses of this psalm employ a chiastic structure, as suggested by Riding:

A  Let us worship our Savior (1, 2),
   B  For He is the Creator of everything (3–5);
   B'  Let us worship our Maker (6)
A'  For He is our Savior (7 a-c)[18]

---

[17] David A. deSilva, *Despising Shame: Honor Discourse and Community Maintenance in the Epistle to the Hebrews*, SBLDS 152 (Atlanta: Scholars, 1995) 215.

[18] Charles B. Riding. "Psalm 95 1–7c as a Large Chiasm," *ZAW* 88 (1976) 418.

The emphasis of the psalmist is on God as Savior[19], especially in the context of the exodus, "YHWH's greatest act of salvation for Israel."[20] It is not incidental that God's swearing that they will not enter His rest is applied in Hebrews to the context of God's greatest act of salvation for *all* people—the sacrifice of His Son. The "lesser" in the Hebrew writer's argument is the exodus; the "greater" is Christ's act of salvation. "For we have become partakers of Christ if we hold the beginning of our confidence steadfast to the end" (Heb 3.14).

Our confidence is in Christ, and His saving grace—a greater act of salvation than even the exodus. If God was justified in rejecting the children of Israel when they departed from Him in the wilderness after He saved them, *how much more* justified is He in rejecting Christians who depart from the salvation in His Son? This is why he calls them to "hear His voice" (Heb 3.7, 15; 4.7)! The argument echoes what the Hebrew writer has already said:

> For if the word spoken through angels proved steadfast, and every transgression and disobedience received a just reward, *how shall we escape if we neglect so great a salvation, which at the first began to be spoken by the Lord, and was confirmed to us by those who heard Him,* God also bearing witness both with signs and wonders, with various miracles, and gifts of the Holy Spirit, according to His own will? (Heb 2.2–4; emphasis added).

And what he would say later:

> Anyone who has rejected Moses' law dies without mercy on the testimony of two or three witnesses. *Of how much worse punishment, do*

---

[19] Riding says, "The present order of these verses, in the form of A B B A parallelism, highlights the fact the YHWH is both our Creator and our Saviour, and that these two are inseparable from each other. Yet while these two themes are firmly interlocked, and both are very important, the structure and arrangement of these verses, as depicted above, suggest strongly that YHWH as our Saviour takes precedence over YHWH as our Creator." Ibid.

[20] Riding's footnote to this structure states: "To justify making v. 7 a-c synonymous with 'He is our Saviour', see Leviticus 26.12, 13 and Jer 11.4, where the phrase 'I will be your God, and you shall be My people' is within the context of the exodus, YHWH's greatest act of salvation for Israel." (Ibid.)

*you suppose, will he be thought worthy who has trampled the Son of God underfoot, counted the blood of the covenant by which he was sanctified a common thing, and insulted the Spirit of grace?* For we know Him who said, "Vengeance is mine, I will repay," says the Lord. And again, "The Lord will judge His people." It is a fearful thing to fall into the hands of the living God" (Heb 10.28–31 NKJV; emphasis added).

The message to the Hebrew brethren is clear: you have more than enough to believe, overcome the peer-pressure and persecution you are experiencing, hold fast to the end, and not drift away or shrink back from what you have heard (Heb 2.1; 3.14; 4.15; 10.23, 38–39; 12.3). In fact, he argues, you have more cause to hear and believe than those who fell in the wilderness.

> For who, having heard, rebelled? Indeed, was it not all who came out of Egypt, led by Moses? Now with whom was He angry forty years? Was it not with those who sinned, whose corpses fell in the wilderness? And to whom did He swear that they would not enter His rest, but to those who did not obey? So we see that they could not enter in because of unbelief. Therefore, since a promise remains of entering His rest, let us fear lest any of you seem to have come short of it. For indeed the gospel was preached to us as well as to them; but the word which they heard did not profit them, not being mixed with faith in those who heard it (Heb 3.16–4.2).

"The quitters who turned back to the wilderness (so the psalm and epistle warn us) may be but pale shadows of ourselves, if we draw back from our great inheritance."[21] Their foreshadowing of our salvation (and possible fall) is expanded upon by Paul in his extended comparison of the Old Testament exodus and our "exodus" from sin:

> Moreover, brethren, I do not want you to be unaware that all our fathers were under the cloud, all passed through the sea, all were baptized into Moses in the cloud and in the sea, all ate the same

---

[21] Derek Kidner, *Psalms 73–150: An Introduction and Commentary,* TOTC 16 (Downers Grove: Inter-Varsity Press, 1975) 378.

spiritual food, and all drank the same spiritual drink. For they drank of that spiritual Rock that followed them, and that Rock was Christ. But with most of them God was not well pleased, for their bodies were scattered in the wilderness. Now these things became our examples, to the intent that we should not lust after evil things as they also lusted. And do not become idolaters as were some of them. As it is written, "The people sat down to eat and drink, and rose up to play." Nor let us commit sexual immorality, as some of them did, and in one day twenty-three thousand fell; nor let us tempt Christ, as some of them also tempted, and were destroyed by serpents; nor complain, as some of them also complained, and were destroyed by the destroyer. Now all these things happened to them as examples, and they were written for our admonition, upon whom the ends of the ages have come. Therefore let him who thinks he stands take heed lest he fall (1 Cor 10.1–12).

| Type of the Exodus | Anti-Type of Our Salvation |
| --- | --- |
| Bondage in Egypt[22] | Bondage in Sin |
| Baptized into Moses | Baptized into Christ |
| Saved/Delivered | Saved/Delivered |
| Blessings in the Wilderness | Spiritual Blessings in this Life |
| Continue in Sin (Lust, Idolatry, Sexual Immorality, Tempt Christ, Complain, etc.) after Receiving Salvation | Continue in Sin (Lust, Idolatry, Sexual Immorality, Tempt Christ, Complain, etc.) after Receiving Salvation |
| Fall in the Wilderness (Lost) | Fall from Grace (Lost) |
| The Jordan River | Physical Death |
| "Promised Land" of Canaan | "Promised Land" of Heaven |

Without going through the specifics of each example Paul uses, his overall picture of type and anti-type comes clearly into focus. "All

---

[22] The elements of bondage in Egypt, the Jordan River, and the Promised Land of Canaan are all implied in the text of 1 Cor 10, though not explicitly stated.

these things happened to them as examples, and they were written for our admonition" (v. 11). God is using the unfaithfulness of His people in times past as a template for us of what *not* to do.

We join with the Hebrews in condemning the wilderness generation, and we too must learn from their example. As Christians we have (a) a more important salvation, (b) from a far worse slavery, (c) following a greater leader, (d) into a more complete rest. "How shall we escape if we neglect so great a salvation?" (Heb 2.3).

## Application to Christians Today

The Hebrew writer draws Psalm 95, and the failures of the children of Israel in the wilderness, to *his* present by quoting, "Today, if you will hear His voice…" (Heb 3.7, 15; 4.7). We would be wise to do the same. "Today" means it is not too late to be who God has called us to be. Kidner strikes at the continued urgency of the Hebrew writer's plea to us when he says, "The 'Today' of which it speaks is this very moment; the 'you' is none other than ourselves…"[23] While that may be somewhat hyperbolic, McClister rightly says, "The author of Hebrews believed that the scriptures were not just historical records of what God said in the past, but that God continually addresses his people through his word."[24] Though the Hebrew writer attributes this psalm to David in 4.7 (cf. Psa 95.1 LXX), he first attributes it to the Holy Spirit in 3.7. This is God's message to His people both then and now. We rightly tend to avoid reading the text as though we are the recipients as a general rule of interpretation, but in this case perhaps we should follow the example of the Hebrew writer and make direct personal application from the things written. Certainly, "Today" refers to the days of David and the days of the Hebrew Christians, but it refers to our days as well. The living and powerful word of God reveals the thoughts and intents of our hearts, just as it did theirs (Heb 4.12). "Let

---

[23] Kidner, *Psalms* 343.

[24] McClister, *Hebrews* 45–46. McClister specifically views "Today" as a reference to the Messianic age. Ibid. 130.

us therefore be diligent to enter that rest, lest anyone fall according to the same example of disobedience" (Heb 4.11).

### What Could Show in Us an Evil Heart of Unbelief?

The first indicator that we may be guilty of unbelief like the exodus generation is that we become dissatisfied with the salvation of God. In the midst of the trials of the wilderness, some of the people talked of all the supposed blessings in Egypt (Exod 16.2–3; Num 11.4–6). The devil wants us to misremember how "great" our life of sin was before salvation. We are tempted to look at social media, watch a commercial, or stream a movie and think a life of slavery to sin is one to be coveted. We even trick ourselves into thinking *that* kind of life can give us the things God promises us, as those wandering in the wilderness did by describing Egypt as a sort of promised land (Num 16.13–14). Ingratitude in our present state as Christians can lead to a rosy picture of our past life of sin that never really existed. Would it have been better for them to receive their wish and return to Egypt? Of course not. Would it have been better for the Hebrews to bend to pressure from the outside world to return to their previous manner of life? Of course not. It is equally foolish to ask, "Would it not be better for me to return to my life of slavery to sin?" May we learn from their example to see our salvation for the precious gift it is.

The second indicator that we may be guilty of unbelief like the exodus generation is that we doubt the goodness of God in his actions and commands toward us. In Deuteronomy 1.27, the people attributed the exodus to the fact the LORD hated them. "Because the LORD hates us, He brought us out of the land of Egypt to deliver us into the hand of the Amorites." The exodus was irrefutable evidence of God's love, but the people forgot that. Sometimes, we forget the irrefutable evidence of God's love in giving His Son. As Paul says in Romans 8.32, "He who did not spare His own Son, but delivered Him up for us all, how shall He not with Him also freely give us all things?" If God did not withhold the greatest blessing that could be given, why would He withhold any lesser blessings if it is for our good? May we learn from their example that God's commands and actions are for our good, always (Deut 6.24; Rom 8.28).

The third indicator that we may be guilty of unbelief like the exodus generation is that we become dissatisfied with the promised blessings of God. Too many are dissatisfied with the blessings God provides: dissatisfied with marriage to one spouse for life; dissatisfied with God's Word as the means of revelation and direction; dissatisfied with a quiet and peaceable life of labor and service; dissatisfied with the church Christ established and the worship He authorizes; dissatisfied with the level of physical wealth we enjoy; or dissatisfied with the spiritual emphasis of the Kingdom. This dissatisfaction leads us into a similar wandering in a wilderness of sin as the Hebrews. We cry out in carnal desire for something other than "every spiritual blessing in the heavenly places in Christ" (Eph 1.3), not realizing the very thing we desire will be a plague to us as soon as we receive it (Num 11.33). The problem of the wilderness generation was unbelief—but it was also ingratitude. Their complaints to God far outnumbered their songs of thanks to Him. God's blessings were never enough and never appreciated. We must make a conscious effort to count our blessings and give thanks lest we forget all we have been given. May we learn from their example to recognize and be grateful for the abundant blessings of God.

The Hebrew writer, through the Holy Spirit, gives us some powerfully timely and relevant Old Testament examples. Like the oaths of God, the examples that apply to us can be positive or negative. Do not imitate those who fell in disbelief and disobedience; imitate those who through faith and patience believed and inherited the promises (Heb 11; 12.1–3; 13.7). Instead of an evil heart of unbelief, maintain a pure heart of trusting faith in God. Thank God, we still have "Today!" to make it so. Thank God a promise remains of entering His rest.

# There Remains a Sabbath Rest
# for the People of God

## Caleb Churchill

In the beginning, God created the world and all it contains. On the sixth day, He created man in His image. On the seventh, he created Sabbath rest so that man and God could enjoy his creation together. The story of Genesis is how man lost that rest; Exodus reveals the work of Yahweh to bring His people out of bondage and back into that rest.[1] This theme of Sabbath rest spans the whole of scripture as God works to bring His stubborn children back into the rest that He first designed for them in the garden. As time passed, many shadows of Sabbath rest came and went. Still, centuries later, the writer of Hebrews wrote, "There remains a Sabbath rest for the people of God" (Heb 4.9).[2] What is that "Sabbath rest" that remains? Did not Joshua give God's people the rest He had promised? Why does the author describe what awaits the people of God as "Sabbath rest"? If there is a Sabbath rest ahead, how should this impact God's people today?

### The Meaning of Sabbath Rest

The Hebrew word *šabbāt*, from which we get our word "Sabbath," is first used in Genesis. After God finished the work of creation, "He *rested* on the seventh day" (Gen 2.2). The significance of that day

---

[1] The terms "people of God" and "Israel" are used interchangeably in this essay.

[2] Unless noted otherwise, all quotations of scripture are from the 1995 update to the NASB.

was only briefly described in the Genesis account. "Then God blessed the seventh day and sanctified it, because in it He rested from all
His work which God had created and made" (Gen 2.3). There are
different senses in which this word *šabbāt* is used, but it is clear that
"to cease from working" is primarily what is in view in the Genesis
account.[3] The author of Hebrews cites this text and comments that
God's works were "finished from the foundation of the world" (Heb
4.3–4). On the seventh day, God began to rest. There is no indication
that God completed his rest and returned to his creative work. Thus,
God's Sabbath rest began at the moment his creative work ceased and
continues still. This rest may be shared by all those who enter into it
through obedient faith in the gospel (Heb 4.1–11).[4]

So why did God rest on the seventh day and what kind of Sabbath
rest does God have in store for his people? It is not as if God became
weary or tired (Isa 40.28). It is also not as if God has ceased all activity
from the seventh day onward (John 5.17). What does it mean that
God rested on the seventh day? Interestingly, the creation of Sabbath
is sandwiched between two accounts of the making of man. God's
final work of creation was making man in His own image (Gen 1.26–
27). Only man is recorded as being an image-bearer of God. After the
creation of man, God rests. Then, the Genesis account describes how
God made man and the beautiful land in which he placed man to
dwell. The sequencing appears intentional. "When God entered into
His rest after creating the world, it was with the intention of enjoying
fellowship with the man He had made..."[5] "The Sabbath was made
for man...," Jesus would later explain (Mark 2.27). Just as the land,
so also the rest was a blessing from God for man to enjoy. This Sabbath rest was more than simply "ceasing from work." It was cessation

---

[3] Gordon J. Wenham, *Genesis 1–15*, WBC 1 (Nashville: Thomas Nelson, 1987;
rep. ed., Grand Rapids: Zondervan, 2014) 35.

[4] F. F. Bruce, *The Epistle to the Hebrews*, NICNT (Grand Rapids: Eerdmans,
1990) 103–111.

[5] David McClister, *A Commentary on Hebrews* (Temple Terrace: Florida College
Press, 2010) 135–136.

with the purpose that man might focus his heart, mind, soul, and strength on his relationship with the Everlasting Creator God.

Sadly, this Sabbath rest did not last. When man sinned, fellowship with God was severed and man was evicted from the beautiful garden and separated from God's presence. While God hinted at his plan and promise to restore that rest when he called Abram out of the land of Ur, [6] it is not until the book of Exodus that the people of God were introduced again to the idea of Sabbath rest. The Exodus story first highlights the lack of rest the people of God experienced in Egypt (Exod 1.11–14). One of the consequences of sin was that man would toil in his work (Gen 3.17), but God never approved of anyone rigorously imposing hard labor on others without rest. Therefore, when the people of God cried out in their anguish and bitterness from their toil, God heard their groaning and remembered the promises he made to Abraham, and he rose up to act. God sent Moses to Pharaoh to rescue his people out of bondage. Pharaoh, ironically, noted that Moses was attempting to "make them *rest* from their burdens" (Exod 5.5 KJV). That is exactly what Yahweh intended. Israel would be delivered from bondage and into rest.

The rest that God prepared for his people certainly included a place. Moses would later write "You have not as yet come to the resting place and the inheritance which the LORD your God is giving you" (Deut 12.9). Still, the rest of God was more than a promised land. This rest included the refreshment, renewal, peace, and security that came from enjoying a relationship with Yahweh himself. When Yahweh recounts before Moses why he called his people out of Egypt, note the destination he desired them to reach. "You yourselves have seen what I did to Egypt, and how I carried you on eagles' wings and brought you to *Myself*" (Exod 19.4–5). The destination intended for the people of God was not primarily a place, but a person. Yahweh rescued Israel so that he could bring them back to find

---

[6] There are hints at this Promised Land of rest in Genesis 12.1,7; 13.14–15; 15.18–21, and 17.8.

rest and refreshment in him. That is how he was able to provide rest for his people even in the wilderness.[7] Just as God rested and was refreshed on the seventh day, so also his presence would go with his people and he would give them rest, the rest that could only come from being present with him (Exod 31.17; 33.14).

When the writer of Hebrews speaks of entering God's rest, it certainly included the idea of a place of rest. This rest is also referred to in Hebrews as a "city with foundations" (Heb 11.10), a "homeland" (11.14), a "heavenly" one (11.16), "the city of the living God" and the "heavenly Jerusalem" (12.22), an unshakeable "kingdom" (12.28). and the "city…to come" (13.14). So there is both a "place" and a "state" in the mind of the author when he writes of rest.[8] Yet there is more. The writer appears to invent a word when he writes "there remains a Sabbath rest for the people of God" (Heb 4.9). This is the earliest known use of the Greek word *sabbatismos*. Since there was no word adequate to describe the kind of rest that awaits the people of God, it appears the author coined his own word.[9] In this word, a clue is given concerning the meaning of the rest God is providing for His people, as all other early uses of *sabbatismos* signify Sabbath observance.[10] Rest is connected to the Sabbath as God originally intended it. Instructions in Judaism concerning the Sabbath emphasized the connection between rest and worship. There are references like this one which stated that the Israelites "observed the Sabbath with fervent praise and thanks to the Lord…" (2 Macc 8.27). By speaking of *Sabbath rest,* the author reminds his readers that the rest of God would be a time for joy and gladness in the celebration and

---

[7] In Exodus 33.14, God promises "My presence shall go with you and I will give you rest." This indicates that rest was plausible even in the wilderness wherever God was present (cf. also Num 10.33–36). Consider also that even in the land there was no rest once the presence of God departed.

[8] Thomas R. Schreiner, *Hebrews,* EBTC (Bellingham: Lexham Press, 2021) 134.

[9] Leon Morris, "Hebrews," in Frank Gaebelein, ed., EBC (Grand Rapids: Zondervan, 1982) 12:42.

[10] William Lane, *Hebrews 1–8,* WBC 47A (Nashville: Thomas Nelson, 1991; rep. ed., Grand Rapids: Zondervan, 2014) 102.

adoration of God. God has prepared one long Sabbath feast in the heavenly sanctuary for his people to rejoice in his presence and enjoy his eternal goodness.[11]

## Seeking Sabbath Rest: Shadows and Substance

Scripture is filled with shadows of rest that increase in substance as the gospel is unveiled. Every shadow gives a glimpse of a greater rest to come, but each is just a foretaste since these shadows proved temporary, incomplete, or both. The fact that God created the world in six days and rested on the *seventh* day hinted that there would one day be a full and complete sabbath rest. The word "seven" in ancient Hebrew is connected to the concept of fullness and completeness.[12] While it is difficult to think of God's rest on the seventh day as simply a shadow of the true rest, it is certainly true that God entered a rest that man would soon forfeit through sin. Therefore God began the work of restoring his people to that ultimate rest. His plan included many shadows of rest that gave his people a taste of what he was ultimately preparing for them.

One of the earliest shadows of rest was revealed in the Israelite observance of the Sabbath day. After God rescued his people from their toil and their groaning in Egypt, he brought them out into the wilderness where he introduced them to rest through the Sabbath day (Exod 16.23–30; 20.8–11). The Sabbath day was first, an opportunity for the Israelites to cease from their daily struggles and strivings, as well as to find refreshment by turning their eyes upon Yahweh their Redeemer.[13] By ceasing their ordinary work, the LORD could have their undivided attention. It was secondly an opportunity for Israel to develop trust in Yahweh as their good and faithful provider. They were ordered not to gather on the seventh day because God would give them bread on the sixth day sufficient to provide for them through the seventh

---

[11] Ibid.

[12] "Sabbath," YouTube, uploaded by the Bible Project, 7 January 2020, https://www.youtube.com/watch?v=PFTLvkB3JLM.

[13] See Exodus 16.25–26: "a sabbath to the LORD"; also 20.8–11 and 23.12.

(Exod 16.29). Thirdly, the Sabbath was a celebration of God's deliverance into rest. These two ideas—deliverance and rest—are revealed in Scripture as the primary reasons for Sabbath observance, as the people of God were called to imitate God's rest and remember his great deliverance (Exod 20.8–11; Deut 5:12–15). When Yahweh gives the "Ten Commandments" on Mount Sinai, he appeals to his rest after creation as the reason why Israel must remember the Sabbath and sanctify it by resting (Exod 20.8–11). Later, when Moses reminds Israel to observe the Sabbath day and keep it holy, he appeals to God's deliverance as the reason. "Remember that you were slaves in Egypt and that the LORD your God brought you out of there with a mighty hand and an outstretched arm. Therefore the LORD your God has commanded you to observe the Sabbath day" (Deut 5.15).

These ideas of "deliverance" and "rest" are not divergent themes but are closely parallel in scripture. In the creation, God labors to create the world and delivers man into his rest to be with him. In the exodus, Yahweh works with an outstretched arm to disarm the most powerful ruler in the world and deliver His people out of Egyptian bondage and into his land of rest. The exodus story is even retold using the phraseology of creation.[14] Most impressively, both the creation and exodus accounts reveal God acting to bring something new so that when he is finished with his work, he can rest in his relationship with man.[15] In order to celebrate this deliverance and rest on the Sabbath day, the Israelites were ordered not only to avoid work, but to sanctify the Sabbath as a "day of sacred assembly" (Lev 23.3 NIV). It was a day to be devoted wholly to the LORD. Thus, every seventh day of the week, the Israelites were granted an opportunity to cease their labors and enjoy a taste of God's rest with him. The Sabbath day, with its sanctified time of rest and worship, became central to the identity of the Jewish people.[16]

---

[14] See the discussion of Psalm 33.7 in connection with Exodus 15.8 as well as Isaiah 43.15–17, etc. in McClister, *Hebrews,* 139.

[15] Ibid.

[16] See Abraham J. Heschel. *The Sabbath: Its Meaning for Modern Man* (New

Of course, the Sabbath day was not the only shadow of the rest to come. The people of God were called to celebrate seven yearly festivals (sometimes called "High Sabbaths" or "High Holy Days"), each of which in some way anticipated the rest of God to come.[17] These holidays served as an opportunity for the people of God to humble their souls before the LORD and focus on worshipping him (Lev 23.32).[18] Additionally, after they entered the Promised Land of rest, they would be required every seventh year to give the land a sabbath rest to the LORD. There would be no plowing, pruning, or reaping. Instead, every man, woman, and beast would rest and enjoy the blessings God provided them. During this year every slave would be set free in remembrance of the time when the LORD redeemed them out of slavery in Egypt (Deuteronomy 15.12–15). This became known as a Sabbath year (Lev 25.8–28). After every seventh Sabbath year, God ordained an additional (fiftieth) year of rest known as the year of Jubilee. In this year, a release would be proclaimed throughout the land. Each would return to their own property and their own family. The jubilee year served as a celebration of freedom, deliverance, and rest. These festivals and Sabbath years suggested that God intended for his people a rest that would last as they were refreshed by God's gracious provisions and devoted themselves to worship in the sacred assemblies.[19]

While God promised his people the possibility of rest even in the wilderness, the greater rest awaited his people in the Promised Land (cf. Deut 12.9–10). He chose Zion for his place of habitation saying, "This is my resting place forever; here I will dwell, for I have desired it" (Psalm 132.13). Though the tabernacle provided some measure of rest as the LORD dwelt among his people in the wilderness, the greater rest would come after the people crossed the Jordan (Numbers 10.33–36). The LORD promised,

---

York: Farrar, Straus and Young, 1951). Heschel describes the Sabbath as "not an interlude, but the climax of living" (23).

[17] "Sabbath," Bible Project.

[18] These feasts are detailed in Leviticus 23.

[19] McClister, *Hebrews,* 142.

> But you will cross the Jordan and settle in the land the LORD your
> God is giving you as an inheritance, and he will give you rest from all
> your enemies around you so that you will live in safety. Then to the
> place the LORD your God will choose as a dwelling for his Name—
> there you are to bring everything I command you: your burnt offer-
> ings and sacrifices, your tithes and special gifts, and all the choice
> possessions you have vowed to the LORD. And there rejoice before
> the LORD your God—you, your sons and daughters, your male and
> female servants, and the Levites from your towns who have no allot-
> ment or inheritance of their own" (Deut 12.10–12).

In the land, God planned to provide a more permanent place where
man could meet with him for worship and fellowship.

Because of their disobedience, most of the first generation coming
out of Egypt did not enter into God's rest.[20] Still, God was faithful to
bring his Promised Land of rest to fruition. He raised up Joshua who
led that second generation into the Promised Land and gave them
rest. Yahweh gave Israel all the land he had sworn to their ancestors
and he gave them "rest on every side, …not one of their enemies
stood before them…. Not one of the good promises with the LORD
had made to the house of Israel failed; all came to pass" (Josh 21.44–
45). However, even the Promised Land of rest could not stop this
stubborn people from abandoning their covenant with the LORD.
In recounting Israel's history, Nehemiah would later pray, "as soon
as they had rest, they did evil" (Neh 9.28). Still, God was long-suffering. Even after the people acted wickedly and broke the covenant
repeatedly, God raised up his servant David as king and gave him
rest on every side. David, responding with gratitude, made plans to
provide a more permanent place for the LORD to dwell. Instead, it
was God who made a house (i.e., dynasty) for David and promised
him rest from all his enemies and a kingdom that would "endure"
and "be established forever" (2 Sam 7.16). The LORD, then, allowed

---

[20] Because of their hardness of heart, God swore "they shall not enter into my
rest" (Psa 95.11).

David's son Solomon to build a temple for him to dwell in. God was faithful to his promise to make Zion his resting place.

Still, living in the Promised Land did not guarantee that the people of God would experience rest. While God assured them he would grant them peace and security and rest in the land, that promise was dependent on whether or not Israel would "follow [God's] decrees" and be "careful to obey [His] commands" (Lev 26.3–6). There were times when Israel did enjoy rest on every side and there were no adversaries or disasters surrounding them. When kings led the people to be faithful to the Lord, they were blessed with rest in the land (e.g., 1 Kng 5.4; 8.56; 1 Chr 22.9, 18; 23.25; 2 Chr 14.6–7; 15.15; 20.30). Sadly, these moments did not last for long. God warned the people, even before they entered the land, that persistent rebellion and refusal to listen would eventually result in exile so that the land could "rest and enjoy its sabbaths" (Lev 26.34). As Israel persisted in unfaithfulness, God called them back time and time again. He spoke through his prophet Jeremiah saying, "Thus says the LORD, "Stand by the ways and see and ask for the ancient paths, Where the good way is, and walk in it; And you will find rest for your souls" (Jer 6.16). Yet Israel responded, "We will not walk in it." Because of the Israelites' repeated willful rebellion, Yahweh their Redeemer who delivered them out of bondage delivered them back into exile to the point that Jeremiah lamented, "We are worn out, there is no rest for us" (Lam 5.5). Even after their return from captivity and rebuilding of the temple, the rest of the returnees was only a dim shadow of what God intended it to be. The people continued to profane the Sabbath, and God's ultimate rest was never achieved with the rebuilding of the temple (cf. Neh 13.17–18). It would only come from the one to whom that temple pointed.[21]

The Old Testament ends on a somber yet hopeful note. Though the true rest is not yet realized, the prophets continued to speak of a rest to come. Isaiah remarked that one day a shoot would spring up

---

[21] McClister, *Hebrews*, 146.

from the stem of Jesse who will "stand as a signal for the peoples" with a glorious "resting place" (Isa 11.10). Again, he predicted that the LORD will again choose Israel and settle them in their own land with strangers who would join them and attach themselves to the house of Jacob. In that day, the LORD will give them "rest from… pain and turmoil and harsh service" in which they were enslaved (Isa 14.3). Ezekiel promised that there would be a shepherd like David who would rescue his people and bring them into their own land and rid the land of all danger so that they may dwell in safety and be showered with blessings (Ezek 34.11–31). Daniel promised that for those who endure until the end, they will "enter into rest and rise again for [their] allotted portion at the end of the age" (Dan 12.13). Thus, there remained a glimmer of hope that these shadows eventually would result in a rest far more substantial than those already realized.

Indeed, something more substantial did arrive with one descendent of Jesse born in Bethlehem. Jesus appeared on the Sabbath day in the synagogue of Nazareth where he opened the scroll of Isaiah and read, "The Spirit of the Lord is upon me, because he anointed me to bring good news to the poor. He has sent me to proclaim release to captives, and recovery of sight to the blind, to set free those who are oppressed, to proclaim the favorable year of the Lord" (Luke 4.18–19; c.f. Isa 61.1–2). After returning to his seat, Jesus sat down and said, "Today, this Scripture has been fulfilled in your hearing" (Luke 4.21). With this Jubilee proclamation, Jesus began his ministry of Sabbath rest. The significance of Jesus beginning his ministry with this scripture cannot be understated. Jesus is indicating that finally the Sabbath rest is being achieved. He has come to restore fellowship between God and man and to deliver God's people out of bondage and into rest. The Sabbath rest is being fulfilled.

And if this event in that Nazarene synagogue was not sufficient to prove the point, Jesus went about deliberately doing healing on the Sabbath day (cf. Luke 4.31, 6.1–11, etc.). Some were so blinded by their Sabbath traditions that they were unable to see that Jesus was proving that he is the Sabbath rest of God who came to restore the relationship between God and man. Those who thought there were "six days" to come and be healed misunderstood the meaning of the Sabbath altogether (Luke 13.14). A proper understanding of Sabbath rest would lead one to the conclusion that there was no more appropriate day for healing than the Sabbath. As Jesus said, "should not this daughter of Abraham, whom Satan has kept bound for eighteen long years, be released from her bondage on the Sabbath day?" (Luke 13.16 Berean Study Bible).

Of course, Jesus had a deeper Sabbath rest in mind than any physical healing could ever provide. "Come to Me, all who are weary and burdened, and I will give you rest," Jesus said. "Take My yoke upon you and learn from Me, for I am gentle and humble in heart, and you will find rest for your souls. For My yoke is comfortable, and My burden is light" (Matt 11.28–30). Rest for the soul is why Jesus came to die. He came to invite Israel and strangers of every nation to enter into God's rest. Each Sabbath day the Israelites looked backward to remember their deliverance out of Egyptian bondage into rest. So also Jesus by healing on the Sabbath pointed his people forward to a time when he by his death would deliver Israel once for all out of their deep bondage to sin and restore to them the rest and refreshment of pure and unadulterated fellowship in the presence of God. When Jesus was resurrected from the dead, God's promise of rest was achieved, as the veil was torn and entrance into God's rest was made possible for all who come to him.

Because of Jesus, there is an already-but-not-yet aspect to this rest.[22] There is a rest for the soul that is already available in Jesus for the people of God. Now something better than the shadows has come, the substance is here, and his name is Christ Jesus. He is the stem of Jesse who has come as a signal for the peoples to prepare for them a glorious resting place. He is the good shepherd who has made a covenant of peace so that whether they live in the wilderness

---

[22] Schreiner, *Hebrews*, 134–137.

or sleep in the forests, those who trust in him will find showers of blessing, fruitful harvests, and security and safety in the land. The rest is here and it is accessible now. Still, there remains an even fuller Sabbath rest ahead that we must press on in order to enter. Jesus declared to his disciples on the night before he died, "I go to prepare a place for you. And if I go and prepare a place for you, I will come again and receive you to Myself, that where I am, there you may be also." This is true and lasting Sabbath rest—to be received by him, to be with him forevermore. Thus, "there remains a Sabbath rest for the people of God" (Heb 4.9).

## The Impact of Sabbath Rest on the People of God Today

So what impact should the Sabbath rest have on the people of God today? Some argue that the Sabbath days and years should still be observed by the people of God. Disputes continue among believers over whether it is the seventh day or the first day that should be commemorated. It is quite true that the Lord Jesus observed the Sabbath each seventh day, being born under the law (Gal 4.4). Even if he was frequently accused of breaking the Sabbath, the only commands regarding the Sabbath day that Jesus violated came from the *Halakhah*, not from the Law of Moses.[23] It is also true though that Paul wrote with the authority of Christ that "no one is to act as your judge in regard to… a festival or a new moon, or a Sabbath, things which are only a shadow of what is to come; but the substance (Gr. *sōma* "body") belongs to Christ" (Col 2.16–17). Just as many Jews in Jesus' day were distracted from the true meaning of Sabbath rest by all the traditions surrounding its observance, so also many Christians today can miss the true meaning of this Sabbath rest: "deliverance into rest." When put in those simple terms, it is obvious that the whole Messianic Age is a Sabbath. "In the Messianic age every day is a Sabbath day, every year is a Sabbath year, and the Messianic age is a spiritual Jubilee

---

[23] *Halakhah* is a reference to Jewish oral rabbinical tradition.

to God."[24] For the Christian, worship is not limited to a certain day of the week. Every day is devoted to celebrating Christ's deliverance, enjoying his fellowship and entering into his rest.[25]

The fact that there remains a Sabbath rest should impact the Christian in several ways. In this portion of the letter, the author of Hebrews insists on at least four ways this promise should affect saints today: (a) fear of falling short of the rest; (b) diligence to enter for self and others; (c) holding fast to one's confession; and (d) boldness to draw nearer to God.

First, let us fear falling short of his rest. (Heb 4.1). "Let us fear" is emphatic because there is an eternal danger at stake. The "fear" he encourages would certainly include the fear of facing eternal condemnation and the wrath of God. But this "fear" would also comprise the fear of missing out on God's promise of the rest to come. Fourteen times, in this brief exhortation—as the author calls it (13.22), the writer refers to the "promise" of God more than any other New Testament book.[26] The writer knew that promises of God would be worth whatever it cost them to endure. Worse than dropping dead in the wilderness was the possibility of not being able to enter God's rest. In the same way today, worse than the fear of hell should be the fear of missing out on this chance to rest with our Redeemer. In life, there are always going to be things we miss out on, but this promise of Sabbath rest is not worthy to be compared to anything else in this world. A rest so great as this demands that we measure our success or failure in life solely in terms of whether we enter it or not.[27] Imagine spending your whole life enduring the wilderness in hopes of reaching the Promised Land, only to fall short in the end. What sorrow

[24] McClister, *Hebrews*, 149.

[25] For discussions on this topic, see D. A. Carson, ed., *From Sabbath to Lord's Day: A Biblical, Historical, and Theological Investigation* (Grand Rapids: Zondervan, 1982; rep. ed., Eugene: Wipf & Stock, 1999).

[26] Morris, "Hebrews," 39.

[27] See David A. DeSilva, *Hebrews: Grace and Gratitude* (Nashville, Abingdon, 2020) 35–52.

could ever compare with that? No fear should compare to our fear of falling short of the Sabbath rest with God.

This fear of falling short must also lead disciples to strengthen their faith in God's promises. The reason the Israelites fell short is not that they had not heard the gospel. They most certainly did hear it, but "the word they heard did not profit them because it was not united by faith" (4.2). Not all Israel was truly Israel, and not everyone who claims to be a believer truly trusts in the Lord. If we do not enter this rest, it will not be because we have not heard the gospel. Indeed, we have. It will be because our listening was not united with faith. We must consider, how is our faith in the promises of God? Throughout Hebrews, a person's faith is measured by their willingness to heed God's call and obey him (e.g., 3.17–18; 5.9; 11.4–31). We must examine ourselves to see if we are following the Lord fully or where we are lacking in our faith. Still, what do we do when our faith grows weak? How might we strengthen our faith in God's promises? Our faith is rooted in the faithfulness of God, so the food that nourishes our faith is God's faithfulness. Later, the writer of Hebrews would urge his readers to "hold fast the confession of [their] hope without wavering." What would help them do this? "For he who promised is faithful" (Heb 10.23). If we want our faith to increase, we must devote ourselves to regularly rehearsing the faithfulness of God in our hearts.

Second, let us be diligent to enter that rest and ensure that no one will fall short of it (4.11). The rest of God should not only move our emotions and intellect but also stir us to action. Diligence (Gr. *spoudazō;* "to make every effort, do one's best") must be applied to ensure we enter and those with us make it, too. As long as we are alive, there is still work to do to enter that rest. Resting from labor is reserved for those whose works are completed.[28] This parallels what John heard from heaven, "'Blessed are the dead who die in the Lord from now.' 'Yes,' says the Spirit, 'so that they may rest from their la-

---

[28] Schreiner, *Hebrews,* 145–146.

bors, for their deeds follow with them'" (Rev 14.13). Since this day of final rest has not yet arrived, we must apply all of our diligence to the pursuit of that future rest.

Note also the encouragement to ensure that "no one will fall." A rest so great as this compels concern not only for self but for others. The writer of Hebrews knew nothing of the rugged individualism rampant in our culture today. Faith is no private matter. Instead, there is a persistent corporate call to faithfulness pervasive throughout the letter. The exhortation "let us..." comes at least fourteen times in the letter (4.1, 11, 14, 16; 6.1; 10.22, 23, 24, 12.1, 2, 28; 13.13, 15). Entering into this rest is something we do together. The reward is too great for our faith to remain a personal pursuit devoid of community. For this reason, the writer stressed the need to "... encourage one another day after day, as long as it is *still* called 'Today,' so that none of you will be hardened by the deceitfulness of sin" (Heb 3.13). Our diligence is not reserved only to ensure that we enter, but also to help others along the way. Therefore, we are moved to offer persistent support, encouragement, and accountability to the people of God.[29] The question we must consider is twofold: What is everything in my power that I can do to enter this rest? And what is everything in my power that I can do to help others to ensure that none of us falls short of this Sabbath rest?

Third, let us hold fast to our confession (Heb 4.14). Since the ultimate fulfillment of the Sabbath rest is still ahead of us, we must not dismiss the one who died to deliver us into this rest. We have a high priest who has passed through the heavens (cf. 7.26; 9.24). This priest surpasses the greatness of Aaron or any other high priest. While Aaron and every other Levitical high priest passed through the veil into the most holy place, Jesus the Son of God has returned into the presence of God.[30] He is already enthroned in the presence of God. To renounce him is to renounce a relationship with God

---

[29] DeSilva, *Hebrews*, 35–52.

[30] Neil Lightfoot, *Jesus Christ Today* (Grand Rapids: Baker, 1976) 100.

himself. Such a beautiful promise of rest inspires saints to hold on even when trials persist, for the reward of entering into his rest will make whatever we must endure worth it in the end.

Finally, let us come with boldness to the throne of grace (Heb 4.16). Our high priest has not only passed through the heavens, he has also passed through the human experience. The Son left behind the perfect Sabbath rest with his Father and came down to enter into our sin-cursed toil and labors so that he would be able to sympathize with our weaknesses and be thoroughly equipped to help us take every step of our journey toward that rest. Though he was tempted in all things as we are, he resisted every temptation and remained faithful to God. Knowing Jesus was tempted in all things gives us assurance that he can relate. Knowing he has passed through the heavens, gives us assurance he can actually help. If we draw near to him when we are tempted, he promises to give us mercy and grace to help us when we need it the most. Because of what our high priest has accomplished, there is no longer any barrier.[31] We have full and open access into the presence of God and we can approach his throne of grace at any time. Knowing what Christ has accomplished on the cross, we can have confidence that it is a throne of grace to which we come. When we come into his presence, he vows that we will receive mercy and find grace to help in our time of need. The people of God are not exempt from the trials and temptations in this world, but neither did God exempt himself. The fact that Jesus overcame every temptation and shed his blood on the cross for us ensures us that we need not shrink back from his presence. This deep rest for the soul remains available for all who come to him.

## Conclusion

The God who entered into his rest on the seventh day also invites his people to enter. The call of Jesus remains, "Come to me all who are weary and heavy-laden, and I will give you rest" (Matt

---

[31] Morris, "Hebrews," 46.

11.28) This rest includes far more than a work stoppage or removal of threats and enemies. This rest is a deeper rest for the soul. Sabbath rest is, above all else, an opportunity to celebrate God's deliverance by devoting ourselves to fellowship, worship, and the enjoyment of our relationship with him. Our Sabbath rest has already begun in Christ. With such a great and gracious high priest, God has created a new Israel in whom his rest is already realized.[32] Yet there remains an even greater lasting rest to come, a more direct and full realization of God's presence and our relationship with him. The Mishnah describes Psalm 92 as "a song for the future, for the day that will be entirely *šabbāt* and rest for everlasting life" (*m. Tamid* 7:4). The Hebrews were longing for another "day" of everlasting rest to come, one that would be entirely *šabbāt*. Here it is. This everlasting Sabbath rest awaits the people of God. For all who trust in him, Christ has prepared this deep rest of the soul. Praise be to Yahweh our Redeemer who has rescued the Israel of God and prepared for us this Sabbath rest where forevermore we will be with him who created us to enjoy him eternally. "There remains a Sabbath rest" for the people of God. "Let us be diligent to enter into that rest."

---

[32] McClister, *Hebrews*, 150.

# Contributors

**V. J. Benson**, a native of India, was baptized in 1980 and started preaching while completing his B.A. and later an M.A. in Telugu literature. He started working as a Radio Station Officer with the Police Communications department in 1984. When he visited the U.S. for the first time in 1987, he was mentored by brothers Billy Raymer and Bernard Bolton. After returning from the U.S. while on extended leave from his job, he started working as a full-time minister in 1988. He preached at four rural congregations in the Guntur area from 1992–1997 and gave up his government job in 1997 to continue working full-time. He met brother Ed Harrell in 1993 and started working with him as his main contact and facilitator which led to a long and ongoing fruitful labor of the Lord's work in India that has expanded into several states and cities. V.J. started working with the church at Moula-Ali in 1997 with five families meeting in a home, now grown to over 200 members, with him serving as an elder since 2012. He also evangelizes widely throughout India. His wife of 33 years is Matilda and they have two grown children, Bernard and Curie. Bernard completed his Ph.D. in Electrical Engineering and works in Birmingham, AL. Curie lives in Chennai, India with her husband Dr. B. Vishal, a vascular surgeon in training, and their three-year-old son Ryan. V.J. first visited Florida College in 2001 with brothers David Owen, Bob Owen, and Brent Lewis, and he was much impressed with the mission and the goal of the college, and he has attended lectures several times since.

**Gianni Berdini** ('80) was born in Rome, Italy to Rodolfo and Lella Berdini. Gianni's father preached for the church in Aprilia, Italy for fifty-five years. After high school at Liceo Scientifico Statale John F. Kennedy in Rome, Gianni completed his undergraduate work in architecture and began graduate work at Sapienza Universita di Roma. However, Gianni interrupted his architectural studies in 1978 to study Bible at Florida College. In 1980, he returned to Italy and completed his doctorate in architecture at the Università di Venezia. After working for a short time with the church in Aprilia, Gianni has worked as an evangelist with the church in Trieste, Italy for the past forty-one years, also serving as an elder there. In addition to his work in Trieste, in 2005 he also began working regularly with the church in Monfalcone nearby. Gianni has written and published numerous religious materials and has preached in Bible conferences for many of the churches in Italy. He and his wife, Giuseppina, have two children, Riccardo (Los Angeles, CA) and Beatrice (Milan, Italy).

**Caleb Churchill** ('08) grew up in Indiana. Caleb graduated from Florida College with a B.A. in Liberal Studies in 2008. It was at Florida College where he met his wife Lindsey (Sams, '09) who he would marry in 2013. It was also at Florida College that Caleb met Roger Polanco and other friends who brought him to New York City and the Northeast. Caleb has spent time over the past 15 years working with churches in the city. After teaching high school for two years in south Alabama, he moved to the Bronx in 2012 and began devoting himself to the ministry of the word. In 2018, he moved to Brooklyn where he works with the Prospect Park Church alongside his wife Lindsey and three boys: Cyrus, Cyprian and Zuriel.

**Andrew Dow** ('13) has been married to Heather (Manz, '13) since 2013. They have three boys—Josiah (6), Amos (4), and Levi (2)—with a fourth child on the way. Andrew has worked as an evangelist with the Olsen Park church of Christ in Amarillo, TX (2013–2015) and the Woodland Hills church of Christ in Conroe, TX (2015–present). His academic education includes an A.A. (2012) and B.A. in Biblical Studies (2013) from Florida College, and a M.A. in Biblical Studies from Faulkner University (2020).

**John Gibson** ('79) grew up in rural Escambia County, FL and after high school attended Florida College from 1977 to 1979. After leaving Florida College he spent a year working with a newly established church in Moody, AL before moving to Beckley WV to work in a preacher training program. While living there he met his future wife Janet Atkins of Charleston, WV. Since their marriage in 1981, John and Janet have worked with churches in Princeton, WV, Selma, AL, Conyers, GA, Seffner, FL, Vinemont and Athens, AL. They have been in the Athens area since 2002 and are currently working with the Jones Road church of Christ. John and Janet have two children Amanda (husband Chad) and Jesse. They have also been blessed with four grandchildren, Bryant, Sutton, Tiffany, and Harper.

**Ben Hall**, his wife Emily ('07), and their four children live in Brooklyn, NY. Ben grew up in north Alabama where his family and friends encouraged him in every way to diligently seek and serve the Lord. After being married, Ben and Emily were part of the work of the Lord in Atlanta, GA until moving to Brooklyn where they now labor alongside the saints there in the preaching of the gospel.

**Tom Hamilton** ('82) and his wife Joy ('84) have been married for 38 years and have 11 children, including 5 by adoption. Seven have attended Florida College: Michael ('08), Bethany ('08, '10), Philip ('11), Sarah ('12), Brian ('17), Stephen ('19, '21), and Aminata ('24). Tom received his formal education at Florida College (A.A., 1982; Advanced Diploma, 1983); Abilene Christian University (B.A., 1984; M.A. in Biblical Languages, 1991); Christian Theological Seminary (M.T.S., 1996); and Knox Theological Seminary (D.Min. in Theological Exegesis, 2015). He has labored as an evangelist with congregations in Hammond, Ind. (1986–90), Muncie, Ind. (1991–2005), and now the 58ᵗʰ Street church in Tampa (2005–present). He has had articles published in *Truth Magazine, Biblical Insights, Focus Magazine*, spoken in several lectureships, authored the Truth Commentary on Joel (2007), and written essays for *Studies in the Psalms: Essays in Honor of D. Phillip Roberts.* (Florida College, 2007), *Blessed Be God: Studies in Ephesians: Essays in Honor of Dr. C. G. "Colly" Caldwell, III* (Florida College, 2010), *From the Pen of Paul: An Introduction to the Pauline Letters* (Florida College, 2019), and *Studies in Church History: Essays in Honor of Daniel W. Petty* (Florida College, 2020). Tom joined the faculty at Florida College to teach Bible in Fall 2005 and serves as the chair of the Department of Biblical Studies since 2021.

**Marc Hinds** ('92) has been preaching for churches of Christ in Texas for 20 years. His wife, Melanie (Gibson, '92) have two children, John Marc and Ginny, and two grandchildren, Jacob (3) and Victoria (8 months). Marc graduated with a M.A. in Biblical Languages from Houston Baptist University in 2017 and is the author of two books, *The Big Picture: A Guide to Learning the Bible's Story* and *Amazed By Jesus: The Big Picture of the Life of Christ* (both published by 21st Century Christian) and is currently working on his third publication, *The Way of Jesus: The Big Picture of the Book of Acts.*

**Chris Huntley** ('03) received a B.A. in Biblical Studies in 2003 from Florida College, where he met his wife Julia. After graduating, he trained under Tom Kinzel with the Vivion Rd church in Kansas City, MO, followed by fourteen years serving as a preacher for the Hazelwood church in St. Louis, MO. While in St. Louis, Chris began work on a Master's Degree in Exegetical Theology at the Covenant Theological Seminary which will soon be completed. In late 2019, Chris and Julia, along with their six children, moved to Salem, OR to begin working with the Market St church.

**Jason Longstreth** ('92) and his wife Stephanie (Stewart, '93) have five children: Hannah, Kira, Jonathan, Alexander, and Olivia. After seven years as Dean of Students at Florida College, Jason has returned to full-time teaching in the Bible department of the college, while also serving as an evangelist with the Forrest Hills congregation in Tampa. Jason received his formal education at Florida College (A.A., 1992; Advanced Diploma, 1994); Johnson University (M.A., 2009); and Amridge University (M.Div., 2012; D.Min., 2014). He has had articles published in *Truth Magazine*, *Biblical Insights*, authored several workbooks, spoken on several lectureships, and written essays for *A Tribute to Melvin D. Curry, Jr.* (Florida College, 1997), *Blessed Be God: Studies in Ephesians: Essays in Honor of Dr. C. G. "Colly" Caldwell, III* (Florida College, 2010), *From the Pen of Paul: An Introduction to the Pauline Letters* (Florida College, 2019), and *Studies in Church History: Essays in Honor of Daniel W. Petty* (Florida College, 2020). Jason is also a member of the Society of Biblical Literature and the Evangelical Theological Society.

**Reagan McClenny** ('06) has preached the gospel since 2004, at the Lindale church of Christ in Lindale, TX from 2004–2010 and at the Timberland Drive church of Christ in Lufkin, TX from 2010-present. Reagan earned his B.A. in Biblical Studies from Florida College in 2006, also being honored with the D. Phillip Roberts Award in Bible. After Florida College, he received an M.Ed. in Educational Leadership from the University of Texas at Tyler. Reagan and his wife Stephanie (Reeves, '06) have two daughters: Madison and Brooklyn. Through the years, he has written for various online and print publications.

**Roger Polanco** ('07) graduated from Florida College with an A.A. in 2007. He is very thankful to the excellent Bible faculty and other professors who helped him grow in knowledge as well as character and played a large role in equipping him to serve God and others. Roger grew up in New York City and has returned there as an evangelist, working for the cause of the gospel in the NY metropolitan area since 2009. Roger lives with his wife Cassie (Churchill) and three children Englewood, NJ just outside NYC.

**Russ Roberts** ('79) and his wife, Elizabeth (Harrell) Roberts have lived in Ponte Vedra, FL since 2017, where he serves as the full-time evangelist at the South Jacksonville church of Christ. They are the parents of Mrs. Randi Roberts Cassel ('04; married to Dan Cassel) and Mr. William Roberts ('05), married to Sarah Towers Roberts ('05). After attending two years at Florida College (1977–1979), Russ received his B.S. degree in Engineering at Texas A&M University. He worked as a civil engineer with the U.S. Army Corps of Engineers for 5 years, and for the U.S. Department of Defense Education Activity for 26 years; holding positions in Texas, Germany, England, and Washington, D.C. In 2017, Russ retired with 31 years of U.S. federal service after acting in the capacity of Facilities and Logistics Directors for the K-12 schools for our military dependents in 10 overseas countries, 8 U.S. states and 2 U.S. territories. Russ and his wife labored with small overseas churches for the over 20 years of their married life that they spent in Germany and England; they continue to work extensively with churches in Germany, India, and Seychelles. Russ served as an elder of the Annandale church in the Washington, D.C. area for eight of the nine years they lived there (2003–2012).

**Mark Russell** grew up in Kentucky and received his B.A. in History and Education from Western Kentucky University in 1987. He married Florida College alum Cindy Dugger ('84) and moved to Valparaiso, Indiana just after their first anniversary in August 1988 to work with the recently formed Valpo congregation as their evangelist, and he now also serves as one of the shepherds there. They have two grown sons, now married, with one granddaughter and another on the way. Mark is very thankful for many faithful men and women connected with Florida College who mentored and encouraged him through the years.

**John Weaver** is a professor of Church History and Biblical Studies at Florida College, where he also serves as the Academic Dean. He and his wife, Vivi, have five children, and he preaches at Mariners Boulevard Church of Christ in Spring Hill, Florida.

www.ingramcontent.com/pod-product-compliance
Lightning Source LLC
Chambersburg PA
CBHW021221090426
42740CB00006B/323